Samuel W. Thomsen

PROGRESS DEBUNKED

The Creation-Destruction Balance
and Ancient Wisdom's Primacy

POISE
PRESS

Copyright © 2017 Samuel W. Thomsen
All rights reserved.
ISBN: 1-947537-00-8
ISBN-13: 978-1-947537-00-2

Poise Press
www.poisepress.com

For my family:
past, present, and future

CONTENTS

Unscientific Preface ... ix

Introduction: The Argument All Too Briefly ... 1

Chapter I
MALTHUS'S PRINCIPLE, EXPLAINED AND EXPANDED

    Misconceptions about Malthus ... 9
    The Birth of Progress ... 10
    Malthus's Principle ... 12
    Not Prophesy, Proof by Contradiction ... 15
    Generalization of Malthus's Principle ... 17
    Malthusian Pressures are Common ... 20
    Summary and Philosophical Implications ... 22

Chapter II
DARWIN'S LAW

    Malthus's Principle and Birth Control ... 24
    Evolution and Birth Control ... 26
    Darwin's Question ... 28
    The Influence of Malthus on Darwin ... 29
    Darwin's Theory in a Nutshell ... 31
    A Note on the Terminology of "Selection" and "Mutation" ... 32
    Eugenics as Tyranny ... 33
    Can Mutation be "Overcome"? ... 36
    Summary and Philosophical Implications ... 38

Chapter III
CULTURAL EVOLUTION

    Biology versus Culture ... 40
    Prototyping Humans? ... 41
    Culture is Subject to Darwin's Law ... 41

The Half-Hearted Debate over Cultural Evolution	44
Our Question: Can Culture Overcome Natural Selection?	47
Eugenics as a Kind of Culture	48
The Current State of Genetic Engineering	51
Cybernetics, Artificial Intelligence, and the "Singularity"	52
Darwin's Law as Universal	56
Cultural Progress Debunked	63
Summary and Philosophical Implications	64

Chapter IV
VALUES AND THE BALANCE OF JOY AND SUFFERING

Joy, Suffering, and Utilitarianism	67
Creation Causes Joy, Destruction Causes Suffering	68
The Rise of Utilitarianism	68
Utilitarianism Evolves	71
The Balance of Joy and Suffering	74
Religion and the Evolution of Values	80
Biological versus Cultural Evolution of Values	84
Summary and Philosophical Implications	89

Chapter V
EVOLUTION AND COMPASSION

Does Human Evolution Equal Social Darwinism?	91
Social Reform versus Property Rights	92
Evolution, Religion, and Greed	93
Evolution, Diversity, and Charity	96
Altruism and "Group Selection"	98
The Ultimate Simulation and the Fate of Civilization	105
Summary and Philosophical Implications	107

Chapter VI
ECOLOGY AND THE FATE OF CIVILIZATION

Civilization and the Biosphere	110
Global Economic Growth and Ecology	112

The Past, Present, and Future of the Biosphere	116
An Eternal Mystery?	118
What We Can Learn	119
Summary and Philosophical Implications	121

Chapter VII
PHILOSOPHY REVITALIZED

How Progress Has Destroyed Philosophy	123
Progress Makes Monocultural Minds	126
How to Think the Ancient, Ecological Way	129
Back to the Classics	131
What is the Task of Philosophy?	132
Ancient Wisdom's Primacy	134
Appendix 1: The Mathematics of Malthusian Equilibrium	135
Appendix 2: The Mathematics of Darwinian Equilibrium	140
Appendix 3: Evidence for Cultural Evolution in the History of Technology	144
Variation	144
Continuity	146
Blindness of Variation	149
Diffusion	151
Natural Selection	153
Appendix 4: Computer Simulations and the Evolution of Compassion	155
Suggested Reading	163
Bibliography	165
Endnotes	177
Acknowledgements	181
Index	183

If the wild south wind churns up the sea, the waves which once were clear as glass, as clear as the bright days, seem muddy and filthy to the beholder. ... So it is with you. If you want to see the truth in clear light, and follow the right road, you must cast off all joy and fear. Fly from hope and sorrow. When these things rule, the mind is clouded and bound to earth.

— BOETHIUS
The Consolation of Philosophy

UNSCIENTIFIC PREFACE

A science fiction magazine once published a list of "Stories We've Seen Too Often." One of them read:

> The future is utopian and is considered by some or many to be perfect, but perfection turns out to be boring and stagnant and soul-deadening; it turns out that only through imperfection, pain, misery, and nature can life actually be good.[1]

The idea that utopia would be lifeless has certainly become a cliché. But there is something eerie about our fatigue with the notion. Isn't it interesting that science fiction magazines receive so many stories of just this sort? Isn't it a little disturbing?

If it is true that utopian perfection—by which I mean the absence of all suffering—would be empty and lifeless, it might be argued that no step toward utopia would be progress. Our status as the pinnacle of history would be thrown into question. Automobiles, airplanes, modern medicine, computers, modern agriculture: none of these would be progress. They would be instead sources of spiritual stagnation.

I will argue in this book that progress, indeed, is nothing more than an illusion.

Science-fiction writers and cultural critics have been critiquing the notion of progress for decades. But where they have used allegory and rhetoric, I will make the case using evidence and logic. The philosophical essence of what I'm getting at is the same: without suffering, uncertainty, and struggle, there can be no joy, novelty, or success.

Our society takes progress for granted. We assume that the world has improved and will continue to improve. But perhaps we've been too hasty in celebrating this supposed victory over the past. The majority of the world remains in dire poverty. The human population is still growing, and resources are dwindling. We are heavily dependent on fossil fuels for our energy and industry. The most disconcerting fact is also one of the best known—it would take five planet earths to support the world population if everyone were to adopt the American way of life.[2] We are flaunting the wealthiest, most exploitative nations as examples of the possibility of progress. Western civilization is unsustainable. Its industry and energy use are growing exponentially, even if its population is not. It cannot survive forever in its current form.

People often claim or imply that human ingenuity will eventually solve these problems. I don't think it can. I will argue that it's impossible to permanently tip the world's balance between joy and suffering.

Why bother writing a book attempting to disprove progress? What's the point if you can't make the world a better place? Indeed, what's the point of anything on my view? To someone used to thinking in terms of progress, the non-progressive view sounds cynical. It sounds like the argument, "Nothing *really* matters in the end, because we know that in a few billion years the sun will expand into a red giant and swallow the earth."

But progress can't be essential to our purpose as humans because it's a very new idea. It's been taken seriously only since the "Enlightenment" period of European philosophy two or three centuries ago. In the meantime, we've had an unusual spike in wealth—the result of our ability to harness coal, oil, and natural gas for vast amounts of energy, many times larger than anything humans have harnessed before. We're in the midst of unsustainable growth, but our long prosperity has spoiled us into thinking that world history is a continual march of improvement. Prior to the modern era, global culture was basically nonexistent, and most philosophers, religious leaders, and scientists assumed that world history was fairly static. They didn't write books to improve the world, but for the humbler purpose of improving themselves and their readers as individuals. Sometimes they hoped to improve their own community, nation, or belief system. When certain rare individuals or societies *did* attempt to improve the entire world, as with Alexander the Great or the British Empire, the actual result was simply to spread their own culture more widely.

My goal with this book is an old-fashioned one, to help bring Western philosophy back to what matters. At the moment we've become obsessed with the notion of improving the entire world based on scientific advances. But this obsession has led our greatest thinkers astray into materialistic calculations, away from the meditations on wisdom that originally made Greek, Roman, and Christian philosophy so profound.

Promises to improve the world inevitably lead us to focus on material goods. Because individuals are diverse in ability, they can't be trusted to provide for themselves, and centralized, industrial production must increase. New children are seen not as wondrous creations, but as new liabilities, dangerous to the stability of the system, which must be regulated from the top down. Ancient cultural traditions are not seen as the treasures they are, but as obstacles to development. In the progressive train of thought, people are eventually demoted from free, responsible, moral beings, to mere consumers, mere members of populations to be fed. Progress means social engineering, and social engineering, I will argue, means dehumanization.

I am neither an authoritarian, nor an anarchist, nor a Luddite. I am not making the classic reactionary argument that our civilization will "regress" unless we reestablish centralized control. Regress is as impossible as progress. Nor am I making the anarchist argument that all government control is dehumanizing and evil. Civilizations will wax and wane, and the best form of government will depend on the phase of society. Nor am I making the Luddite argument that all technology is bad. But I do think that modern Western culture overemphasizes science, technology, and industry, to the detriment of the humanities, religion, high culture, folk culture, and those rural values that we will need as our civilization wanes.

So what is the point of life without progress? My answer, in brief, is to live in the most romantic and heroic, virtuous and compassionate way possible. That's all. The point is not to save the entire world. You can't save the world. It's not creating a world government. It's not redistributing all wealth to feed all the poor. No such victory would last. In the past, such schemes (including the Soviet Union and the Third Reich) have done more harm than good. It's better to fix yourself first. Then when you've got your own life in order, help your family members. Help your close friends. Help your local community. I guarantee you will be more fulfilled than if you throw yourself heart and soul into Utopian idealism, as so tragically many young people have done over the past 150 years, to the detriment of their minds and souls.

Some tell me my skepticism of progress comes from cynicism. Quite the contrary—my skepticism of progress comes from idealism. The "perfect" society we are building is indeed "boring and stagnant and soul-deadening." I write this book not out of despair, but out of resolute protest. I find it hard to believe that people would prefer a closed, controlled world without struggle or meaningful danger, to an open world of wild adventure and freedom. My ideal is the ecology of nature, a system of manifold diversity and unpredictable novelty, filled to the brim with both horror and elation, each vitally intertwined with the other. The realities of nature are the fundamental moral realities. Traditional morality has its source in human evolution. Our oldest philosophical, literary, and religious traditions have been tested to their core through the successive growth and collapse of previous civilizations. It is in these traditions that our most vital principles and values live, not in the changeable fashions of social science. The idea of progress—that science, technology, or any other means can produce a better world than what we've had—is an illusion. The proper goals for a society are to grow and create, not mechanize and control. Modern ideas are untested in their long-term effects; we should have more confidence in the traditional ideals that have helped our ancestors thrive during centuries and millennia of hardship. We need to start valuing longstanding ideals again, not short-lived "progress."

This book is somewhat unusual. It's not a textbook. It's not a plea to policy makers. It's not a work of postmodernism. It's not a series of literary essays. Rather, it is a work of *systematic philosophy* in the *traditional* sense. Let me explain what I mean by this.

Philosophy is—or *should be,* regardless of what they presently teach at the universities—an attempt to understand humankind's place in the world and to determine what ideals and principles to live by while we are here. It is concerned with the big picture, with the whys of human existence. Historians investigate *events*—their order, causes, and effects. Scientists investigate *mechanisms*—the ways that nature produces cause from effect. Philosophers investigate *meaning*—the significance of all these scientific facts and historical events. Is there such a thing as long-term, worldwide progress? This question has historical and scientific components, but it is essentially philosophical.

If you mistake my argument for a scientific or historical argument, you will misunderstand it. Science and history are about discovering and demonstrating novel facts. Philosophy is about questioning and reconciling facts we already accept, and assumptions we already make. Whether you already believe in progress or not, this book is supposed to challenge your view of the world. This book is not just one argument and one conclusion. It's many arguments stemming from the multifaceted insight that progress is a mirage.

Systematic philosophy argues using reason. The first component of reason is *logic,* which is the connecting and deducing of facts and principles using still more basic facts and principles. Pure logic is simply mathematics. Logical reasoning is found throughout the sciences and in all systematic philosophy. There will be mathematics in this book, though where it gets complex I will put it in an appendix.

The second component of systematic reason is *evidence,* which is simply a term for observed facts. Evidence gathering is the essential activity of science. It is an important part of any systematic investigation because it provides context, examples, and statistical support. I will present a great deal of secondary evidence in this book. I'm not attempting to present new evidence, as a scientific or historical book does, but rather to present the evidence in such a way as to reveal the big picture of what it means. I am seeking to critique, promote, and unite extant, well-tested ideas into a panoramic collage that shows a more coherent picture than the progressive one that is currently the fashion. My argument may have its foundation in research done by others, but this is precisely what allows it to do the neglected job of synthesis.

When I call my philosophical style **traditional**, I mean to emphasize that I reject the modern notion that real philosophy is the critical dissection of language and argumentation that occurs in most current academic books and articles. This notion leads to a collection of microscopic, overspecialized texts that do almost nothing to help anyone—especially non-philosophers—understand humankind's place in the world.

Traditionally, synthesis was considered the essence of philosophy. It was the primary task of the most highly regarded classics, including Plato's *Republic*, Aristotle's *Politics*, Aquinas's *Summa Theologica*, Descartes' *The World*, Rousseau's *Social Contract*, and Darwin's *Origin of Species*. Science itself used to be considered a branch of philosophy—"natural philosophy"—that focused less on human purpose and more on objective reality. In recent times, since we've enthroned technological progress and the technical science it depends on as the summits of human intellectual achievement, we've come to neglect the task of synthesis and demean it as inexact and unreliable. But this is to dismiss what is most essential simply because its investigation involves unique challenges.

In short, I attempt to develop arguments supported by science and logic for a new big picture of world history and our place in it. This picture necessarily has aesthetic, poetic, and moral components. But I've attempted to ground my view as well as I can in the physical and material realities of the human condition. This book is an attempt at systematic philosophy, in the traditional sense of these terms.

What needs to change, in my view, is not a certain isolated collection of policies, theories, or practices. What needs to change is the entire modern picture of world history and social ecology. We need to abandon the notion that human history consists of an accelerating series of technological and political innovations that make our lives better. Instead, human history has been a process of diversification and natural selection, involving both rapid changes and gradual adaptation. Disruptions brought on by technology have led to the growth of some societies and the decline of others. Prosperity has come in spurts and led to the flowering of civilizations, each of which eventually outstrips its resources or grows luxurious and corrupt, ending in decline and collapse.

This is not a new picture of history. Stories of growth and decline are what you find in Edward Gibbon's *Decline and Fall of the Roman Empire,* in the writings of the Greek philosophers, and in the *Bible*. Scholars had taken this view of history for granted until fairly recently. It's the view Gibbon

UNSCIENTIFIC PREFACE

alludes to in 1776 when he begins a sentence with: "Notwithstanding the propensity of mankind to exalt the past, and deprecate the present ..." It's only been over the last two centuries that our ideology has taken a radical twist, deprecating the past and exalting the present. But the resulting logical, physical, and aesthetic inconsistencies have led our philosophy widely astray of what is natural, ecological, beautiful, and good. And progress has made us blind to certain hard realities. Human beings are mortal and fallible. Sometimes they are evil and sometimes they are incompetent. The freedom and individual diversity that make humanity beautiful are *in their essence tied* to the possibility of evil and incompetence. One thing that separates this book from most others of its kind is that, rather than romantically avoiding such facts—as most "back to nature" rhetoric does—it will plunge right into their heart to gain a clearer view of the fundamental, unshakable principles of nature that are at work. In fact, the principles that eliminate the possibility of progress will turn out to be those of Malthus and Darwin.

What is really important lies on the other side of the veil of progress. Ancient wisdom. A connection with the past. A connection with nature and the earth. Most of the issues I focus on in this book (population growth, DNA mutation, world government) should be forgotten, not tackled harder; this book is a long-winded critique of the pernicious and widespread idea that these issues are "problems" that must be solved. I don't write it to fuel more discussion of how to curb population growth, feed the entire population of the world, and eliminate all violent struggle everywhere, but to ridicule our persistent obsession with these utopian goals, and to bring ideals of nature, romance, and virtue back into philosophy.

Those progressives who disagree with my argument tend to listen to the end, skirt the veil, balk, and pull back because they see that one of the implications is that our civilization cannot achieve perfect sustainability, and will thus eventually collapse and billions will die. This is indeed part of what I'm saying. It may take a couple of decades, maybe a couple of centuries. But ten thousand civilizations have fallen before ours and ten thousand civilizations will fall after. The collapse of ours won't be fatal to what matters. Human culture has always managed to renew itself. Whatever books and music and knowledge and belief systems survive the next

1000 years will truly be treasures, because they will be what got people through the most formidable of all adventures: an apocalypse.

INTRODUCTION: THE ARGUMENT ALL TOO BRIEFLY

Before debunking progress, we need to define progress.

The first thing to eliminate is the idea that we can identify progress as an increase in capability or technical means, such as energy, money, power, numerical advantage, or complexity. It is actually easy to see why this approach would be absurd. If having greater concentrations of energy is better, then we should all want to collapse into a black hole. If power is most important then we are forced to the conclusion that Stalin was the greatest man who ever lived. If having a larger population is better, then the most advanced organisms are microbes. If you mean complexity, then a teaspoon of soil with its millions of species of bacteria is many orders of magnitude more progressed than all of human computer technology combined.

More generally, any quantity that attempts to capture how *capable* something is neglects the point, which is what that capacity is to be used for. It's a means without an end. We admire not large populations but happy populations. We value energy not for its own sake, but because we can use it for so many ends. Once the means in itself is considered good, you end up with the absurd goal of having an enormous capacity to no purpose.

We might be tempted to define progress as the loftiness of one's culture, in terms of science, philosophy, and art. But the success of our science is measured in terms of technology, which brings us back to mere capacity. The success of modern philosophy is usually alleged in terms of science. It's true that we've produced a lot of art, but to determine whether it is genuinely better than that produced in other cultures or in previous ages only brings us back to the question of how we define improvement.

The most common view among intellectuals, perhaps because it most evokes feelings of compassion and indignation to injustice, is that progress is the increased satisfaction of every human's material needs—food, clothing, health, and shelter. This view makes sense because material satisfaction is an end, not a means. A hundred schemes for progress have been proposed along these lines, starting with eighteenth- and nineteenth-century philosophers such as the Marquis de Condorcet and Karl Marx, and continuing today in the writings of Amartya Sen and Jeffery Sachs. Here we have a notion of progress that is widely influential and has been around for centuries. Here we have a worthy antithesis.

In short, this kind of progress means a decrease in the sum total of human suffering. I think this is very close to what most people mean by "progress," but it leaves out something important: human joy. If we only count suffering, a negative quantity, we can't account for all the things people do not out of fear but out of desire for reward. Going to work is a kind of suffering, but it pays off in the joy of prosperity. Childbirth can be agonizing, but people do it for the joy of family. Fighting in wars is terrifying, but it is often done for the joy of victory. So if we are to define progress in terms of suffering, I will have to side with the utilitarian philosophers: what matters is the sum total of happiness, minus the sum total of suffering. The founder of utilitarianism, Jeremy Bentham, first introduced the idea of measuring total happiness in the late eighteenth century. We will come back to the details of his theory in later chapters. For now, here is the definition of the kind of progress we will debunk:

> **Progress** *is a permanent increase in the ratio of the total happiness of all people to their total suffering.*

And the thesis of this book can be stated:

> *The ratio of the total happiness experienced in the world, to the total suffering, converges to one when each is summed over a long-enough period of time.*

INTRODUCTION:
THE ARGUMENT ALL TOO BRIEFLY

Happiness and suffering can fluctuate over time, as resources become scarce or plentiful. So I'm not saying that this quantity will always balance exactly. But similar to the way flipping a coin repeatedly will eventually lead to an even ratio of heads and tails (a phenomenon called the Law of Large Numbers by probability theorists), overall happiness and suffering, as I will argue in later chapters, will also approach an even ratio over time.

This definition of progress may not be satisfying to everyone. Perhaps you already disagree with the utilitarian way of looking at this, or you are already skeptical that such progress is possible. But by analyzing exactly what is wrong with utilitarianism and its notion of progress, we will come to a much clearer view of the human condition. As I've said, this book is not simply a single argument with a single conclusion. It's a critical exploration of the idea of progress and what it means for the fate of humanity. Utilitarian theory will form a useful locus for this discussion, because it is relatively simple and involves the central notions we'll be concerned with: happiness, suffering, population, and progress.

Utilitarians such as Jeremy Bentham and John Stuart Mill were in fact among the first to argue that progress was possible, that total happiness could be increased and total suffering decreased. They believed that using birth control could achieve this result. Their ideas became widely implemented after about 1900, when birth rates in Europe and America began to plunge. Since then, prosperity in the West has increased and hunger has declined, and it is generally believed that the ratio of happiness to suffering is getting higher and higher.

I'm glossing over the question of how exactly to measure happiness, to be discussed in Chapter 4. For now, it suffices to note that modern utilitarians, such as Peter Singer, measure happiness according to how people would rank their preferences. This sort of measurement can be made quantitatively using surveys. And it gives us a very general and democratic definition of progress, one that adds together each individual notion of progress to get a total, self-declared happiness. In Chapter 4 we will see how this preference-rank measure converges, in the long run, to that of evolutionary fitness. Just as importantly, this definition of progress is utilitarian, and for the last two centuries utilitarianism has formed the core of progressive ethical theory. Modern decision theory, for example, assumes that human decisions are based on ranked preferences in terms of *utility* or *happiness*, which are taken to be the same.

There may already be good reasons to reject utilitarianism as a foundation of ethics. But it is still critical to debunk its notion of "progress," because it has become a universal assumption in our culture—a sort of religion—even if many of us don't realize it. Even when people pay lip service to "stagnation" or "doom and gloom," they assume that progress is our ultimate goal and do not challenge our basic utilitarian world-picture. Almost every intellectual discussion about the future implicitly takes the possibility of progress for granted. We believe that human happiness *has* increased, and *should* continue to increase, at least if we make the right policy decisions and recycle.

Birth control is an essential component of this modern notion of progress. Since the time of Malthus, we all understand that when the population grows exponentially, food and water become scarce. By curbing population growth, it is believed, we eliminate this basic source of distress.

Family planning is often taken to be *the* cornerstone of progress, the *one thing needed* that will do most to eliminate suffering. If the population doesn't grow, it is argued, food production can remain steady and no one will go hungry. Reducing population growth, by itself, is often touted as the most sustainable way of doing things.

I'd like to offer an alternative view. According to this view, birth control is in fact an unnatural and unsustainable policy. According to this view, civilization *itself* is fundamentally unsustainable. The fact is that there have been thousands of civilizations over the course of history, and the vast majority have collapsed. Many of these civilizations, including the ancient Greeks and Romans, used population control. Limiting the population is not, contrary to what many experts say, a cure-all.

If it eliminates suffering, birth control does so by eliminating the struggle to flourish that's at the root of the creativity of human evolution, which produces so much diversity in our species. We know this instinctively. The fertile energy of sexual passion is part of what makes life life: a holy mixture of joy and sorrow, triumph and tragedy.

Life *should* be such a mixture, I will argue. If it is not, we should conclude that something is wrong with our perception of it. Life is worthwhile because we must strive toward the best, happiest outcomes, and avoid the worst and saddest. It's why we have a mind in the first place, to be able to consider these contrasting possibilities and learn from the pain of mistakes. Paul Valerie, a French poet and aphorist of the early twentieth century, was correct to point out, "Happy peoples have no mind. They have

INTRODUCTION:
THE ARGUMENT ALL TOO BRIEFLY

no great need of it." Even before Darwin, Malthus argued that, "To avoid evil and to pursue good seem to be the great duty and business of man ... and it is by this exertion, by these stimulants, that mind is formed."

The fundamental inconsistency in the idea of progress is easy to state, if not to fully grasp. If we imagine a world where the worst forms of suffering have been eliminated, we are necessarily imagining a world with that much less challenge, that much less triumph, and that much less mind. Life and joy are thus extinguished along with suffering. Progress means that by degrees the need for the business of living disappears. Life disappears.

But this way of putting it sounds surreal and fantastical. And we are left with a no less abhorrent picture of our present world, with its growing human population, and untold suffering due to lack. Are we to simply turn up our noses to the miseries of the poor and say, "Such is life"?

Absolutely not. Life is, as Malthus argued, essentially a struggle against evil. The struggle must continue. What should cease is the idea that this struggle can somehow be won once and for all. Such a victory would mean the destruction of life itself. This book is about how to understand this abstract insight from a practical, physical point of view. What can we and can't we realistically expect for the future of our civilization? To address this question systematically I will be applying Malthus's theory of population (Chapter 1), Darwin's theory of evolution (Chapters 2, 3, and 5), and utilitarian decision theory (Chapter 4). We will look at some evidence concerning the short- to medium-term survival of our industrial civilization (Chapter 6), and suggest that intellectual life should be reoriented toward tradition and the classics rather than scientific progress (Chapter 7).

Thomas Robert Malthus was the first to argue that the basic ecology of populations will strictly prevent any long-run improvement of the world. The joy of procreation causes population growth, and this growth causes resource limitations, famine, and suffering. In this way, Malthus believed that human life remains in an overall equilibrium, never getting better or worse on the whole. This idea is a good start toward a theory of what I call "creation-destruction balance." Roughly speaking, population growth is a kind of creation, and limits to growth mean destruction. Since population growth is always balanced by limits, total creativity and total destruction must balance in the long run. In **Chapter 1**, I will attempt to extend and refine Malthus's version of this theory.

However, most modern progressives view birth control as a final "solution" to Malthus's dilemma. In **Chapter 2**, I argue that this view neglects the effect of evolution on the human population. Recent studies suggest that mutation has been increasing the rate of congenital diseases in industrialized countries, and that if the trend continues the effect will be catastrophic within two centuries.[3] Chapter 2 will go on to explain the theoretical core of this book, evolution by mutation and natural selection. Evolution is essential to life. Without mutation, there would be no diversity, and without selection over this diversity, no new structures can be formed or preserved. Selection means that some organisms succeed and others do not. Here again we'll see an aspect of the evolutionary balance, a mutual dependence of creation and destruction. I will state in this chapter the fundamental trilemma for the human population: if we rid ourselves of selection, we must choose either uncontrolled mutation or stagnation, and if we accept selection then we accept the Malthusian balance.

Also in Chapter 2, I discuss the idea of eugenics, that selection should be brought under the control of the government. I finish this discussion in **Chapter 3**, arguing that, rather than ridding us of selection, eugenics would merely shift the level of selection up to breeding programs themselves, short-circuiting the healthier, naturally evolved processes of love, marriage, and family. This chapter will argue, more generally, that humans cannot overcome the forces of Darwinian selection by *any* means, whether by using reason, science, or technology. The process of selection is not special to biological life, but applies with equal force—whether we like it or not—to ideas, knowledge, and culture. "Mutation" in human culture can mean the generation of new ideas, random or not; "selection" can mean the competition among these ideas, whether it takes place rationally, economically, or by violence; and strictly speaking, Darwinian evolution will still be occurring. Because some ideas reproduce themselves faster, and it takes physical resources to store them, the generation of new ideas will necessarily reach a creation-destruction balance just as the generation of new biological progeny does. This process can easily be seen in countless instances, including the struggles between Islam and the West, the competition among social theories, and the universal endeavor by writers and artists to become admired and emulated. Darwinian selection is a universal law, applying to any system that reproduces with heritable variations, including culture. We can no more overcome selection, I will argue, than we can break the laws of physics.

INTRODUCTION:
THE ARGUMENT ALL TOO BRIEFLY

A common objection to evolutionary arguments is that joy and suffering do not always correspond to reproduction or failure to reproduce. In **Chapter 4**, I will argue that, on the contrary, joy and suffering are essentially the mental sensations of evolutionary success and failure, whether of our genes or our ideas. When we succeed in spreading our genes or ideas, we feel pleasure. When our ability to survive or reproduce is diminished, we feel pain. The fact that modern technology allows us to trick our inborn perceptions of reality by using such things as contraception or psychoactive drugs only strengthens the force of this insight. In the long run, our perceptions of success and failure should track our actual evolutionary success and failure, because those whose perceptions are discordant are eliminated by selection. (An example of this process would be the extinction of the practice of infanticide in antiquity, a way to enjoy the pleasure of sex without having to raise the child.) The upshot is that the Malthusian balance between creation and destruction implies an overall balance between joy and suffering.

The view that natural selection applies strictly to humans is often derided as "Social Darwinism." It is criticized as being a heartless and brutal view of the human condition, pitting us all against each other in a perpetual struggle for dominance. In **Chapter 5**, I argue that a proper understanding of evolution shows that selfish behaviors have no special selective advantage over non-selfish behaviors. Charity, kindness, and benevolence can and do have evolutionary benefits. Biologists may disagree on what the mechanism is behind such evolution, but none seriously doubt that non-selfish behaviors can evolve by natural selection. Evolution shapes and enhances human compassion.

In **Chapter 6**, I'll attempt to anticipate where our current civilization is going, and how this should affect the way we live our lives. It appears that our exponential economic growth, coupled with fast-depleting non-renewable resources, will cause the decline or collapse of our industrial civilization within the next few centuries, if not decades. Even without resource limitations, this outcome would be inevitable due to the effects of cultural and biological mutation. Our population and its diversity have been growing rapidly for a couple of centuries, but a return to a creation-destruction equilibrium, as in the last dark ages and the nonindustrialized world, is inevitable, and we should aim for cultural achievements in science, philosophy, art, and religion, that will be able to stand the test of future dark ages and benefit generations less affluent than our own.

Chapter 7 will argue that our philosophy should focus less on ways to perpetuate modern unsustainable world civilization, and more on how we can improve as individuals, families, and local communities. Modern science is a good source of facts, but doesn't supply reliable, tested principles for living a successful life. Tradition and ancient wisdom—classic literature, sacred texts, and canonical philosophy—are the most reliable sources of truth, analogous to the oldest parts of our DNA, tested over centuries or millennia of natural selection on culture.[i]

---

[i] The **Appendices** provide more technical arguments that supplement the main argument of the book. If the reader is interested in whether the principles I state can be proven rigorously, they should consult the Appendices. Otherwise, they are inessential to my main conclusions. **Appendix 1** uses calculus to prove a rigorous version of Malthus's Principle, showing that even though populations may grow exponentially for brief periods, these periods will approach zero length with time, even for a civilization growing at the speed of light. **Appendix 2** demonstrates mathematically that some force of selection is needed to counter mutation. **Appendix 3** presents historical evidence, taken from secondary literature, that the evolution of technology is constrained by Darwinian selection. **Appendix 4** describes a series of computer simulations I ran showing that both selfishness and unselfishness can easily be favored by selection, depending on the details of the context, and that unselfish adaptations need not be directed exclusively toward genetic relatives.

I

MALTHUS'S PRINCIPLE, EXPLAINED AND EXPANDED

MISCONCEPTIONS ABOUT MALTHUS

Everyone is familiar with the idea of overpopulation, that human numbers are increasing exponentially, endangering our shared resources. Most likely a graph springs to mind, showing how the human population has exploded in the last few centuries, along with an absurd image of an overcrowded earth with too little room to stand. The name Malthus probably accompanies all this, and something about a prophetic essay he wrote two hundred years ago warning that humans were breeding too fast and would run out of food. The truth is, Malthus never used the term "overpopulation" in his *Essay on the Principle of Population*, nor did he prophesy that the human population would grow exponentially. He did not believe our resources were in danger, nor that we would all starve at some point in the future. He did not predict that the earth would become too crowded. In fact, he was not attempting to predict any future calamity at all.

If you take the time to read Reverend Malthus's *Essay*, you will see that his point was quite the opposite. According to Malthus, the human population cannot grow exponentially because limited food production will always keep it in check. He concluded that the population would never greatly exceed the ability of the land to support it. He believed that there would always be a balance between the joy of procreation and the suffering caused by hunger, and that this constant pressure of distress and sorrow was essential to human life, a force that tended to soften and humanize the heart, and lead the mind to greater heights. The concluding paragraph of the *Essay* summarizes his philosophy nicely:

> Evil exists in the world, not to create despair, but activity. We are not patiently to submit to it, but to exert ourselves to avoid it. It is not only the interest, but the duty of every individual, to use his utmost efforts to remove evil from himself; and from as large a circle as he can influence; and the more he exercises himself in this duty, the more wisely he directs his efforts, and the more successful these efforts are; the more he will probably improve and exalt his own mind, and the more completely does he appear to fulfill the will of his Creator.

Malthus attempted to start a philosophical dialogue on the place of suffering in human life, to challenge the worldview that was then forming, and that has now come to dominate: the belief that evil and suffering *can be* and *are being* gradually eliminated from the world. That is, the belief in *progress*.

THE BIRTH OF PROGRESS

The theory of progress arose in the 1700s, also known as "The Enlightenment," a period of social upheaval in the West. Monarchy ultimately gave way to democracy, feudalism to capitalism and socialism, fundamentalism to free thought, tradition to science. These transformations did not come without a price in violence. A Revolution in the Thirteen Colonies soon helped inspire the still more bloody Revolution in France, where the philosophical debate over utopia reached unprecedented heights of brutality.

The Marquis de Condorcet was a brilliant polymath whose radical notion of progress had made him many enemies. Living in exile, hiding from a death sentence pronounced by his political opponents (soon to be carried out), he penned perhaps the most influential argument for progress written so far, *Outlines of an Historical View of the Progress of the Human Mind*.

He wrote, somewhat prophetically, that "truths appertaining to the sciences of observation, calculation and experiment, may be perpetually augmented" so that "instruments, machines, looms, will add every day to the capabilities and skill of man" and "the same manufactured or artificial commodity will be produced at a smaller expense of raw materials." Steam engines and textile factories were already improving standards of living in England and France, and promised a brighter, more prosperous future.

But objections to progress based on population growth were already common currency. Condorcet addresses them briefly:

> [I]t may, I say, be demanded ... [w]hether the number of inhabitants in the universe at length exceeding the means of existence, there will not result a continual decay of happiness and population, and a progress towards barbarism, or at least a sort of oscillation between good and evil? Will not this oscillation, in societies arrived at this epoch, be a perennial source of periodical calamity and distress? In a word, do not these considerations point out the limit at which all farther improvement will become impossible, and consequently the perfectibility of man arrive at a period which in the immensity of ages it may attain, but which it can never pass?

Malthus would later take these doubts to heart. He would not be consoled reading Condorcet's two-sentence dismissal:

> There is, doubtless, no individual that does not perceive how very remote from us will be this period: but must it one day arrive? It is equally impossible to pronounce on either side respecting an event, which can only be realized at an epoch when the human species will necessarily have acquired a degree of knowledge, of which our short-sighted understandings can scarcely form an idea.

Few writers felt this "question of population" to be important enough to face directly. William Godwin called the debate "considerably curious." In his own book on the future social progress of Europe, *An Enquiry concerning Political Justice*, he wrote:

> Several writers upon these topics have treated it in a way calculated to produce a very gloomy impression, [but] [t]here is a principle in the nature of human society, by means of which everything seems to tend to its level. ... There are various methods by the practice of which population may be checked; by the exposing of children, as among the ancients, and, at this day, in China; by the art of procuring abortion, as it is said to subsist in the island of Ceylon; by a promiscuous intercourse of the sexes, which is found extremely hostile to the multiplication of the species; or, lastly, by a systematical abstinence, such as must be supposed, in some degree, to prevail in monasteries of either sex. But, without any express institution of this kind, the encouragement or discouragement that arises from the general state of a community, will probably be found to be all-powerful in its operation.

Like Condorcet, Godwin didn't find population doubts particularly troubling. He concluded his brief chapter on population by saying, "however ... to reason thus, is to foresee difficulties at a great distance."

As Malthus would come to see it, these "difficulties" were not remote at all, but ever present in all nations throughout history, for all animals, plants, and humans. He believed a mathematical principle, which he would call the Principle of Population, absolutely barred the way to progress and utopia.

MALTHUS'S PRINCIPLE

In Chapter 1 of his *Essay on the Principle of Population* (1798), Malthus laments: "The really good arguments on each side of the question are not allowed to have their proper weight. Each pursues his own theory, little solicitous to correct or improve it by an attention to what is advanced by his opponents." His goal was to finally put the question on solid ground:

> I think I may fairly make two postulata.
>   First, That food is necessary to the existence of man.
>   Secondly, That the passion between the sexes is necessary and will remain nearly in its present state.

Malthus chose these "postulata" or "assumptions" to be as simple and self-evident as possible. From the standpoint of physics, they do lack

MALTHUS'S PRINCIPLE, EXPLAINED AND EXPANDED

mathematical formulation. For example, "passion between the sexes" is not obviously a measurable quantity. But from what follows it becomes clear enough what he means, and his theories on population growth are still widely cited by biologists, sociologists, and other scientists:

> Population, when unchecked, increases in a geometrical ratio. Subsistence increases only in an arithmetical ratio. A slight acquaintance with numbers will shew the immensity of the first power in comparison of the second.
>
> By that law of our nature which makes food necessary to the life of man, the effects of these two unequal powers must be kept equal.
>
> This implies a strong and constantly operating check on population from the difficulty of subsistence. This difficulty must fall somewhere and must necessarily be severely felt by a large portion of mankind.

Population has a tendency to grow exponentially. If every couple has four children, for example, and this trend continues, you're doubling the population every generation. Exponential growth means your rate of increase *is itself increasing*. The more people you have the more people you add each generation. Two grows by two, four grows by four, eight grows by eight.

Food production, on the other hand, depends on the availability of land. The more land is used, the less land is available. At best, in Malthus's view, your food resources will grow "arithmetically," that is, by adding a constant value. Two grows by two, four grows by two, six grows by two.

Since population grows faster, Malthus's theory says that there will be a "strong and constantly operating check on population." A *check on population* may be defined as anything that may cause (1) death before old age, or (2) reduced fertility. How such a "check" occurs will depend on the details of the situation. It could be disease, violence, lack of food or shelter, lack of water, or lack of space. Malthus focuses his discussion on food, because limitations in food production alone are enough to prove that the population cannot grow indefinitely.

For Malthus, this dilemma determines whether you can create a utopian society without any misery. As long as the dilemma stands, progress toward utopia is unsustainable. He wrote, "All other arguments are of slight and subordinate consideration in comparison of this."

Malthus notes that population checks are seen throughout nature:

Through the animal and vegetable kingdoms, nature has scattered the seeds of life abroad with the most profuse and liberal hand. She has been comparatively sparing in the room and the nourishment necessary to rear them. The germs of existence contained in this spot of earth, with ample food, and ample room to expand in, would fill millions of worlds in the course of a few thousand years. Necessity, that imperious all pervading law of nature, restrains them within the prescribed bounds. The race of plants and the race of animals shrink under this great restrictive law. And the race of man cannot, by any efforts of reason, escape from it.

Many trees produce thousands of seeds at a time, and every garden plant produces several seeds, if not dozens or hundreds. Cats and dogs breed in litters. Every animal wild or domesticated, left to breed freely, will over time produce more than two offspring per mother. We know that if these populations were not checked by limitations on resources—such as food, water, and space—they would grow out of control. What we have, then, is a law that applies to all of animate nature, including humankind.

Malthus estimated that the human population, without any checks from famine or disease, would double every 25 years. That meant that no

Illustration 1: How population would grow if unchecked by food shortage, according to Malthus. (Hypothetical scenario.)

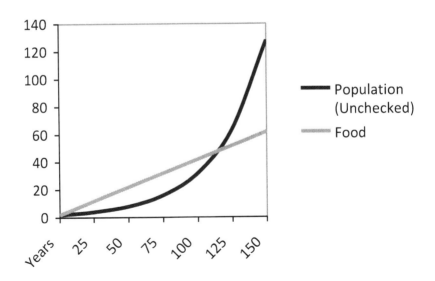

matter how fast your food supplies grew initially, eventually your doubling population would catch up.

NOT PROPHESY, PROOF BY CONTRADICTION

Malthus's argument may seem clear enough, but it is widely misunderstood. He introduced his principle to refute the idea of progress, to debunk "the perfectibility of man." But charts like *Illustration 1* have led to the popular belief that he was predicting a future calamity, where the population will become so great that everyone must starve. This "prophetic" reading has been encouraged by pseudo-Malthusian works with titles like *The Population Bomb* (Ehrlich, 1968), and over the last century his relevance to the question of progress has been largely forgotten. For instance, Nobel-prize-winning economist Amartya Sen (*Development as Freedom*, 1999) writes:

> Is the world food output falling behind world population in what is seen as a "race" between the two? The fear that this is precisely what is happening, or that it will soon happen, has had remarkable staying power despite relatively little evidence in its favor. Malthus, for example, anticipated two centuries ago that food production was losing the race and that terrible disasters would result from the consequent imbalance in "the proportion between the natural increase of population and food." He was quite convinced, in his late-eighteenth-century world, that "the period when the number of men surpass their means of subsistence has long since arrived."

Ironically, the latter quotation ("the period when ... long since arrived") is actually taken from a context where Malthus is arguing against Condorcet's tendency to treat population arguments as prophetic. Malthus writes (Sen's quotes shown in bold):

> Mr. Condorcet's picture of what may be expected to happen when the number of men shall surpass the means of their subsistence is justly drawn. The oscillation which he describes will certainly take place and will without doubt be a constantly subsisting cause of periodical misery. The only point in which I differ from Mr. Condorcet with regard to this

picture is the period when it may be applied to the human race. Mr. Condorcet thinks that it cannot possibly be applicable but at an era extremely distant. If **the proportion between the natural increase of population and food** which I have given be in any degree near the truth, it will appear, on the contrary, that **the period when the number of men surpass their means of subsistence has long since arrived**, and that this necessary oscillation, this constantly subsisting cause of periodical misery, has existed ever since we have had any histories of mankind, does exist at present, and will for ever continue to exist, unless some decided change take place in the physical constitution of our nature.

In other words, the human population is already subject to continual Malthusian checks, and has been throughout history. A graph better illustrative of his view would look like *Illustration 2*.

What, then, is the point of passages like this in Malthus's *Essay*:

[T]he human species would increase in the ratio of—1, 2, 4, 8, 16, 32, 64, 128, 256, 512, etc. and subsistence as—1, 2, 3, 4, 5, 6, 7, 8, 9, 10, etc. In two

Illustration 2: How population is checked by food shortage, according to Malthus. (Hypothetical scenario.)

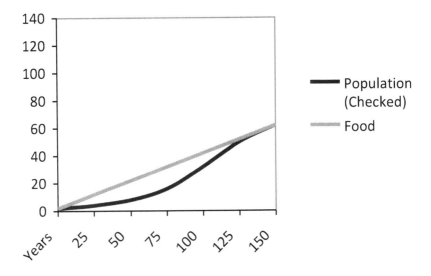

centuries and a quarter, the population would be to the means of subsistence as 512 to 10: in three centuries as 4096 to 13, and in two thousand years the difference would be almost incalculable.

What is being mistaken for a prophecy here, is really what logicians call a *reductio ad absurdum*, (Latin for "reduction to absurdity") against his opponents' view. He is saying that there *must* be checks of some sort operating on the human population, because if there were not there would already be far more people than you could feed. His conclusion to the above argument is that "the increase of the human species can only be kept commensurate to the increase of the means of subsistence by the constant operation of the strong law of necessity acting as a check." He's referring to existing poverty, hunger, disease, and vice—obstacles to survival and successful childrearing. He wasn't speaking of the increase of such things in the future, but rather their constant quantity throughout history up to the present, representing what is imperfect in humankind that cannot be eliminated.

Even today, we can't say that we've overcome this limitation. About 45 percent of deaths in children under five are caused by poor nutrition, and one in four of the world's children are stunted.[4] While people in industrialized countries enjoy widespread food security, most of the world's population lives in nonindustrialized countries that are vulnerable to famine. It is often argued that per-capita food production has never been higher, but modern food production and transportation is heavily dependent both on fossil fuels, which are nonrenewable, and the availability of arable land, which is shrinking faster than it can be replenished.

GENERALIZATION OF MALTHUS'S PRINCIPLE

The truth is, since the time of Malthus our population *has* grown exponentially. This has only been possible because his *postulum* that food resources grow linearly at best has proven false. There was nothing wrong with his mathematics, but his physical assumptions were faulty: our crop yields have grown exponentially—not linearly as he thought—due to new agricultural technology and more widespread land cultivation.

It would seem that *something* like Malthus's Principle is true. That a population could grow exponentially forever seems absurd. Even if food resources grew indefinitely (which is unlikely), you will eventually have to contend with lack of water, lack of space, lack of building materials, and so on. Exponential growth is fast, and there must be some way to show that it cannot go on and on.

Let's generalize Malthus's Principle of Population so that we can apply it with more confidence to scenarios involving dramatic increases in technology and resources.

Surprisingly few have attempted this. In *The Population Bomb* (1968), Ehrlich makes a rough-and-ready generalization of Malthus. Some were saying that space travel might alleviate population pressures. Ehrlich replied that "at the current growth rate, in a few thousand years everything in the visible universe would be converted into people, and the ball of people would be expanding with the speed of light!"

Let's make this idea more precise. It is true that we could never spread colonies through space faster than the speed of light. That means that the space we could have for this growth would be bounded by a sphere expanding at this speed. The volume of a sphere is proportional to the radius

Illustration 3: How population would be checked even if it could expand outward in three dimensions.

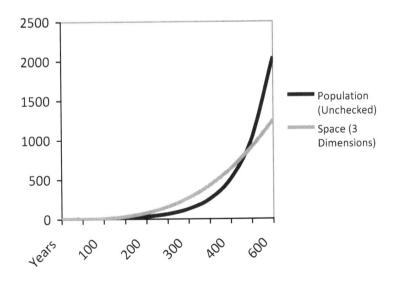

cubed. It is a mathematical fact that an exponential curve will always overtake even cubical growth. We cannot overcome Malthusian pressures even if we grow in three dimensions (see *Illustration 3*).

Exponential curves will overtake *any* polynomial curve—that is, any curve that grows like a power, x^2, x^3, x^4, etc.—whether it's squared, cubed, or to the power of four or more. That's because an exponential curve grows with a rate proportional to its size, which means that its rate of growth will grow faster as it grows, and even its acceleration will grow faster, etc. But polynomial growth does not compound in this way. (If there is any doubt in the reader's mind, know that for centuries mathematicians have been able to prove the faster growth of exponential curves rigorously using Calculus.)

Thus, we only need to make three *postulata*.

First, every human being takes up finite space.

Second, population grows exponentially if unchecked by birth control or pre-reproductive death.

Third, the speed of light cannot be exceeded. This is a principle of Einstein's Special Relativity, whose predictions have been confirmed exhaustively by experimental physicists.

From these three assumptions, it follows that there must be checks on a growing human population. As long as you cannot travel faster than the speed of light, the space you have available grows proportionally to the time cubed. And an exponential curve will always intersect such a curve, leading to constant checks on the population. These checks must occur the vast majority of the time, because exponential growth is fast. We may be experiencing exponential population growth now, but in the long run such spurts of growth must be rare and short-lived. Perhaps our current growth will last centuries. But however long it lasts, it will be small relative to how much time humanity spends at equilibrium. (For a detailed mathematical derivation, see Appendix 1.)

Do I actually believe that the human population will grow outward at the speed of light? Maybe someday we could come close. But the point of this argument is to present a *reductio ad absurdum* of the view that the population can grow indefinitely without any Malthusian population pressures. Any population experiencing continued growth will also necessarily experience misery and premature death. This is how populations are checked throughout nature, and in most human societies for most of history. Not even space travel can change this.

MALTHUSIAN PRESSURES ARE COMMON

We don't have to wait for interstellar travel to see the effects of Malthus's Principle. Amartya Sen argues that the total food production of the world is enough to feed everyone. But as he also points out, this food is unevenly distributed and most local populations on earth still suffer from hunger. In other words, Malthusian checks are already operating locally in most places. We frequently refer to these places as "the third world" as if they were the exception, but in terms of total population, wealthy countries without significant population checks are the exception.

Sen and others frequently claim that all we need to do to feed the world is to more widely distribute the food we already produce. True, such redistribution may provide a temporary respite, but as long as the world population is growing, production would eventually have to increase as well. And even if it did increase, we would still face shortages of water, space, and other resources. The question of distribution is ultimately irrelevant to the validity of Malthus's argument.

Historical evidence shows that almost all societies throughout history have been subject to population checks due to limited resources. The historian Gregory Clark found in his research that before 1900 the entire world was in what he calls "the Malthusian Trap." Birth rates averaged between five and eight, and income per person remained approximately constant since our prehistoric years. The invention of fire did not alleviate our population pressures, nor did the invention of the wheel, agriculture, or the plow. Compiling data from before 1790, Clark estimates that the average birth rate in Europe ranged from seven to eleven. The only thing that brought certain societies out of the Malthusian regime, according to Clark, was the rise of birth control during the nineteenth century.

Spoiled by fossil-fuel-driven prosperity, Westerners are used to saying things like, "Food *used to* be really expensive," or "Life was harder *in the past*." Too often it is forgotten that places like Africa have seen little improvement and in some ways have gotten worse. The popular picture of progress—that everywhere things have been getting better and better—ignores how things are across most of the globe, and forgets that most of our recent growth is unsustainable.

Western countries have birth rates from one to two children per woman. Native populations in places like the United States, Canada, England, and Germany are in fact shrinking. But this is relatively uncommon. Most third world countries have birth rates between two and seven per woman. Afghanistan, Kenya, India, Bolivia, Mongolia, and most other countries are still experiencing Malthusian pressures. Their populations are growing exponentially and are thus checked periodically by lack of food and water. These pressures are more intense in some countries than in others. Resources being equal, the higher the fertility rate the stronger the population checks.

Far from being a prophesy of future calamity or a theory of rare exceptions, Malthus's Principle applies to most societies throughout most of history, right up until today. Shortages of water, food, and natural resources cause poverty and suffering throughout the world, checking population growth. But somehow Malthus's original message was lost. Today it is taken merely as an argument for widespread birth control. We now think that there is something unnecessary about the ubiquity of struggle in human existence. But Malthus's original point was the opposite. He claimed that the world is not a test or "state of trial" that can be won or lost, but a process for forming the human soul:

> I should be inclined, therefore, as I have hinted before, to consider the world and this life as the mighty process of God, not for the trial, but for the creation and formation of mind, a process necessary to awaken inert, chaotic matter into spirit, to sublimate the dust of the earth into soul, to elicit an ethereal spark from the clod of clay.

His view verged on the evolutionary, and as we will see his principle was pivotal in the development of Darwin's theory. As Malthus saw it, it was struggle that not only produced mind but maintained it against decay:

> From all that experience has taught us concerning the structure of the human mind, if those stimulants to exertion which arise from the wants of the body were removed from the mass of mankind, we have much more reason to think that they would be sunk to the level of brutes, from

a deficiency of excitements, than that they would be raised to the rank of philosophers by the possession of leisure.

We will be in a better position to examine these claims once we have discussed, in Chapter 2, Darwin's theory of evolution and how it might be applied to the human condition.

SUMMARY AND PHILOSOPHICAL IMPLICATIONS

Most people understand Malthus's *Essay* as a prophecy of future calamity resulting from an exploding population. But Malthus himself warned against such a misreading. His argument was that there have always been, and will always be, limits to human population growth—such as famine and disease—that will lead to suffering. Since population growth is exponential, it will be continually checked by resource shortages. As a result, he argued, human society will never achieve perfection, and life is an unceasing struggle against evil.

Though Malthus's prediction that food supplies would not grow exponentially has proven false in the short run, in the long run there can be no doubt that Malthusian checks will continue to occur. Not even space travel can remove all checks, because space colonization, limited by the speed of light, cannot occur at an exponential rate. Whatever the future holds, at present most populations on earth are in fact growing exponentially and checked by limited supplies of food and water, vindicating Malthus's conclusion.

Like Malthus, I do not offer this analysis to show that there is a world crisis that needs to be solved. On the contrary, the analysis is supposed to show that there is no silver bullet that will solve all crises indefinitely. Resource limitations guarantee that all societies will experience periodic difficulties. In fact, suffering and crisis are ineliminable components of the human condition. Without them, there would ultimately be no impetus for people to adapt, struggle, feel, or think.

As I see it, Malthus discovered a deep philosophical principle. Evil is necessary to life, because it is only through the struggle to overcome it that we become fully human. It is absurd to suppose that the right political or economic system will one day eliminate all evil and struggle from every society in the world. This is not supposed to discourage us from doing good and charitable deeds, but encourage us to pursue them on a local scale. Between us and Malthus lie the twin catastrophes of Fascism and Communism. If Malthus's Principle was prophetic of anything, it was that progressive, utopian ideologies like these are fundamentally irrational.

II

DARWIN'S LAW

MALTHUS'S PRINCIPLE AND BIRTH CONTROL

Granted that all of nature and most societies have been subject to the Principle of Population, might it still not be possible to rationally convince the world to use birth control, and finally rid ourselves of this obstacle to progress? Aren't organizations like Planned Parenthood already trying to do this?

As urbanization continues across the globe, average fertility rates are falling. According to the UN, between 1950 and 1955 the total fertility rate (births per woman) was about 4.95. Between 2010 and 2015, it was 2.36. It is declining and it doesn't seem unreasonable, on the face of it, that this trend will continue and eventually free the world from the "Malthusian Trap."

I'd like to argue that this is an irrational hope.

Malthus originally assumed that the "passion between the sexes" could never be overcome. It is ubiquitous in nature. Every plant and animal species produces, on average, more offspring than can reproduce themselves. This is no surprise on Darwin's theory of natural selection.

Other factors being equal, populations that reproduce more rapidly will always come to predominate.

Creative evolution requires mutation as well as natural selection. Mutations add diversity to the gene pool. Natural selection whittles down this diversity to what is best adapted. Without natural selection, mutation leads to uncontrolled variation. Without mutation, a species has no adaptability.

Many see natural selection's way of doing things as unnecessarily cruel. In order for it to work, most offspring must fail to reproduce. In the modern Western world, we try to challenge this perceived cruelty by reducing the number of births. Birth control, it is believed, is simply a rational way to reduce overall pain and suffering. Many scientific authors like to say that we've *overcome* Darwinian evolution. "If each family had only two children," writes biologist Cavalli-Sforza triumphantly, "there would be no natural selection."[5] Richard Dawkins writes in *The Selfish Gene* (1976): "We are built as gene machines and cultured as meme machines, but we have the power to turn against our creators. We, alone on Earth can rebel against the tyranny of the selfish replicators." Steve Jones, in *The Language of Genes* (1995) writes: "It may even be that economic advance and medical progress mean that humans are almost at the end of their evolutionary road, that we are as near to our biological Utopia as we are ever likely to get."

The reality is that most of humankind is still subject to natural selection. Most ethnicities have fertility rates above two. In fact most preindustrial cultures explicitly discourage birth control.[6] During the period 2000-2005, there were 33 nations (totaling 720 million inhabitants) with average birth rates of at least 5 children per female, 17 nations (totaling 240 million people) with average birth rates of at least 6, and 3 nations (totaling 45 million people) with birth rates of at least 7. These birth rates are comparable to those in the preindustrial West. These nations are growing significantly faster than the rest of the world, with annual growth rates between 2 and 4.5 percent, compared to the world average of 1.17 percent. Even within the United States, there are religious groups, such as the Amish, who oppose birth control on principled grounds and thus have a consistently higher fertility than the rest of the country.

At the same time, many industrial countries have birth rates below replacement levels, so that their populations are in fact declining at exponential rates. Countries with fertility rates below 1.5 children per female include China, Japan, South Korea, Lithuania, Ukraine, Spain, Italy, Hungary, and Austria. In fact, the European Union as a whole has an average fertility rate of about 1.50. Assuming that children tend to adopt the birth control practices of their parents, it appears that natural selection will eventually lead to the elimination of those cultures that use birth control.

The tendency of humans and animals to reproduce exponentially is the result of evolution. Instincts that favor reproduction are needed for a species to continue to spread, diversify, and adapt. In this chapter we'll explore Darwin's theory in more detail and formulate it as a strict law of nature that mandates a balance between creativity and destruction. We'll see how it follows from such a law that neither progress nor regress is possible in the long run, whether we are talking about plants, animals, or human civilization.

EVOLUTION AND BIRTH CONTROL

Many express the hope that by industrializing and educating other nations we may eventually reduce the average fertility rate to two. It usually isn't mentioned that every society in the entire world would have to consent to this. If only one society of, say, a million people retained a birth rate of three children per family, this society could number in the billions within four centuries. If the Amish maintain their current rate of population growth, German-speakers will outnumber English-speakers in North America within two hundred years. This is natural selection at work. The same explanation may account for the disappearance of Pagans and Gnostics who used abortion and infanticide as means of family planning in late Antiquity, and the spread of early Christians who discouraged these practices.[7]

However, I'm not sure you can *prove* that birth rates can't be lowered to replacement levels in every society worldwide. It is conceivable that a world government might be put in place that sterilizes all women after two children, for example. Rest assured if that happened you could count me among the freedom fighters. But to gain a better understanding of the principles of evolution, let's assume for the sake of argument that birth rates have been reduced to two everywhere and indefinitely.

In such a scenario you still have a hitch: inheritance is not perfect. When DNA is copied, there are sometimes mistakes. It is estimated that about 400 mutations occur between each generation of human. Most of these mutations don't make any difference. A few are harmful, and a very rare few are beneficial. It is much more common for mutations to have detrimental effects than beneficial ones.

In nature, harmful mutations are eliminated by natural selection. The more frequent the mutations, the stronger the force of selection must be (as I argue mathematically in Appendix 2). And a stronger force of selection requires that some individuals have a correspondingly higher rate of reproduction. In a world where everyone survives to adulthood and has two children, there is no natural selection. Everyone would reproduce at the same rate, so there would be no differences in fitness. New mutations would arise, but they would give no one any advantage or disadvantage. Instead, every generation would accumulate more random mutations and pass them on.

Mutations are more often harmful than helpful for the same reason that cars tend to run worse, and not better, as they get older. Random changes to any structure will tend toward disorder.

There is a much-abused principle from physics called "The Second Law of Thermodynamics." It states that in a closed system, the total disorder—"entropy" is the precise term—tends to increase over time. This law is based on statistical reasoning: carefully place a few dozen dice in a box, sixes up, shake the box, and you'll quickly lose the sixes to a random mixture of numbers. Spell out a message in Scrabble letters and shake it up, and you'll lose the message. DNA is the same way. Random mutations will tend to disorder its message.

But we shouldn't be hasty in drawing conclusions from this law. Scientists hesitate to apply the Second Law to biological organisms because they are not closed systems but "open systems" that can trade entropy with other systems. Plants, for instance, are constantly taking ordered energy from the sun to maintain their structures. Consuming ordered energy is how all species resist the increase of entropy. In the case of DNA, Darwinian selection is the source of order. Most harmful mutations are eliminated by selection, and beneficial mutations are often preserved by it.

To put it concisely, mutation is a source of entropy or disorder in DNA, and it is only by selection that this disorder is suppressed.

As we know from Malthus's Principle, most plants and animals produce many more offspring than can survive to adulthood and reproduce. In this way mutation and natural selection keep each other in check. Mutation provides new variety, natural selection eliminates unfit varieties.

Birth control, we may conclude, would appear to disrupt the balance between mutation and natural selection. That this might be so has been feared for over a century. A shallow understanding of these principles of evolution, however, led to the infamous eugenics movement. Before we look at the history of that movement, let's get clearer on what the basic principles of Darwinian evolution are.

DARWIN'S QUESTION

Along with social upheavals, the eighteenth-century Enlightenment created tremendous scientific upheavals. As Europe became wealthy on transoceanic trade, specimens of plants, animals, and minerals were brought back from around the world, overthrowing previous theories in geology and biology. Scientists began to speculate that the world was at least millions of years old, that species might have changed over these vast periods of time, and that different species might have even descended from a common ancestor.

The question of the origin of species was divisive. On the one hand you had Biblical history, in which each species was specially created a few thousand years ago. All had to fit on a wooden ark to survive the flood. On the other hand you had views like those of Lamarck, who argued that when any animal used an organ or limb, it would become enlarged, and that if it did not use it, it would shrink and eventually disappear. In this way he supposed that every species had evolved toward greater and greater complexity over millions of years. Neither view seemed satisfactory. The Biblical view didn't accord with the evidence, and Lamarck's "use and disuse" could only explain size—not things like shape, color, or instinct.

In the mid-nineteenth century, under the influence of Malthus's *Essay*, a new theory began to emerge. Young Darwin, as he voyaged from continent to continent as the naturalist on board the *Beagle*, had made special note of how species were distributed across the globe. For instance, finches on the Galapagos Islands were partially adapted for niches usually filled by other species in other places. In fact, the Galapagos had almost no birds besides finches. There were insect-eating finches, nut-eating finches, cactus-eating finches, and several other kinds, each with specially adapted beaks, feathers, and colorings. If a creator had placed these birds here, why only finches? Why not use better-adapted varieties seen elsewhere? Evolution seemed a simpler explanation. Finches were more common on the mainland of South America. If they had migrated to the Galapagos it would explain why there were only finches there, who had adapted to local conditions and now came in so many unusual varieties.

From this observation and several others, Darwin began to speculate on evolution. Taxonomy and comparative anatomy also provided good evidence that most or all species had evolved from a common ancestor. "What can be more curious," he wrote, "than that the hand of a man, formed for grasping, that of a mole for digging, the leg of a horse, the paddle of a porpoise, and the wing of a bat, should all be constructed on the same pattern, and should include the same bones, in the same relative positions?" The big question was how this evolution had happened. What process had allowed species to change and adapt so meticulously over time? Geologists had been able to explain dramatic geological change through the action of wind, waves, and dust over millions of years. But biology was missing a theory of how complex adaptations arose. Use and disuse didn't explain much. Why would using an organ make it grow larger rather than smaller? How had a device as complex and intricate as the eye arose by the chance influence of the environment?

THE INFLUENCE OF MALTHUS ON DARWIN

Prior to his reading of Malthus, Darwin "perceived that selection was the keystone of man's success in making useful races of animals and plants. But how selection could be applied to organisms living in a state of nature remained for some time a mystery" (*Autobiography*, 1887). Animal breeding by humans had succeeded in creating animals as different as dachshunds and Great Danes from a single common ancestor. Could there be a similar process by which nature built up new varieties? But how could the random processes of blind nature compare with careful selection by animal breeders?

In his *Autobiography*, Darwin explains his breakthrough reading Malthus:

> In October 1838, that is, fifteen months after I had begun my systematic enquiry, I happened to read for amusement Malthus on *Population*, and being well prepared to appreciate the struggle for existence which everywhere goes on from long-continued observation of the habits of animals and plants, it at once struck me that under these circumstances favourable variations would tend to be preserved, and unfavourable ones to be destroyed. The result of this would be the formation of new species. Here then I had at last got a theory by which to work; but I was so anxious to avoid prejudice, that I determined not for some time to write even the briefest sketch of it.

He called this process by which favorable variations were preserved *natural selection*, by analogy with the process of artificial selection that humans use to make new breeds of animals and plants.

Because all animal and plant populations grow exponentially, they are subject to constant pressures from lack of resources. These pressures cause the less well-adapted to die or have fewer offspring than others. If a certain plant produces a hundred seeds, on average only one can grow to maturity to produce its own seeds, and this one will tend to be better-adapted. In this way, the better-adapted survive and pass on their traits.

But Darwin knew that natural selection alone could not account for evolution. Selection was a purely destructive force. It did not create new varieties but only destroyed the ones that were less well-adapted. In order for natural selection to produce new species, it needed a constant supply of new variations to work on. And these variations had to be heritable, or they could not lead to permanent change in the species.

Today we know that heritable traits are coded in DNA. Mutations in DNA create new variations, providing raw material for natural selection. In Darwin's day, the mechanisms of inheritance were obscure. He devoted several chapters of the *Origin of Species* to arguing, using evidence from animal breeding and natural history, that heritable variation was common throughout the plant and animal kingdoms, even if its details were still unknown. This is important to remember, because it will come into play later in our argument: Darwin's theory says nothing about how traits are inherited. It does not require DNA. And this is why, as we will discuss in Chapter 3, the theory of evolution by natural selection applies with equal force to culture and technology, though they are coded in brains and not DNA. Darwin's theory applies whatever the system of inheritance.

DARWIN'S THEORY IN A NUTSHELL

Biologists have since refined Darwin's theory to a set of three conditions, known as Lewontin's Criteria. They are based on a mathematical formalization of Darwin's theory by Mary Williams published in 1970. In the same year, the biologist Richard Lewontin published a paper, "The Units of Selection," in which he points out that natural selection is guaranteed to occur in any population which satisfies the following three criteria:

1. Different individuals in a population have different mental and physical traits ("Variation").
2. This variation is heritable ("Heritability").
3. Different variants have different rates of survival and reproduction ("Differential Fitness").

It is widely recognized among biologists that all systems which satisfy these conditions undergo natural selection.

Variation is also referred to as diversity. If all the individuals in a population have the same traits, there can be no evolution. Natural selection only works on differences.

Heritability just means that traits are passed from one generation to the next. If the traits aren't passed down, then new variations will be lost.

Differential fitness refers to the fact that some traits will spread more quickly than others. *Fitness* is a biological term meaning expected number of offspring an organism with the trait will have over its lifetime. Among humans, if the average for a trait is two children, that will be fitness one, because children are shared with one other parent. If the average is four children, that's fitness two. An average of one child means fitness of one-half. Traits with a fitness above one will quickly spread and come to predominate. Traits with a fitness below one will quickly disappear.

From here on out I will refer to this principle—that Lewontin's conditions imply natural selection—as "Darwin's Law."

When these three conditions hold over a period of time, you get evolution by natural selection. Certain variants will disappear, and others will become widespread. What keeps evolution going in the real world is the appearance of new variations, which we call "mutation." In fact one can combine these conditions and state a single condition for evolution:

Evolution occurs when heritable variations (mutations) arise that make a difference to how many offspring are produced.

This is Darwin's entire theory of evolution in a nutshell.

Say you've got a mutation that causes a certain organism to produce slightly more offspring. If this mutation is passed down, then its offspring will also have more offspring. The spread of this variant will thus be exponential. Since there are limited resources, by Malthus's Principle, other variants will decrease in the population until they disappear.

Ultimately, Darwin's theory explains the mystery of why every species tends to reproduce at an exponential rate.

Armed with this theory, we can now introduce the fundamental trilemma for human populations. The next several chapters will be devoted to arguing that we cannot escape this trilemma. Option (1) is to rid the human population of selection. But without selection our DNA would eventually decay by mutation. Option (2) is to rid ourselves of both selection and mutation. But this would mean stagnation – no evolutionary change, no ability to adapt. Option (3) is to accept the Malthusian balance, including both mutation and a high-enough fertility rate for natural selection to balance it.

A NOTE ON THE TERMINOLOGY OF "SELECTION" AND "MUTATION"

Differential fitness is commonly referred to as "selection" by biologists, and I will use the same term here. Originally, Darwin drew a sharp distinction between *natural* and *artificial* selection, because his challenge was to argue that species could evolve without the intervention of a higher being. It was well known that animal breeding—"artificial selection"—could produce from the same species animals as different as St. Bernards and Terriers. Darwin had to show that this process was possible in the wild, and he called this "natural selection."

In this book, we are discussing selection among humans. When the distinction between natural and artificial selection is unnecessary, I will simply use the term "selection," which refers to either kind. "Natural selection," as with animals, will refer to selection due to untimely death, individual mate choice, or difficulty reproducing. However, to maintain continuity with past literature on human evolution, artificial selection of humans will be referred to as "eugenics." This term will be used for any scenario where mate choice or family size are deliberately restricted by law or decree.

The term "mutation" also carries some ambiguities that will need to be cleared up before we proceed. Biological mutations, as we must define them, come in four major types. On the smallest scale, you have the *substitution* of one base for another, the *insertion* of extra base pairs, and the *deletion* of base pairs. The fourth major type we need to consider occurs on a larger scale. *Recombination* happens during sexual reproduction and involves the cutting and splicing of entire chromosomes. Because it does not introduce or eliminate base pairs, it is not always classed as a kind of mutation. But since it does introduce novel *combinations* of genes, it must be counted as a source of new variations, and thus counts as a kind of mutation for the purposes of our discussion.

EUGENICS AS TYRANNY

Eugenics was a widespread social movement responsible for the sterilization of millions in the early- to mid-twentieth century, and was used by the Nazis to justify the murder of millions. There are still eugenic societies around the world, though most have been forced to keep a low profile in the wake of the atrocities of World War II.

Let me clarify my personal views before we go any further. I am not a eugenicist in any sense of the word. Eugenics is based on the idea that humankind as a whole can be improved or degraded. I don't believe either is possible. Freedom, family, and universal love are held as sacred values by all religions. In order for these to be possible, each individual must be valued as the incomprehensibly complex, creative, and spiritual being that he or she is. Any and all state-run programs that seek to control human reproduction—one of the highest expressions of human love and creativity, the bringing into the universe of a new incomprehensible being—are intrinsically evil and should be opposed. This includes any program that impedes a human's right to reproduce, whether for the purpose of limiting the world population, or for the purpose of "improving" its genetic stock. Both of these goals have been integral tenants of the eugenics movement.

The origin of the most influential eugenic theories lay in the late nineteenth century, before the mechanisms of heredity were well understood. Francis Galton, a statistician and sociologist, worried that the poor were outbreeding the "gifted" in his influential book *Hereditary Genius* (1887). Karl Pearson, another statistician, agreed that we needed to "check the fertility of the inferior stocks" (*The Grammar of Science,* 1892).

Reactions varied. Many put up stalwart resistance. In his 1893 essay "Evolution and Ethics," T.H. Huxley, an ardent supporter of Darwin's theory, condemned the idea of eugenics because it failed to take into account both its impracticality and the immoral effects it would have on society. Arguing for its impracticality he wrote:

> I doubt whether even the keenest judge of character, if he had before him a hundred boys and girls under fourteen, could pick out, with the least chance of success, those who should be kept, as certain to be serviceable members of the polity, and those who should be chloroformed, as equally sure to be stupid, idle, or vicious. The "points" of a good or of a bad citizen are really far harder to discern than those of a puppy or short-horn calf; many do not show themselves before the practical difficulties of life stimulate manhood to full exertion.

And against its morality he argued that it would require "preternatural ruthlessness" and "drastic thoroughness" and that "human society is kept together by bonds of such a singular character, that the attempts to perfect society after [the animal breeder's] fashion would run serious risk of loosening them."

But the movement only grew in strength. In 1922, the social critic G.K. Chesterton was moved to publish a lengthy and brilliant—if somewhat unscientific—refutation of eugenics entitled "Eugenics and other Evils." He argued that love is personal and should not be regulated by the state. He called any such regulation "tyrannical" and rhetorically asked *to whom* "such risks of tyranny could be trusted." He pointed out, quite rightly, that the "complexity [of heredity] must be nearly unfathomable ..."

But the heavy mathematical artillery, as it unfortunately happened, fell into the lap of eugenics. Mathematicians J.B.S. Haldane and R.A. Fisher—who were skeptical of eugenics—were the first to develop a mathematics describing natural selection among discrete (Mendelian) genes. They finally developed one model covering processes of both natural selection and mutation, an important step in filling in the gaps in Darwin's theory of inheritance. But the most influential mathematical biologist was the eugenicist Julian Huxley, who wove together Fisher and Haldane's theories, field biology, social anthropology, statistics, and genetics into his masterwork, *Evolution: The Modern Synthesis* in 1942. Huxley was vice president of the British Eugenics Society from 1937-1944 and President from 1959-1962. He encouraged many of the mass sterilizations that happened throughout Europe and North America during this time.

After World War II eugenics became associated with Nazism, so Huxley coined the term "Transhumanism" for it in his 1957 essay of the same name, and the society changed its name to the Galton Institute in 1989.

In 1964, Huxley published *Evolutionary Humanism*, which argued:

> To effect [future improvements of our species we] must first of all check the processes making for genetic deterioration. This means reducing man-made radiation to a minimum, discouraging genetically defective or inferior types from breeding, reducing human overmultiplication in general and the high differential fertility of various regions, nations, and classes in particular. Then [we] can proceed to the much more important task of positive improvement.

Nevertheless, eugenics continued to decline in the wake of the horrors of Nazism, though few attempts at scientific, quantitative refutation were attempted. Stephen Jay Gould's *Mismeasure of Man* (1981) did challenge the use of IQ testing that the eugenic program depended on. Gould argued that people were attempting to reify a concept that had no objective basis, and that rank-ordering complex things like intelligence was inherently nonsensical. Political tracts such as *Not in Our Genes* (1984) by R.C.

Lewontin, Steven Rose, and Leon J. Kamin offered woefully indecisive objections that nevertheless few dared to publicly question:

> We reject [the nature-nurture] dichotomy. We do assert that we cannot think of any significant human social behavior that is built into our genes in such a way that it cannot be modified and shaped by social conditioning.... Yet, at the same time, we deny that human beings are born *tabulae rasae* ..."

Despite the lack of rigorous analysis, the view that heredity is irrelevant to discussions of the human population has become the public consensus among scientists. This consensus has made itself plain by the indignant reactions to Herrstein and Murray's 1994 book *The Bell Curve*, which presented evidence that IQ was heritable, differed among races, and had a measurable effect on future income.

The debate over IQ measurements and race is ultimately what logicians call a *red herring*, a distraction from what was originally at stake. What of the eugenicists' original concern, namely, that modern Western society lacks natural selection to check mutation? The fear of raising further outcries has discouraged critical discussion. As far as I can tell no reasoned consensus about human evolution has been reached.

CAN MUTATION BE "OVERCOME"?

Let's return to Julian Huxley's original question, which was whether humanity can reach utopia when our DNA is constantly mutating in ways that are usually harmful. Huxley believed that we must control our population to avoid running out of food. At the same time, he saw that birth control would weaken the force of natural selection, which was why he wanted a program of eugenics to eliminate harmful mutations from the human gene pool.

A few subsequent authors seconded this proposal. In his 1978, Pulitzer-prize-winning *On Human Nature*, biologist E.O. Wilson brought up the apparent problem of human mutation and said that eventually we will have the knowledge to put in place a "democratically contrived eugenics" to counteract it.

Harvard biologist Stephen Jay Gould made a spirited attempt to challenge this assumption in his posthumous tome *The Structure of Evolutionary Theory*:

> This situation supposedly raises a forest of ethical questions about double-edged swords in the cure of diseases arising from genetic predisposition, the spread of genes for poor vision in a world of cheap eyeglasses, *et cetera ad infinitum*. (Pardon my cynicism based on some knowledge of the history of such arguments, but the neo-eugenical implications of these claims, however unintended in modern versions, cannot be ignored or regarded as just benignly foolish.)
>
> ...
>
> This entire line of fallacious reasoning, with all its burgeoning implications, immediately collapses under a speciational reformulation. Once people understand *Homo sapiens* as a biological species, not a transitory point of achievement, the apparent paradox disappears ... Most species—especially those with large, successful, highly mobile, globally spread, environmentally diverse, and effective panmictic populations—remain stable throughout their history .... Change occurs by punctuational speciation of isolated subgroups, not by geologically slow anagenetic transformation of an entirety.

Gould is referring to a theory in evolutionary biology that large populations do not show very much evolutionary change. But many population biologists argue that this theory neglects the greater flux of new mutations that a large population can select from.[8] And in any case Gould's objection does not apply to the case of humans using birth control. There are no examples of any species aside from humans that are not continually subject to natural selection. For a species to remain "stable" as Gould puts it, natural selection must act continually to counter mutation, as all elementary textbooks in population biology teach. (For a simple mathematical argument, see Appendix 2).

In fact, recent scientific studies on mutation show that reduced selection in industrialized societies is causing a cumulative fitness reduction that will become serious within two centuries.[9] While humans have a higher mutation rate than any other well-studied species, many human populations today have a much lower rate of natural selection than what traditional societies and other species typically experience. We are getting more mutations and there is less selection to prune them. The above-mentioned studies have attempted to measure the detrimental effects of mutation in humans and animals, and the consensus is that the human mutation rate produces a 1-5 percent fitness reduction per generation in industrialized societies.[10] This may not sound like much, but in the span of 200 years, or eight generations, this would mean a fitness reduction of 5-34 percent due to genetic diseases and other heritable deficiencies.

So Julian Huxley and E.O. Wilson are correct to point out that mutation is harmful when unchecked by selection, as it is for the most part in our society. Are they and the rest of the eugenicists then in the right? Are we bound to control human mutation lest it spiral out of control?

Nonsense. Once again we're forgetting about the "third world." In reality, it follows from Darwin's Law that more traditional populations with higher birth rates will come to predominate by natural selection, as they have in the past.

So far in this book we've shown that the only conceivable path to progress is to reduce average fertility to two, and somehow—whether by eugenics or genetic engineering—counteract genetic decay by mutation. This would mean either universal eugenics, or genetically engineering every new baby on the planet. In the next chapter we will discuss some evolutionary reasons to think that no social or genetic engineering, nor any kind of new technology or social system, can achieve progress, even hypothetically. I will argue that human culture is subject to the same Darwinian and Malthusian forces as human biology.

SUMMARY AND PHILOSOPHICAL IMPLICATIONS

Natural selection is currently favoring all those societies—most of them nonindustrialized—that are having large families and growing exponentially. Even if we could force everyone in the world to use birth control we would leave them prone to genetic deterioration by mutation, a consequence that is already happening in industrialized nations.

Darwin's theory emerged as an extension of Malthus's, showing that exponential growth is the basis of natural selection, the force that checks mutation in nature and works raw diversity into exquisitely adaptive structures. Seeing that humans were at risk without some form of selection, the eugenicists of the early twentieth century encouraged state-run programs to sterilize or kill people they deemed "unfit" for reproduction. As a result, the eugenics movement has been rightly villainized and marginalized. But there is a continued absence of any decisive scientific refutation of their original concern.

In fact, the evidence appears to vindicate their theory that continued mutation in the absence of natural selection leads to genetic deterioration. Nevertheless, most societies on earth are still reproducing at an exponential rate. Natural selection is ongoing, so the eugenicist fear is ultimately unrealistic. Humans, it appears, will continue to be subject both to mutation and natural selection.

Where does this leave us? Is humanity hopeless? Quite the contrary. We are back to Malthus's original conclusion. You cannot completely eliminate suffering and evil from life. Mutation carries with it both good and bad. It is the source of new talent, new genius, and new diversity among humans. To rid ourselves of mutation would be to rid ourselves of what is unique and creative about individuals. And in our universe there is no free lunch. The benefit of mutation comes at a price. Many mutations are bad and lead to vice and incompetence. Part of what makes humankind beautiful is that the good and evil in us are fast intertwined.

III

CULTURAL EVOLUTION

BIOLOGY VERSUS CULTURE

So far our discussion has focused on the *biological* evolution of humans. Is it any surprise then, you might ask, that progress appears to be impossible? If we limit ourselves only to the evolutionary resources at the disposal of every plant and animal, namely DNA replication, mutation, and natural selection, why shouldn't we expect the same Malthusian fate as the rest of nature? But what about our ability to pass down traditions from brain to brain via speech, books, and imitation? We can't do much to improve our DNA, maybe, but aren't we free to ruminate, discard, adopt, and refine when it comes to culture?

Or could it be that *anything* that evolves must do so through mutation and selection, including culture and technology? I want to argue that this is true. Relying on our culture alone for adaptability will run into the same "problems" (I'd prefer the term *realities*) as relying on biological evolution. Under the heading of culture I mean to include technology, science, and all human ideas and artifacts—anything that humans pass down from generation to generation that is not in our DNA. In this chapter I will expand on the idea that culture is subject to natural selection. In brief, Lewontin's criteria apply to culture and thus culture is constrained by

Darwin's Law as strictly as biology. All self-replicating systems, in fact, are subject to both Darwin's Law and Malthusian resource limitations. Ultimately, this principle will provide us with a general theory to describe the fundamental logical inconsistency in the notion of progress.

PROTOTYPING HUMANS?

Transhumanists and other neo-eugenicists argue that human DNA could simply be engineered like any other technology, and thus could continue to change and evolve without having to worry about mutation and selection. Such fantasies are farfetched on close inspection. The human genome is incredibly complex, and it isn't clear that anyone could understand the human genome well enough to alter it at will without error. We are nowhere near being able to predict the fitness of all new mutations or alterations in a human genome. Most machines that we make, including computers and cars, are far less complex than the human body, but when we are designing new versions, it is always necessary to build prototypes and test them to see if they will work. Invariably they do not work except after a lot of testing and redesigning. It seems that nothing like this would be ethical for humans. We would obviously not want to raise an entire human being as a "prototype" to be destroyed if he or she does not function properly.

As a matter of fact, it is almost never possible to calculate the functionality of a new technology before it is built and implemented, not with full certainty. Any engineer will tell you this. Human invention, it would appear, depends on selection as essentially as biological evolution does.

CULTURE IS SUBJECT TO DARWIN'S LAW

I'd like to put this forward as a principle: All of human culture is essentially subject to Darwin's Law.

Let's see why this principle is tautological by looking at what we mean by *culture*.

To start with, anything that is the same among all societies and all individuals would not be considered culture. It would be considered, rather, "basic human nature." Culture is part of what makes societies different. Thus, culture always shows *variation*.

Culture can be passed down. If it couldn't, once again, it wouldn't be culture. The word "culture" has the same root as the Latin word for farming, and refers to the raising of a new generation. To be "cultured" is to receive these traits from the previous generation. Anything that is not gained from other humans is not called culture, but experience. So cultural variation shows *heritability*.

Some ideas are better than others. I regret to say that it is impossible to disagree with me on this point. Because if you disagree, you hold your view to be better than mine—as one should expect. The same reasoning holds for all elements of culture. If they were not liable to judgment—a kind of selection—then we would not care to discuss them. We would not care to pass any culture down to our children if we did not think it worthy. And "worthiness" is a selective measure, even if you only mean that your idea is better than no idea. It is inconceivable then that some ideas and some teachings would not be better at spreading themselves than others. Like biological organisms, cultures tend to reproduce themselves as fast as they can, because the ones that do not tend to die away. Authors, scientists, religious leaders, and artists are all constantly striving to show that their ideas are worth having. And some do this better than others, so you have *differential fitness*.

Culture satisfies Lewontin's criteria: *variation*, *heritability*, and *differential fitness*. It is selected, whether naturally or artificially. People have different ideas, and we take it for granted that some are better than others. Some ideas proliferate, some do not, whether you're talking about technology, beliefs, or fashions.

Do Malthusian resource constraints apply to culture? Of course they do. Just as for biological evolution, selection leads to exponential proliferation whenever there are enough resources. Ideas that are taught only to one's children have the same rate of proliferation as biological replication—which is exponential. Ideas that are also passed to peers spread even more quickly—still at an exponential rate.

Ideas require brains, and brains require bodies, which suffer all the population constraints we've already discussed. What if we went completely digital and uploaded ourselves onto computers, hoping that we could proliferate our ideas without any worry of competition? It would make no difference. Computers take space and energy as well. Even a civilization of computers alone would eventually reach the thermodynamic limit of how much information can be stored using a given amount of energy.[11] At that point it could only expand outward at the speed of light, which as we've discussed would be slower than exponential growth.

What about faster-than-light travel? With so much at stake for progress, it might seem like a worthy project. Some physicists do believe that it is possible. But even if it were somehow achievable, I'm not sure that faster-than-light travel would resolve the heart of the self-contradiction in progress. If your hope is to jettison all new ideas into space at faster-than-light speed, you're asking for a scenario without selection. And as we've just discussed, it doesn't seem possible to have what we call "culture" without some kind of differential fitness among ideas.

In any case, we don't have to wait for interstellar travel to see Malthusian limitations in full effect. Agricultural methods *would* spread exponentially, but their growth is already limited by the supply of land. Novels, too, already compete for a limited supply of readers. Scientific theories compete for a limited supply of people who care enough to learn them. Religions compete for a limited supply of converts. Hard disk space is growing fast, but even then, it is not easy or common for a new indie computer game to get widespread downloads.

And this all implies an ongoing balance between proliferation and defeat, creation and destruction, joy and suffering.

Since it's been so neglected, cultural evolution may sound like a revolutionary concept. But that's not actually my point. I'm not saying it overthrows our current conception of the world at all. It doesn't by a long shot. It's merely another way to look at it. The only thing I mean to overthrow, ultimately, is the inane conception of some future worldwide state of bliss. Bliss will probably continue to occur, but just as it always has—balanced by its opposite.

THE HALF-HEARTED DEBATE OVER CULTURAL EVOLUTION

That *all* of human culture, without exception, is subject to the principles of Malthus and Darwin is not a new contention, though the history of the debate is far less riveting than the history of Malthusianism or Darwinism. In the 1960s the psychology professor Donald Campbell proposed a kind of universal Darwinism that would apply to all human knowledge:

> A blind-variation-and-selective-retention process is fundamental to ... all genuine increases in knowledge, to all increases in fit of system to environment.[12]

The obvious retort here was, what if I see a comet in a telescope and calculate its trajectory? What if I notice storm clouds on the horizon? What if I feel a cold wind? In all these cases we are getting knowledge, and it's not clear where the blindness comes in. Campbell's answer was that telescopes, mathematics, eyes, and nerves all themselves originate by evolution. In his words, "The many processes which shortcut a more full blind-variation-and-selective-retention process [contain] wisdom about the environment achieved originally by blind variation and selective retention." But Campbell wasn't very adamant about applying his theory to processes outside of scientific practice, and he didn't do much to develop it outside of a psychological context. His question was "Where does science come from?" and he wasn't too concerned about progress, Malthusian pressures, or the fate of civilization.

Karl Popper would, more famously, promote a similar idea about the generation of scientific theories. His Falsifiability Thesis—that no good scientific theory is safe from being disproven—would become a dogma among many scientists over the course of the twentieth century. He considered himself an evolutionary epistemologist along with Campbell. But like Campbell he didn't try to apply the theory universally to all of culture, and wasn't concerned with disciplines outside of academic science.

In the social sciences, the idea of universal Darwinism has found its occasional supporters over the last few decades, though again no consensus has been reached, and few seem to care. E.O. Wilson viewed cultural evolution as ultimately shaped by biological instinct. "The genes hold culture on a leash," he wrote in his 1978 *On Human Nature.* Other social scientists took up a different point of view. Cavalli-Sforza and Feldman, in *Cultural Transmission and Evolution* (1981) argued that culture could evolve by natural selection too. But they seemed unsure to what extent:

> The mechanism of natural selection retains ultimate control, but only in the long run, and for cultural adaptation to be possible, at least some delegation of control is necessary. Control is delegated to a system of poorly understood internal drives and rewards.

Boyd and Richerson, in *Culture and the Evolutionary Process* (1985), were at least univocal: "[W]e believe that the empirically known properties of culture virtually guarantee that cultural variation is subject to natural selection (p. 11)." Both William Durham (*Coevolution,* 1991) and D.S. Wilson (*Darwin's Cathedral,* 2002) would employ cultural selection as an explanatory principle, but in neither case did they treat it as a strict law.

Recently, "memetics" and "Universal Darwinism" with a capital "U" have gained a few outspoken proponents. Richard Dawkins famously coined the term "meme" to mean the cultural version of a gene in his 1976 *The Selfish Gene*, and later promoted the idea of cultural evolution in his 1983 article "Universal Darwinism." In the meantime more books have been published along these lines, including Daniel Dennett's *Darwin's Dangerous Idea*, Susan Blackmore's *The Meme Machine*, and more recently Matt Ridley's *The Evolution of Everything*. But this field has never become a very active area of scientific research, nor has it gained much ground among philosophers, cultural critics, or most social scientists.

You might wonder why such movements—cultural evolution theory, memetics, Universal Darwinism, and the like—have never gathered any steam. I think the main reason is that they all lack one essential thing: *motivation*. It almost seems as if everyone is trying to apply Darwin's theory to culture simply for lack of a better idea. In every case we've discussed, the ultimate goal is "explanation."

Malthus proposed his theory not merely to explain, but out of exasperation with an idea—"the perfectibility of man"—that he felt had grown to ridiculous proportions. He offered his Principle as a strict rule and challenge to his opponents.

Darwin was so thorough with his theory of evolution because he had to overcome centuries of Biblically excused bias. This is why he needed a strict, generally applicable theory. He did not have the luxury of providing just a few unconnected explanations.

The problem is that none of Campbell, Popper, nor even Dawkins has recognized Darwin's Law as a law, let alone asked whether it is possible for human culture to escape this law. In fact, it looks like every cultural Darwinist I've mentioned still assumes it is possible to achieve sustained worldwide progress. Cavalli-Sforza and Feldman end their book with this statement:

> In spite of [our lack of knowledge concerning precise mechanisms and coefficients of selection], there would be a consensus that positive cultural evolution of human society is possible, and, at least for technology has certainly occurred.

Matt Ridley also ends his book on this note:

> Incremental, inexorable, inevitable changes will bring us material and spiritual improvements that will make the lives of our grandchildren wealthier, healthier, happier, cleverer, cleaner, kinder, freer, more peaceful and more equal—almost entirely as a serendipitous by-product of cultural evolution.

D.S. Wilson, in his book on cultural evolution, endorses the idea of worldwide progress with equal unconcern:

> If there is more to religion than belief in supernatural agents, then perhaps science is not as hostile to religion as it is often taken to be. One reason that I admire some aspects of religion is because I share some of its values. I have not attempted to hide this fact, and I hope that it has not intruded upon my science. Nor have I attempted to conceal my basic optimism that *the world can be a better place in the future than in the past or present*—that there can be such a thing as a path to enlightenment. Being a scientist does not require becoming indifferent to human welfare (*Darwin's Cathedral*, italics mine).

Let me be clear that my only issue with this passage is the statement in italics—otherwise I am in agreement with the values D.S. Wilson's expresses. Stephen Jay Gould, in *Full House*, affirms a belief in progress, at least in theory:

> But human cultural change is an entirely distinct process [from biological evolution] operating under radically different principles that do allow for the strong possibility of a driven trend to what we may legitimately call "progress" (at least in the technological sense, whether or not the changes ultimately do us any good in a practical or moral way).

Richard Dawkins, the original "Universal Darwinist," finally stated it this way in *The Selfish Gene*: "We are built as gene machines and cultured as meme machines, but we have the power to turn against our creators. We, alone on earth, can rebel against the tyranny of the selfish replicators."

But can we? So far it seems that even the most ardent Darwinists assume so. But the truth is that we can no more defy Darwinian selection than defy the laws of physics.

OUR QUESTION: CAN CULTURE OVERCOME NATURAL SELECTION?

In the last chapter we established that mutation, selection, and resource limitation are natural, unavoidable factors for any biological population. Mutation creates new variation, some variation reproduces faster, and this growth causes population pressures and natural selection. This is the trilemma for humans as biological creatures: if we rid ourselves of selection, we must choose either uncontrolled mutation or stagnation, and if we accept selection then we accept the Malthusian balance that comes with it.

I will argue that there is no way out of this trilemma, whether through eugenics, genetic engineering, cybernetics, artificial intelligence, or *any* other intelligent—that is, *cultural*—means. Cultural evolution is subject to the same Darwinian logic as biological evolution. To really understand this principle, let us consider each of these progressive schemes in turn in the next several sections.

EUGENICS AS A KIND OF CULTURE

Recall that eugenics is the idea that the government should regulate who gets to breed, so that "unfit" genes are eliminated from the gene pool *without* relying on biological selection. The idea is that biological selection means premature death, and that sterilization would be preferable.

This is the strategy we use when breeding animals. Eugenics, stripped of its scientific facade, is nothing more or less than the suggestion that humans should be bred like cattle. Most people instinctively abhor the idea, but we need to get to the bottom of what is wrong with it. Let's have a look at animal breeding to get a handle on what it would mean to breed humans.

Why exactly do we breed animals? According to Charles Smith in *Animal Breeding: Technology for the 21st Century* (1998),

> The purpose of animal breeding is to improve genetically the economic efficiency of livestock production.

We breed animals to make more money, in other words. Obviously, the goal would have to be different in the case of humans. Or would it? What is the goal of being human? Is it making money? Making scientific discoveries? Practicing a true religion? I have met people who believe in any one of these. But how would we choose which goal to work toward in breeding humans? Perhaps we could have multiple breeding programs with multiple goals? Would we need a goal? According to animal breeders, we would: "Note that a clear evaluation of the breeding goal is essential to all methods of improvement," Charles Smith writes.

In any case, animal breeding is a way to select biological traits on the basis of cultural ideals. It may be seen as a subordination of biological to cultural evolution. So if human breeding is to be modeled on the science that has already been developed, it would essentially be the replacement of our natural biological values (our natural attractions to the opposite sex) with whatever cultural values the breeders deem more important. The government would choose your spouse.

Fine. Perhaps it would be weird to have our mates chosen for us, but arranged marriages are common in some societies, so it wouldn't be too bad, would it? Well, successful animal breeders actually use a couple of additional methods. Rice, Andrews, and Warwick discuss Robert Bakewell's success in breeding beef cattle in their 1953 *Breeding Better Livestock*:

> [Robert Bakewell's] success in improving his stock is said to have been due to three things: (1) He had definite ideals—in beef cattle, for example, a low-set, blocky, quick-maturing animal almost unknown at that time; (2) he leased rather than sold males and returned them to his own farm if they transmitted desirable qualities; and (3) he bred the best to the best regardless of relationships, which often meant rather close inbreeding.

All right, so in addition to clear ideals we need to make sure we keep track of our best males and breed them as often as possible. Sounds tolerable (if not always for the females). And we'll need to make sure that we disregard interrelatedness in choosing matches. You don't want to lose those good genes just because the two were brother and sister, right?

Okay, fine. I mean, heck, we're breeding a perfect race to populate a utopia where nothing bad happens. Maybe it *would* be worth the sacrifice. Wouldn't it? Well, according to Rice, Andrews, and Warwick:

> As we look back we can easily see that a better job could have been done [in American animal breeding over the previous century]—more rigid selection and refusal to register inferior purebreds would have strengthened all breeds and much of the breed promotional activity was not genetically sound. Nevertheless, the purebred contribution to improved animal husbandry in America is beyond calculation. This is not to say that every breed has shown a steady march to perfection. Most of the breeds have had ups and downs and some breeds seem to be in a downward trend at the present time as regards the efficient production of their respective products. In short, breeds can, and do, go up and down just as herds do.

Apparently, breeding is never a surefire thing. Sometimes it works and sometimes it doesn't.

So, not surprisingly—but very unfortunately for the eugenicist—it appears that there are currently no breeding programs that guarantee progress, and in animal breeding any advances in say milk production generally come at the cost of new weaknesses in other areas. For example, in the same book they point out, "In the past, many cows that ... became breed champions for production also became sterile in the process." Others become short-lived or produce watery milk.

If it's such a crapshoot, why then do humans breed animals at all?

In a few cases, animal breeding has been successful. And these breeds have become widely adopted. There's a kind of natural selection going on here. Not every breeder has to succeed for there to be some good varieties out there.

In fact, animal breeding is a clear-cut case where Lewontin's criteria for natural selection can be applied. Different breeding programs (variations) are passed between farmers (heredity) and some do better and spread (selection). There are only so many dairy farms, and thus these ideas are competing for a limited resource (Malthus's Principle of Population), which implies that the success of some means the failure of others. Ultimately, there is a balance between the creation of new breeding schemes and the extinction of bad ones.

Note that this operation of selection is not optional. If some breeding programs spread, others will disappear. This is a mathematical truth given limited resources. E.O. Wilson might like to claim, based on his "leash" principle, that it is all ultimately due to our genes, but it is no consolation to the failed animal breeder that his ideas do not reside in DNA and therefore aren't *really* subject to accepted evolutionary theory.

I hope to have shown two things from this argument. First, if we applied the science of breeding—as it stands today—to humans it would be an immoral and even monstrous policy. Second, and more importantly for arguments to follow, the science of breeding is a form of culture, and is therefore constrained by Darwinian selection like all other forms of culture.

It may my argued that one day this science will advance to a stage where we *can* anticipate the consequences of a breeding program well enough to prevent genetic decay. Perhaps we could, it might be suggested, sequence the genome of fetuses and selectively abort those that are unfit. In this particular case, you would have a form of genetic engineering, discussed in the next section. Any other conceivable breeding program for humans or sentient beings will be considered more generally in Section 3.8, where I argue that even if we had the power to design new sentient beings from scratch, we still cannot escape the logic of Darwin's Law as applied to culture.

THE CURRENT STATE OF GENETIC ENGINEERING

Genetic engineering is no longer science fiction. It is currently used as a way to introduce new traits into stocks of animals and plants for agricultural breeding. Genetic engineering programs, like other breeding programs, do not guarantee success, and in fact many of them, it has been argued, may be causing environmental, ecological, and health problems.[13] In any case, the current methods of genetic engineering use trial and error in an essential way. Applying them to humans would be risky. Gene therapy *is* currently being used on humans, but only for somatic cells, whose DNA is not passed on to children. In 2015, biologists called for a worldwide moratorium on human germline modification, which would introduce heritable variations into sperm and egg cell DNA, citing our current lack of knowledge of what the effects would be. It is currently illegal in dozens of countries to tamper with any DNA that may be passed on to one's children.

We may have sequenced most of the human genome, but we do not know most of the details of how it works to produce an adult human. There is no general theory of how a certain DNA alteration will affect the life of a human. The processes involved are so complex that in every successful case of genetic engineering, the organism must be born and reach maturity before success can even be provisionally declared. Even now, after years of genetically modifying crops, we still see controversy over their effects on the environment and on health. Human chemical physiology, and the ecosystems of bacteria that help us stay healthy, are many, many times more complex than what we currently understand.

As of 2017, there is no silver bullet in genetic engineering. The current reality is, we do not yet have a cure for cancer, let alone every possible heritable disease. But does our present lack of knowledge prove that we will *never* have the knowledge needed to engineer better humans, or at least protect against mutations? If we could only prevent harmful mutations from occurring, couldn't we then stall the harmful long-term effects of birth control and finally achieve our utopia? Possibly. What remains to be discussed is whether such a utopia would signify genuine progress.

Preventing all harmful mutation by genetic engineering remains in the realm of science fiction. It is unlikely to happen soon, but we haven't shown it to be impossible. Let's move on to more such science-fictional schemes, and consider the hope of a perfected art of genetic engineering along with the rest.

CYBERNETICS, ARTIFICIAL INTELLIGENCE, AND THE "SINGULARITY"

Pretend we find a way to fix all problems with our DNA. Or pretend that we simply improve ourselves with cybernetic enhancements. Maybe we replace our muscles and bones with robotics that are stronger and faster. Or we put computer chips in our brains to make us smarter, or maybe even more compassionate. Maybe we prevent our DNA from decaying, or maybe we simply become more robotic as it does, replacing biology with technology.

As if technological evolution were ever so simple. But where exactly do these schemes for progress go wrong? Humans do get artificial joints and organs, even neurological enhancements such as pacemakers. If steroids and other performance-enhancing drugs may be considered cyber-technology, perhaps we have already have transcended our biology to some small degree. Of course, none of these technologies come without their worrying side-effects, but where's our decisive evidence that progress is or is not possible along these lines?

Equally nebulous, it seems, is the prospect of Artificial Intelligence. That true AI is only 10 years away has been maintained by AI researchers for 50 years. The project may seem silly. *I* think it's silly: Have we even agreed on a definition of "intelligence?" Doesn't intelligence come in many forms? When scientists predict that computers will soon be smarter than humans, do they mean smarter than all of us? Measured how? Smarter than Einstein even? But do we even understand what made Einstein smart? Do we even understand what precisely makes humans smart? What exactly *is* the goal of AI?

But perhaps those of us with such questions are being too skeptical, like those who said humans would never fly, or visit the moon. How do we know that some computer smarter than us can't figure out how to achieve progress? Ray Kurzweil and other believers in the coming "Singularity" claim that there is no way to understand what is in store for us, because once computers exceed human intelligence the progress of history will simply be too complex to entirely comprehend. (As if it were ever simple enough to entirely comprehend.)

In any case, I think a proof *can* be made that no intelligence, no matter how advanced, can achieve progress. Just as the laws of thermodynamics, physics, and probability cannot be "overcome" by any super intelligence, but must rather be obeyed by it, so too the laws of population and evolution would constrain its behavior.

Let's debunk this last holdout of progress.

First, let's consider the question of whether cybernetic humans or artificial intelligence would come in multiple varieties. We would certainly want them to. How would it be progress if suddenly all people were engineered to be exactly the same? Or if we were all replaced with a civilization of identical robots? These possibilities would be terrifying if they weren't so implausible.

We've got two choices, the same two choices we faced in considering whether mutation was a good or a bad thing for humans. The first option is to allow for different transhumans or robots to be different from each other. The second option is to wipe out all diversity and have a uniform society with no differences.

The second option—eliminating all human diversity—would certainly not be progress.

So let's choose the first option. Our new transhumans, whatever percent machine they are, come in a great diversity of forms and (we would hope) personalities.

But now we're starting to satisfy Lewontin's three criteria for evolution by natural selection.

We can now tick off Lewontin's first condition: **Variation**. We have a population of transhumans with differences and diversity.

1. Different individuals in a population have different mental and physical traits ("Variation"). *(CHECK)*
2. This variation is heritable ("Heritability"). *(?)*
3. Different variants have different rates of survival and reproduction ("Differential Fitness"). *(?)*

Let's consider 2., heritability of variation. Would these transhumans be able to pass on any of their unique traits to the next generation, or would every generation have completely new variations in body and mind? In modern human civilization, traits are passed from generation to generation, whether by DNA or by culture. If we learn something new, we can teach it to our children. If there were no cultural or biological heritability, then every generation would be completely new and utterly oblivious to all history that came before it.

It seems like again our utopia is left with two options. First option: each generation is some random selection among preordained possibilities (no heritability of variation). Second option: the diversity in one generation is to some extent passed on to the next one (heritability of variation).

It should be clear that the first option, no heritability, would mean a world without history and without choice. Every point in time is some random combination of possibilities that cannot affect the future, and is disconnected from the past.

The second option, allowing for heritability as in the real world, where we allow some dependence of one generation on the last (i.e. some ability to make choices based on past experience) is obviously the only sane choice.

So we can tick off the second criterion, **Heritability**.

Finally, we get to Lewontin's third criterion. Whether we satisfy this criterion will determine whether there is selection occurring (and hence suffering). It will determine whether destruction is a necessary part of our envisioned future. The first option, what Lewontin and other biologists call "differential fitness," is that some transhumans will be different in ways that will affect how successful they are in influencing future generations. The second option, no differential fitness, would mean that every transhuman has exactly the same chance of influencing others.

Again, satisfying this criterion is the only real option. Without it, you are stuck in a situation where nothing better can replace the worse, no meaningful change can happen, a society frozen in time, exactly the same from generation to generation—or at best drifting from one indifferent mutation to the next.

Therefore, we have to tick off the third criterion, **Differential Fitness**, because some transhumans will pass down their ideas or DNA more readily than others, and these will prosper and others will eventually disappear. This would be Darwinian selection. And here we once again see our Malthusian balance between triumph and tragedy.

For the world to be at all interesting, suffering cannot be avoided. To say that suffering can be eliminated is to say you can have a world where no value judgments whatsoever could be made about which forms or personalities or intelligences or traits were "better" or "worse." But if there were no difference between good and bad, we could have all the diversity you want but none of it would make any difference. It would be like being doomed to eat a thousand flavors of potato chip and no other food.

It is extremely hard to imagine that you could have a significant diversity, whether humans or intelligent robots, that did not show any differences among individuals in how well they would pass on their traits. Humans tend to imitate certain people more, and others less. Imitation leads to the spread of some habits, and the disappearance of others. For example, habits of racism are on their way out, and ideals of diversity are on their way in. It would be a sign of hopeless and nihilistic relativism to say that this shouldn't be the case simply because there should never be any advantage of one idea over another. And here we have the crux of the question of whether Darwin's theory applies to culture. Of course it must, if we value the existence of meaningful cultural diversity. Because no true diversity exists if no value judgments—that is—*selections* can be made. And selection—as has only been neglected because it is such a simple and obvious truth—is the essence of evolution. And thus value difference—the desire for one thing over another—is the root cause both of suffering and of joy, as the Buddha realized two millennia ago:

> "What, O Monks, is the origin of suffering? It is that craving which gives rise to ever fresh rebirth and bound up with pleasure and lust, now here, now there, finds ever fresh delight." (Dīgha-Nikāya XXII)[14]

And this is why no Artificial Intelligence, no transhuman, no Singularity, no culture or biology no matter how advanced can tip the long-run Malthusian balance between joy and suffering, creation and destruction.

DARWIN'S LAW AS UNIVERSAL

Since the discovery of DNA, cultural evolutionism has been dismissed as a second-rate theory, lacking the scientific evidence and mathematical rigor of biological evolutionism. All changes in an organism could now be traced back to mutations in its DNA, a long but relatively simple molecule to describe, made up of various combinations of only four basic parts. No similar locus has been found for cultural heredity.

A few decades ago, in the *Selfish Gene*, Richard Dawkins famously coined the term "meme" for the genetic element of cultural heredity. As genes were to organisms, so memes would be to culture. In the *Blind Watchmaker* he vividly describes its proposed role as the locus of cultural evolution:

> DNA replicators built 'survival machines' for themselves—the bodies of living organisms including ourselves. As a part of their equipment, bodies evolved on-board computers—brains. Brains evolved the capacity to communicate with other brains by means of language and cultural traditions. But the new milieu of cultural tradition opens up new possibilities for self-replicating entities. The new replicators are not DNA.... They are patterns of information that can thrive only in brains or the artificially manufactured products of brains—books, computers, and so on. But, given that brains, books and computers exist, these new replicators, which I called memes to distinguish them from genes, can propagate themselves from brain to brain, from brain to book, from book to brain, from brain to computers, from computer to computer. As they propagate they can change—mutate. And perhaps 'mutant' memes can exert the kinds of influence that I am here calling 'replicator power.' Remember that this means any kind of influence affecting their own likelihood of being propagated. Evolution under the influence of the new replicators—memic evolution—is in its infancy. It is manifested in the phenomena that we call cultural evolution.

From a scientific point of view, the notion of memes has, unfortunately, floundered. Genetic sequencing labs have sprung up around the world, busily sequencing the DNA of many organisms, including humans. But there are no memetic sequencing labs, for the simple reason that memes are not so simple. As Dawkins says, they can spring from brain to book to computer and back again. But we don't just learn from books and computers. We can also learn simply by observing human artifacts such as tools, machines, and works of art. So "memes" can even spring from tool to picture to computer to book. It would be pointless to set up a lab to study these because these are things we interact with at a fundamental level every day.

There is no science of memetics, at least not with the prestige of genetics. But I think that our celebration of the discovery of DNA has made us forget that Darwin's theory was originally designed to be independent of the mechanism of inheritance. The reason for this was that in the nineteenth century they had no idea exactly how traits were passed from parent to child. Darwin defended his principle of inheritance in *The Origin of Species*:

> No breeder doubts how strong is the tendency to inheritance: like produces like is his fundamental belief: doubts have been thrown on this principle by theoretical writers alone.

The same thing can be said about culture. We know that cultural traditions are passed down. This is how there can be different cultures in different parts of the world and these differences persist for centuries and sometimes millennia.

When Lewontin proposed his three logical criteria for selection, these criteria still did not depend on substrate. And that was the point. Lewontin was trying to argue that *groups* of organisms, and not just individuals, can be loci of evolution. As a logical structure, the theory of evolution has no dependence on *what* is being selected. In fact, there are organisms that replicate and evolve through non-DNA mechanisms. Some use RNA. And some replicators are simply proteins that copy themselves. Most evolutionists believe that DNA itself was not the original locus of evolution, that there must have been simpler ways that organisms copied themselves in the early history of life. Clay crystals have been proposed, and self-sustaining chemical reactions. These theories of the origin of life are still controversial, but what is not controversial (or at least shouldn't be) is that DNA has never been the exclusive locus of heredity and evolutionary change.[15]

Evolutionary theorists have not only studied evolving viruses and bacteria and verified the operation of natural selection in nature, but over the past several decades they have been studying the evolution of self-replicating computer programs, what they like to call "domesticated computer viruses."[16] What evolves in such artificial organisms is not even molecules but instructions on the hard disk of a computer.

We must begin to see Darwin's theory as a logical theory instead of an hypothesis. Some of its opponents (famously Ann Coulter[17]) have criticized it for being *too* logical, for being what logicians call a *tautology*. A tautology is something that cannot possibly be false. For example, the statement, "Rain is wet," is true no matter what the weather conditions. Rain is falling water by definition. And water is wet by definition. According to Intelligent Design theorists, "survival of the fittest" is similarly an empty tautology. We define the fittest to be those that survive, and thus it is inescapable that the fittest will survive.

This logical inescapability, I would argue, is a good thing. It makes the theory very general.

What such critics overlook is the power of their own logic. The "survival of the fittest" actually always means the survival of the *heritably fittest variants*. To say that one type is "fittest," that is, to make any comparison at all, there must be *variants*. So that part is tautological also. To say that these variants are *heritable* means they are capable of passing down their traits, and this is exactly what is meant by evolutionary "survival" in the first place.

Survival of the fittest logically contains all of Lewontin's conditions, all the ingredients for evolution. And it applies to every system you can conceive of because *of course* the fittest will survive. In situations where nothing survives or everything survives fitness cannot be compared anyway, so there are no fittest. As soon as you can define "fittest" in a given situation, that is, "best at surviving," then you automatically, logically, have evolution. What we have here is something a lot like Newton's Second Law, $F=ma$, his seemingly empty definition of force as mass times acceleration. That it's so empty is part of the reason that it can be applied to every particle in the universe as it is pushed and pulled by gravitational, electric, magnetic, or whatever force you can imagine. Any change in speed whatsoever in any object is governed by Newton's Second Law. Similarly, any heritable change in fitness whatsoever in any population is governed by Darwin's Law.

You cannot escape this law, whether you're talking biology or culture or anything else. Let's do a thought experiment. Let's see if we can satisfy Lewontin's criteria yet see no selection at all. Imagine something trivial and inert-seeming, say, a collection of rocks. Grant them variability—they come in many shapes and sizes. Fine. Now grant them heritability. In fact, let's get technical and malicious and say, all right, the variability in these rocks is heritable in the sense that these rocks are virtually immortal. They pass down their traits simply by surviving. Is this cheating, when they don't even have the ability to self-replicate? I don't know, I can't think of any reason why it is cheating. But there's no evolution here yet—we just have rocks sitting there.

Now let's add the third criterion, differential fitness. How would this be possible for rocks? How could some of these rocks be better at surviving? Well, let's choose something from real life. Say all the rocks containing gold are taken and melted down by humans.

Do we have evolutionary change? Yes. It's rudimentary, but there. Because now over time our population of rocks will change to contain fewer and fewer gold-bearing rocks. Since these rocks don't reproduce we can't imagine this evolution as occurring in the long term, but we can't deny that such a change is occurring. It's inescapable. It's a consequence of logic.

Darwin's Law is completely general. We just need to be faithful in applying Lewontin's conditions, just as Newton was faithful in applying his own rules to every system, whether a falling apple or the moon.

Let's take a rationally justified leap of imagination and apply Darwin's theory to the whole universe:

Atoms. Do they evolve? They come in different varieties: carbon, hydrogen, silver, argon, etc. You've got *variation*. Like the rocks in our example they tend to persist through time, which gives us *heritability*. But do they show differences in fitness? True, certain radioactive atoms tend to decay. Over time we can deduce that these variants will die out. But there is no long-term evolution here, because atoms have no tendency to self-replicate. The situation is the same as with the rocks above—short term selection can happen, but eventually nothing in the long run, once all the unstable kinds have decayed.

Clouds. These come in different variants but they are always changing, and don't show any heritability. Mountains, same, though in slow motion. Star clusters, same, though in even slower motion.

This sort of logic seems to cover most inanimate objects. Some show the ability to experience short-term evolution, but none reproduce so none show any long-term evolution.

What about fire? It can reproduce itself in a sense. But we don't see any heritable variation here. Different flames may come in different temperatures and have different material components, but this depends on the material being burned and not on the fire itself. Once the fire spreads to a new area its characteristics will be determined not by its parent fire, but by the materials in the region. With fire we do have self-reproduction, but we are missing heritable variation and thus do not satisfy Lewontin's criteria.

DNA. The one example almost every scientist agrees on. It comes in many varieties, caused by mutation. Every human has a different DNA sequence, and this is why none of us, except identical twins with the same DNA, look quite the same. It shows *variation*. It is passed from parent to child, with only about one-in-a-million base pairs mutated. So it is extremely *heritable*. Finally, some people are stronger, or have better resistance to heat, or lactose tolerance, or any number of heritable strengths and weaknesses that will affect their ability to pass on their DNA. We've got *differential fitness,* and thus we have evolution. All plants and animals on the planet have DNA satisfying these conditions, and thus they all evolve. And this evolution is long term because every generation the population is replenished by reproduction. Selection, caused by Malthusian pressures, checks the population, while exponential reproduction fills the population back out. This constant replenishment has kept species evolving for billions of years.

Acquired muscle. Here's an interesting one. Lamarck originally thought that evolution involved the passing down of "acquired characteristics." He believed that "use and disuse" could affect the size of an organ, and this change could be passed down. But biologists have failed to confirm that this theory holds in almost every study they've done. Using a muscle does typically make it grow, but this makes it no more likely that one's children will have larger muscles. They will have to work out themselves, so the *heritability* condition fails in this case.

Cars. These don't reproduce, so like rocks perhaps they can only show short term selection. But wait a second. Doesn't it sometimes happen that an automobile engineer sees a design on the road that he likes, and takes certain elements from the design to use himself? Say he sees tail fins on a competitor's model, and decides that he should jump on the bandwagon. Now you've got a trait that is being *inherited*, it's a *variation*, and in this case it is more popular so shows *differential fitness*. Here we have an example of technological evolution. Since Darwin's theory is so general, and technology surely does show persistent change in the long run, we should expect it to fall under Darwin's Law.

Incest taboos. Certain royal families in history have not had the same taboos concerning incest as other societies. There's been *variation*. Taboos against incest (or lack thereof) are taught to new generations, so there is *heritability*. Biologists believe that incest taboos help a gene pool stay healthier. In this case you would expect biological fitness to be affected. But is the fitness of the incest taboo *itself* affected? It must be, because the fewer healthy children one has the less the chance there is of passing down a cultural tradition. In this way biological fitness almost always makes a difference to cultural fitness. It should be clear that cultures that encourage reproductive health would be fitter in the long run. And this would explain why societies without incest taboos have tended to die out, and why almost every culture has these taboos. It's the long-term effect of Darwin's Law, of selection. Historically, birth control, infanticide, and abortion taboos have shown essentially the same pattern. In the modern world—as in the Roman world—cultural fashion has spread some of these practices widely, but in the long run it does not appear that any of them will be able to survive the effects of Darwin's Law. In the case of the ancient Romans, they did not.

Scientific theories. Decades ago Donald Campbell, Karl Popper, and others introduced the idea that scientific theories evolve in a Darwinian way. Among scientists and philosophers this idea remains controversial, and has failed to reach consensus. But it shouldn't be controversial at all. Scientific theories are quite *heritable*, and in fact some, like Archimedes' Law of Displacement, have been passed down from the time of the Greeks. They come in many varieties. Physics is generally considered the most mathematical and precise of the sciences. But there is *variation* even here. Hundreds of different grand unified theories have been proposed. There are multiple hypotheses for many unexplained phenomena. And is there *differential fitness*? Of course there is. Otherwise you would have to argue that the ascendancy of Newton's Laws as the best account of motion was purely the result of chance.

If it is so self-evident that scientific theories are subject to evolution, why is there so much resistance to the idea among philosophers and scientists? Philosopher of science David Hull discusses one such objection in his article "The Naked Meme":

> According to Rescher (1977: 157), cognitive evolution is not a "blind groping amongst *all conceivable* alternatives, but a carefully guided search among the *really promising* alternatives." This he takes to be a "crucial disanalogy between biological and cognitive evolution." Rescher is surely right about cognitive development. ... [Yet] he is wrong about biological evolution. Biological evolution does not result from selection of all possible gene combinations. There are more possible combinations of genes in *Homo sapiens* alone than there are atoms in the universe.

Nicholas Rescher's objection is probably the most commonly heard objection in academia to applying Darwin's theory to science, or to any human culture for that matter. In biological evolution, DNA mutations are random. You might say they are "blind." And this is why you need selection to weed out the bad ones. Rescher and others would like to argue that new scientific ideas are not random at all. Stephen Toulmin calls them "pre-selected."[18]

Entire scholarly books have been written arguing this point, but the whole debate is irrelevant. In *The Origin of Species*, Darwin made a sharp distinction between *natural* selection as it occurs in nature and *artificial* selection as employed by animal breeders. Everyone at that time already agreed that selection was essential to creating new breeds of animals. What Darwin needed to show was that new species could arise without any breeder at all. This is why he introduced the term *natural selection*.

But the logic of Darwin's theory doesn't care whether selection has its source in humans or not. He wanted to argue you could replace artificial selection with natural selection and it would make no substantial difference to the process. Sure, many of our ideas are artificially selected, but they are selected nonetheless, and thus subject to Darwin's Law.

If it were true that all new scientific ideas were entirely "pre-selected," there would be no competition at all. Every theory would spring into being fully-formed and no theory would have a rival. In Thomas Kuhn's book *The Structure of Scientific Revolutions*, he famously illustrates through historical examples that scientific change almost always arises from the competition of rival paradigms. While the details of his account have been disputed, the historical evidence does show that new theories are forced to compete.

This competition need not be irrational. Some read Kuhn as saying that new theories are adopted for political reasons. If this were so, science would have little credibility as a source for truth. But Kuhn himself denies that authority alone decides paradigm shifts. Historically, most scientific revolutions are resolved by appealing to evidence and reason, and this is why we call them "scientific." I think Newton's laws of motion do describe the world truthfully. But this is not to say that Newton's theory wasn't selected among a number of rival theories. You had Aristotle's theory, Descartes', Galileo's, Leibniz's, and a dozen others. Selection definitely occurred. Call it artificial selection, call it rational selection, call it empirical selection, it doesn't matter. Selection is selection, and it implies that one theory succeeded and another theory failed.

Once we accept that science is subject to the laws of evolution, it is needless to go through this argument for each additional element of human culture: literature, art, politics, technology, religion, and even values. All of these elements obviously show *heritable variation* and *differential fitness,* and thus they are all subject to Darwin's Law. (For more detailed evidence, please see Appendix 3, which presents examples I've gleaned from the secondary literature of Darwinian selection among technologies.)

CULTURAL PROGRESS DEBUNKED

As with the population of every animal and plant, and the human population itself, the population of ideas (whether stored in books or brains or computers) is incapable of "overcoming" Malthus. Perhaps, like Malthus's swarm of misinterpreters, some will panic because more ideas are being created than can ever survive. Perhaps they will begin to preach "creativity control," that we must stop thinking of new ideas so that the population of ideas can remain constant and never run up against the limited resource of brains to hold them. And then a group of Cultural Darwinians will arise, once again misunderstanding their own theory, worried that without natural selection our ideas will mutate out of control, and propose a scheme of idea-eugenics (eumemics?) such that only fit ideas will be allowed to breed to create new ones, and books with unfit ideas shall be burned. And then it will be realized that this solution too is no good, and that we must pioneer memetic engineering and make designer ideologies. But then ... who will design the ideologies for designing ideologies ...?

Enough. Let us accept that culture, like biology, will always remain poised in Malthusian balance between creation and destruction, mutation and selection, subject to the Darwinian laws that constrain all animate phenomena.

Since creation means joy, and destruction means suffering—even for culture—I will argue that there is a long-run balance between joy and suffering in both cultural and biological evolution. But to get absolutely clear on what this balance between joy and suffering really means, we need to develop an unequivocal theory of value, the topic of the next chapter.

SUMMARY AND PHILOSOPHICAL IMPLICATIONS

The thing that humans have that animals don't, that would seem to give us a special ability to progress is *culture*. Culture may be defined as everything passed down from generation to generation by nonbiological means, which includes technology, science, religion, art, philosophy, language, literature, and values.

To genetically engineer humans would be to bring our DNA under the control of culture. If done like any other kind of engineering, it would involve trial and error. But are trial and error necessary to cultural evolution, or is there any way to overcome the need for Darwinian selection? This was the central question of this chapter.

Culture always varies, it is inherited, and some forms of culture spread better than others. It satisfies all of Lewontin's criteria and must, in fact, experience selection. Culture seeks to grow exponentially, and because it must inhabit physical brains, books, or computers it is ultimately limited by resources. It will also see a creation-destruction balance.

The idea of cultural evolution has long been ignored in academia, and even ridiculed. But evidence of cultural evolution is everywhere if you know how to look. Nearly all ideologies, belief systems, theories, and religions strive to spread themselves as widely as possible. The reason that cultural evolution is not taken seriously is that—so far—it has had nothing important to explain and no real motivation. *Our* goal is to determine whether progress is possible, and armed with this motivation we have a use for the fact that culture is strictly an evolutionary system. It is subject to Darwin's Law, which means a choice of (1) Malthusian resource limitations, (2) uncontrolled mutation, or (3) evolutionary stasis.

We applied this reasoning to various transhumanist schemes for progress. Eugenics would have to draw on the state of the art of animal breeding, which actually does not eliminate the need for selection, since not all breeds are successful. Genetic engineering is likewise fallible, and thus cannot, at present, eliminate the need for selection.

If we attempt to imagine a world where we can design a perfect species of cybernetic beings or robots, without any limitations, it is difficult to imagine that this new species will be in any way interesting unless it is subject to Lewontin's conditions and thus Darwin's Law. If the new species lacks variation it will be completely homogeneous, a society of identical robots. If it lacks heritability it will have no memory of the past and no history. And if there are no differences in fitness the population will be trapped in eternal stasis and will lack any notion of better or worse. It will be unable to adapt to new conditions. From these considerations, we can see that selection is essential to our concept of life, and we cannot get rid of it without ridding ourselves of life itself. Life—being life—will always have fit and unfit, creation and destruction, joy and suffering. Even if it is comprised of superintelligent robots.

Darwin's theory of natural selection is actually a logical tautology. That the fittest variants will spread follows from the biological meaning of the term "fit." It is not something that culture can "overcome," but a logical condition of its existence. This logic is universal and can be applied to all systems in the universe, even ones normally thought of as inanimate. The main difference between animate and inanimate is that animate systems show persistent, long-term evolution as new mutants arise and spread by reproduction. Inanimate systems still show selection, but never perpetually. Culture and technology obviously show proliferation and selection in a way that produces long term evolutionary lineages, even in science. Selection has been disregarded so far because scientists have demanded that it be "blind." However, Lewontin's criteria do not care whether the source of variation is blind or not, only that there *is* variation, and even scientific theories show variation.

Cultural evolution is, therefore, subject to the principles of Malthus and Darwin, just as biological evolution is. Humans may be set apart from animals by culture, and it may give us new evolutionary avenues and sources of novelty, but it does not allow us to "transcend" the logic of Darwinian selection to produce progress.

IV

VALUES AND THE BALANCE OF JOY AND SUFFERING

JOY, SUFFERING, AND UTILITARIANISM

You may have noticed that I keep making this sort of inference: creation and reproduction imply *joy*, destruction and infertility imply *suffering*. You may challenge me here and ask why selective destruction must always imply suffering, whether we can't find some kind of selection that satisfies Darwin's Law but is somehow less painful. You may ask how the death of an idea (cultural death) could be as bad as the death of your genes (biological death).

My thesis, if you recall, is that total joy and suffering across the entire human race over the long term must always converge to an even ratio. They must be precisely balanced in the long run. But for me to argue this I must be able to measure joy and suffering as quantities, as *numbers*.

The idea that we can measure joy and suffering in such a precise way is a primary tenet of utilitarianism, a widespread theory among philosophers who believe in progress. I don't believe it to be a very good ethical theory. But I've been using it to have a common basis of argument with my opponent, and these assumptions should be made explicit.

CREATION CAUSES JOY, DESTRUCTION CAUSES SUFFERING

Our original definition of progress was:

Progress is an increase in the ratio of the happiness of all people to the total suffering.

So far our discussion has proceeded in terms of Malthusian and Darwinian theories, which focus on the balance of births and deaths, that is, creation and destruction. Though I've made some implicit assumptions that death and destruction cause suffering, and birth and creation cause joy, these connections remain obscure and need to be clarified.

In short, I think that joy is a mental perception of the occurrence of evolutionary success—"creation"—and suffering is essentially a perception of evolutionary failure—"destruction." Joy and suffering were evolved specifically to reward or punish organisms for reproducing or failing to reproduce. In the long run, joy should track ability to have offspring and suffering should track failure to have offspring. So—in the long run—the Malthusian balance implies a simultaneous balance between joy and suffering. If we can show this, we have the final component needed to prove our thesis that progress is impossible.

THE RISE OF UTILITARIANISM

Modern views on how to measure joy and suffering originate in the philosophical theory known as "utilitarianism." The founder of utilitarianism was a political philosopher by the name of Jeremy Bentham (1748-1832). As France was being rocked by revolutions, the British undertook to reform their laws to prevent a similar catastrophe. Bentham led the "Philosophic Radicals" in their quest to transform the government—as quietly and bloodlessly as possible—to be consistent with the more scientific, more rational principles of the Enlightenment.

Bentham was extremely sensitive as a child and his primary source of pleasure was in books. By the age of four he was reading Latin. At the age of fifteen he graduated from Queen's College, Oxford. He studied law for a time but became frustrated because he felt English laws were impractically complex and inconsistent.

In 1776 Bentham published an essay lampooning the American Declaration of Independence, mocking it for attempting to secure rights to "life, liberty, and the pursuit of happiness," by instituting a government when "nothing which can be called Government ever was, or ever could be, in any instance, exercised, but at the expence of one or other of those rights."[19] During the same year he wrote a response to William Blackstone's *Commentaries on the Laws of England*, in which he first introduced the principle of utility.[20]

In his *Comment on the Commentaries*, Bentham argued that Blackstone was too complacent with English law as it stood. Bentham thought that along with scientific progress society should be pursuing *moral progress* as well. "Correspondent to *discovery* and *improvement* in the natural world, is *reformation* in the moral; if that which seems a common notion be, indeed, a true one, that in the moral world there no longer remains any matter for *discovery*. Perhaps, however, this may not be the case ..." It is here that he introduces the "fundamental axiom" of utility as a discovery that could lead to such progress:

> It is the greatest happiness of the greatest number that is the measure of right and wrong.

He called the "grand and fundamental" blemish of Blackstone's book its "antipathy to reform." According to Bentham, it contained many defenses and justifications of the laws of England, but made no effort to criticize even the most unreasonable laws. For too long these laws had been used to benefit the few wealthy over the many poor. Bentham felt he needed an external criterion to prove the absurdity of this. So he used the notion of utility.

It is relevant to our discussion that Bentham introduced the notion of *utility*—the greatest happiness of the greatest number—to defend a kind of *progress*. The two notions are both historically and conceptually linked. It is not clear how you would measure progress if you didn't somehow take into account total happiness, summed over all people in question. What began as a reasonable assumption for England would eventually spread throughout the West. By the twentieth century, social reformers would routinely (if dubiously) apply the principle of the greatest happiness for the greatest number of people to the entire world.

When the French Revolution was at its height, a man named Honoré Gabriel Riqueti, comte de Mirabeau—a Jacobin—became interested in Bentham's ideas. He wanted France's new laws to be modeled after English Law. He and Bentham corresponded for many years. Once Mirabeau rose to power, he was so grateful to Bentham that he granted him French citizenship. Mirabeau died shortly after; it is suspected he was poisoned by his political opponents.

Bentham sought clarity and precision in expressing his ideas, and his book, *Principles of Morals and Legislation,* laid out his theory of utility as a "calculus."

> It is not to be expected that this process should be strictly pursued previously to every moral judgment, or to every legislative or judicial operation. It may, however, be always kept in view: and as near as the process actually pursued on these occasions approaches to it, so near will such process approach to the character of an exact one.
>
> To a number of persons, with reference to each of whom to the value of a pleasure or a pain is considered, it will be greater or less, according to seven circumstances: to wit, the six preceding ones; viz.
>
> 1. Its intensity.
> 2. Its duration.
> 3. Its certainty or uncertainty.
> 4. Its propinquity or remoteness.
> 5. Its fecundity.
> 6. Its purity.
>
> And one other; to wit:
>
> 7. Its extent; that is, the number of persons to whom it extends; or (in other words) who are affected by it.

Though as precise as he could make it, the point of the framework was not to make an exact calculation of the balance between pleasure and pain for a given population. This would be impractical. The point was to have a perspective in mind that is useful in making social judgments. If a certain law benefited a few wealthy individuals but made life more miserable for many workers, the law was clearly unjust.

In 1823 Jeremy Bentham and James Mill founded the *Westminster Review*, a periodical for "Philosophic Radicals." James Mill's son, John Stuart Mill, was brought up a "utilitarian" from a young age, and would go on to become the most famously brilliant of the utilitarians, a philosopher of science and politics whose books would be widely influential.

UTILITARIANISM EVOLVES

Many readers of Bentham considered his calculus offensive or useless. Holding up bodily pleasures as the ultimate good of society was deemed hedonistic. The popular reactionary philosopher Thomas Carlyle ridiculed it unsparingly, satirizing it as "Pig Philosophy":

> Supposing swine (I mean four-footed swine), of sensibility and superior logical parts, had attained such culture; and could, after survey and reflection, jot down for us their notion of the Universe ... Pig Propositions, in a rough form, are somewhat as follows:
> 1. The Universe, so far as sane conjecture can go, is an immeasurable Swine's-trough, consisting of solid and liquid, and of other contrasts and kinds;—especially consisting of attainable and unattainable, the latter in immensely great quantities for most pigs.
> 2. Moral evil is unattainability of Pig's-wash; moral good, attainability of ditto.

By the twentieth century utilitarians would go to great lengths to distance themselves from Bentham's so-called hedonistic calculus. The academic philosopher G.E. Moore urged what he called "ideal utilitarianism" which sums all *objective* positive qualities, including beauty, courage, truth, and goodness. Clearly a life of pain that was lived in service of Truth and Beauty was preferable to a life of pleasure lived in service to the Ugly and False. But this way of looking at things was difficult to make precise, and utilitarians remained divided.

At present, most serious utilitarians such as Peter Singer and Richard Hare calculate total utility in terms of preferences. According to preference utilitarianism no assumptions need to be made about whether people value pleasure, beauty, truth, or whatnot, as long as we simply take into account what outcomes each person would prefer. The resulting utilitarian calculus ends up looking like democratic voting, and modern utilitarians claim that circulating surveys is among the best ways to practically measure what would give the greatest happiness to the greatest number.

Whether utilitarianism has come very far since the time of the French Revolution is open to debate. Either way, our society has certainly absorbed utilitarianism into its overarching myth of progress. It's the most objective-seeming way to measure the greater good, and when people argue for the benefits of technology and industrialization they tend to make utilitarian claims. "Sure, technology has its downsides," people tend to say, "but hasn't it made most of our lives more pleasant? Isn't it raising standards of living in most countries?"

Modern utilitarians tend to be neo-Malthusians, that is, they believe that we must reduce birth rates in order to achieve worldwide progress. In Peter Singer's widely used textbook, *Practical Ethics*, it is assumed without argument that overpopulation is to be avoided by controlling family size. For example, he criticizes one argument against abortion—that it ends a *potential* life—simply by pointing out that it "does not provide any reason for thinking abortion worse than any other means of population control. If the world is already overpopulated, the argument provides no reason at all against abortion." He takes it for granted that "overpopulation" is to be combated with population control of some kind.

Jeremy Bentham believed utilitarianism to urge the exact opposite conclusion, at least for the England of his day. In his essay "Of Population" (1843) he wrote "Increase of population is desirable, as being an increase of—1. The beings susceptible of enjoyment; 2. The beings capable of being employed as instruments of defense. It results of course from the increase of the means of subsistence, and cannot be carried beyond them." Bentham's view thus had some close similarities to Malthus's. A population will always be checked so that it does not exceed "means of subsistence," that is, production of food. Because it naturally grows at an exponential rate "next to nothing is required to be done by the government." His advice is simply to "[r]ender men happy, and trust to nature."

At what point then, did utilitarianism go from being Malthusian to neo-Malthusian? At what point did it stop urging population growth and start preaching population control? In a 2008 article in *Revue d'etudes benthamiennes,* Michael Quinn identifies the key turning points in this transformation. One of Bentham's unpublished manuscripts states:

Sooner or later the earth itself, if the play of the planets suffer it to last thus long, will have reached the same period of maturity and repletion. Thence will the policy of the statesman be directed to the arrestment of population, as now to its encrease: and what is now stigmatized under the name of vice will then receive the treatment, if not the name, of virtue.[21]

John Stuart Mill would later recall the Philosophic Radicals' developing views on population:

Malthus's population principle was quite as much a banner, and point of union among us, as any opinion specially belonging to Bentham. This great doctrine, originally brought forward as an argument against the infinite improvability of human affairs, we took up with ardent zeal in the contrary sense, as indicating the sole means of realizing that improvability by securing full employment at high wages to the whole labouring population through a voluntary restriction of the increase of their numbers.[22]

In other words, where Malthus saw an absolute barrier to progress in terms of population growth, the utilitarians eventually saw the only possible route to progress. Quinn explains Mill's ardency in this quest:

For a secular utilitarian, the obvious alternative to moral restraint was contraception, and Mill was certainly associated with Francis Place in his campaign in the 1820's to advocate the practice, and to publicize a means for its achievement. Mill himself had pseudonymously written three articles arguing in favour of birth control, and was briefly arrested for involvement in distributing handbills providing practical instruction.

What the Philosophic Radicals were lacking, as I argued in Chapter 2, was an understanding of Darwin's Law as an ultimate barrier to the success of global progress. Populations that reproduce more slowly are gradually eliminated by natural selection—as occurred during the late Roman Empire. Furthermore, when growth is reduced and selection diminished more mutations will enter the population, leading to nonequilibrium.

Can we set absolute constraints on the increase of worldwide happiness? I believe we can, but to do it we must somehow define "happiness." Utilitarianism provides some important clues. Our notion of happiness appears to be related to tipping the balance between pleasure and pain. It would seem to depend on how different people would, in an ideal situation, rank their preferences.

These are ultimately philosophical questions, since they concern value-laden terminology. But let's do what we can to develop principles that are generally-applicable, logical, and objective.

THE BALANCE OF JOY AND SUFFERING

Let's consider the notion of *value* in its most abstract and general sense. Moral values distinguish right from wrong. Aesthetic values distinguish beautiful from ugly. Philosophical values distinguish rational from irrational. In every case of value judgment, most generally, *good* is distinguished from *bad*.

In all cases, if a person calls something *good*, it is preferable to something *bad*. Given a choice, that which you would choose is what you would call the "better." That which you would reject you would call the "worse."

It's not controversial to say that a happier state of affairs is one that a person would call better, and that a sadder state of affairs is one they would call worse. By *joy* we mean the experience of something better. By *suffering* we mean the experience of something worse.

So far, so good. But now we do come to a controversial question: What kind of creature must you be to experience joy or suffering? In other words, what kind of creature is capable of making value judgments of better and worse? Do plants experience joy? Insects? Fish? Higher mammals? Or is value the sole province of humans?

A more fundamental question is this. From a psychological point of view, why do we experience joy or suffering at all? Why do we bother making value judgments?

There is only one answer to this question that makes any sense: to learn. Let me explain why.

First, note that joy and suffering are *mental* states. They are processes of the brain.

Second, recall our principle that, given a choice, an individual will always choose the better over the worse. An individual will always choose joy over suffering.

Third, in order for choice to be possible, foresight is necessary. Choice #1 leads to joy. Choice #2 leads to suffering. If choice #1 is intrinsically better we would expect it to be a matter of instinct. Your heart pumping blood, for example, requires no choice because it is intrinsically better, that is better in every case. On the other hand, tilling a field is harder than doing nothing and is only preferable if it pays off in later satisfaction. This is why people choose to till a field but do not choose for their heart to pump blood.

Finally, foresight implies learning. Foresight cannot be the result of instinct or tradition. It must be the result of experience. One might imagine a race of humans who have evolved an instinct to till their fields on the day of the spring equinox, something they do without thinking the way birds instinctively migrate south. Such humans would not be making a choice to till their fields. The same is true if they are simply following tradition without any reflection. If there is any meaningful choice at all there must be some expectation of what outcomes their choice might bring. If a farmer decides to break tradition and plant at a different time, for this decision to make sense it must be based on an experience. The old way of doing things didn't work. The old way of doing things was worse. This change of opinion implies that the farmer *learned* to anticipate a certain outcome.

So, value judgments always involve learning. When a certain kind of choice leads to suffering, that kind of choice is now categorized as bad. In evolutionary terms, it is usually *selected against*. When a certain choice leads to joy, that kind of choice is now categorized as good. In evolutionary terms, good ideas are normally *selected for*. No one would honestly say, "That was bad and painful, so let's do it again." No one would ever say, "That was a pleasant outcome, always to be avoided." Pleasure and pain, joy and suffering are psychological functions designed by evolution to allow a mind to select good decisions among bad. This becomes obvious if we look at organisms without brains, such as plants. Many plants do have the ability to move. Sunflowers, for example, track the movement of the sun. But there is little reason for plants to learn because usually they do not need to adapt their strategies. They absorb water and nutrients, grow, and seek out sunlight. None of these processes require choice. They are simply done. Perhaps some rudimentary learning is possible. Plants are known to exchange chemical signals in certain cases to trigger the release of pesticides, for example. But to be learning there would have to be a system of value in place, such that some outcomes are considered bad (for example lack of sunlight) and others are considered good. And in order for these systems of value to operate the plant would need a way to perceive good and bad, i.e., to experience joy and suffering.

If a cow were to strip the leaves off the branches of a tree, we don't imagine that tree would suffer if there were nothing to do about it, if the tree were to continue as before. But what if we assume the tree can change the way it grows so that its leaves are more thorny and worse to eat? Only in such a case—when adaptive learning is possible—can we imagine that the tree might feel pain. Without learning, suffering has no function. And the same must be true for joy.

Joy evolves as perceived *gain* in evolutionary fitness, and suffering evolves as perceived *loss* of evolutionary fitness. If it were the other way around, organisms would have evolved to seek out pain and avoid pleasure. And if there were no difference in fitness, as with the tree that can't react to its leaves being eaten, there would be no selective advantage and the perception of pleasure and pain would never evolve in the first place.

If you had an organism that took pleasure when its evolutionary fitness decreased, and another organism that took pleasure when its evolutionary fitness increased, then natural selection would eventually lead to the extinction of the first and the predominance of the second.

Again, value judgments require choice. Choice requires foresight. Foresight requires learning. And as we've seen, such learning requires experience. (Learning from tradition counts as a kind of instinct, in this discussion.) In short, *value judgments require experience*.

Experience is the formation of a memory that something was either better or worse than usual. If experience is possible, joy and suffering are possible. I'd like to argue, furthermore, that joy and suffering must balance one another with increasing exactness in the long run.

Humans have evolved a capacity to learn only because the best courses of action may depend on time and place. Adaptation is important because conditions change. If conditions did not change we would not need learning and we could act purely according to instinct and tradition.

Changing conditions mean some unpredictability. If the changes were entirely predictable there would be no reason to make a choice. We would not need minds at all. We have minds so we can take our experiences—some good, some bad—and use them to make better choices in the future.

VALUES AND THE BALANCE OF JOY AND SUFFERING

Now I'd like to make a key point of this book, perhaps my most important point. It will take a little more work, but bear with me.

Take any given value distinction. Any dichotomy between joy and suffering will do. Let's say skinny versus non-skinny. Choose an arbitrary body-mass index and call it "too skinny." This is our negative value judgment, our "worse," or condition for suffering. Our positive value, our "better," or condition of joy, is to have a body-mass index higher than this number.

If none were below the threshold, or none above, it would be a meaningless distinction to make. Assuming we are speaking of a meaningful value, it is unavoidable that some people will be below, and thus "suffer" by our definition, and that some will be above the threshold, and thus "rejoice." True, those that suffer may later change their lifestyles and achieve a "better" body-mass index. But all we want to calculate is the fitness, that is the reproduction rate, of the entire population on average.

In the long run, the average growth rate of a population must be very close to zero. Even if the growth rate is slightly above zero, this is exponential growth and will eventually outstrip available resources. And if the growth rate is slightly below zero, this is exponential decline and the population will die out before long. So the average growth rate will converge to zero in the long term.

And as we've seen, the suffering members of this population, those with a too-low body-mass index, must be less fit. Their reproduction rate is lower. Those who have a high-enough body-mass index must be more fit, and their reproduction rate must be higher.

Since the two growth rates must add to zero, one must be positive and the other must be negative. If there are only a few people suffering, they must have a much lower fitness to balance out the high reproduction rate of the many people rejoicing. Or if there are only a few people rejoicing, then they must have a much higher fitness to make up for all the people reproducing slowly.

All we have left to do to prove that Bentham's measure of happiness sums to zero, is to show that the amount of suffering must be proportional to the amount of fitness loss, and the amount of joy must be proportional to the amount of fitness gain. If this is true then the sum of happiness and joy over an entire population, for any value, must sum to zero in the long run.

Here's why it is true that happiness must be proportional to fitness. Imagine that some people in our population have a choice: either they can be too skinny by not eating a certain grain, or they can have a healthy weight by eating this grain. And let's say the grain takes a lot of time to grow. If you grow it, you spend more time working and have less time for reproducing.

Which option is better? Being skinny makes it harder to reproduce, but so does growing the grain. The question is which practice has highest fitness overall. Assuming our population has reached an adaptive solution to the dilemma, the higher fitness option must lead to joy and the lower fitness option must lead to suffering. For this to work out, being a healthy weight must be more pleasant than growing the grain is unpleasant *exactly when* being a healthy weight is fitter than growing the grain is unfit. In other words, the adaptive optimum occurs when joy and suffering are exactly proportional to the associated fitness gain and loss. Joy, it would appear, is simply our perception of a gain in fitness; just as suffering is our perception of a loss in fitness. *And it is in our evolutionary interest for these perceptions to be as accurate as possible so we can best weigh our options.*

That isn't to say the best choice is always obvious. In particular, the Western world is filled with so many new choices that our instincts haven't evolved for, from eating junk food to learning quantum physics to using condoms, that we quite often choose what would be obviously less fit according to Darwinian selection. But this is an unstable state of affairs in the long run. We would expect that eventually our pleasures and pains would evolve to more accurately track what is better and worse for our progeny.

And more to the point, it would be absurd to argue that progress is possible merely because our pleasures and pains might have difficulty reflecting fitness and unfitness exactly. The promotion of birth control is a good example of such a difficulty. Nations with high birth rates almost always place a higher social value on large families. The larger the family the more admired the parents, and the more widely imitated. Western society was the same for thousands of years. To think that the current state of our culture, where children are discouraged, will somehow miraculously pass the evolutionary test is unrealistic. Societies whose values are more in line with evolution are almost certain to predominate in the future, just as those Roman and Greek cultures that encouraged infanticide eventually gave way to those who developed the value judgment that such practices were worse.

But let's return to our theoretical discussion, because I think we've hit upon a very important law, the Law of the Balance of Joy and Suffering. We know from Malthus's Principle that birth and death—that is, creation and destruction—must balance out with asymptotic exactness in the long run. From Darwin's Law we know that our values, our very notions of what is good or bad, happy or sad, are subject to the constraints of natural selection. We know that they will tend to track fitness and unfitness, that their evolutionary purpose is to track them with as much precision as possible.

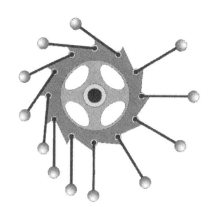

Illustration 4: The overbalanced wheel, a classic perpetual motion scheme dating at the latest from the writings of Bhaskara in the 12th century (Dims, 2005, Wikimedia, public domain).

We are logically assured, then, that progress is impossible. All joy is, in the long term, balanced by suffering. But we also know that all suffering is eventually balanced by joy. Not only progress, but regress too is impossible. In fact, many of the fears of the reactionaries and eugenicists are as irrational as the hopes of the utopians and progressives.

Take a moment to examine *Illustration 4*. Such a device, known as the "overbalanced wheel," has often been thought to be a perpetual motion machine. If you'll count the weights to each side of the middle line it will appear that there are more on one side than the other. You might expect that this perpetual imbalance would cause the machine to turn forever. Can you figure out what is wrong with this expectation?

The easiest way to see the problem is to use Archimedes' theory of the lever. Even though one half has more weights, those weights are closer to the center and thus exert less force. The weights on the other half have more leverage, and if you do the calculation you will see that this makes up for there being fewer of them.

But simply doing this calculation is not enough to explain why *no* perpetual motion device is possible. To show this we need the principle of Conservation of Energy, which can be proven using Newtonian physics.

Similarly, to show that progress is in general impossible, I'd like to argue that the Balance of Joy and Suffering is a law of evolution. Putting the argument above in mathematical form is unnecessary, because the basic reasoning is very simple. Organisms that prefer a higher-fitness outcome will be fitter in the long run. The optimal preference rankings should track fitness rankings. Fitnesses must always average to one in the long run, so the average preference for the actual state of affairs should equal the preference ranking for fitness equal to one. It follows that the average preference for the current state of affairs, taken over all people, cannot increase or decrease on any permanent basis.

RELIGION AND THE EVOLUTION OF VALUES

One is reminded of the passage from Lao Tzu's *Tao Te Ching*, an ancient Chinese book of philosophy: "All the world knows good. But if that becomes good, this becomes bad. The coexistence of have and have not ... is endless."

Implicit insights about evolution, selection, and reproduction can be found in many philosophies and religions, suggesting that these ideas themselves, even when they are unproven, have evolutionary fitness.

Ideas of population control rarely survive for more a few centuries. Both Plato's *Republic* and Aristotle's *Politics*, the two most influential political tracts of Antiquity, endorsed population control as a means of preventing hunger and revolution in the populace. The Romans and Greeks had no reliable methods for abortion or contraception, however, so infanticide was generally used alongside certain crude and dangerous methods of abortion. This was especially common in cities, among the nobility, and in cases where individuals sought to advance their careers unhindered by family duties.

Within centuries, however, infanticide and abortion were universally acknowledged as wrong. What happened?

Christianity has often been blamed for this change of heart, but there are no surviving quotes from Jesus weighing one way or another on the matter. The apostle Paul merely encouraged abstinence and discouraged sex outside of marriage. Many early Christians, notably a number of Gnostic sects, practiced infanticide or discouraged families altogether. It was only later, after several generations, that Christians who valued families rose to predominate.

There is evidence that a higher value was placed on families as the Roman Empire declined and Christianity ascended. In his 1984 article "Latin Funerary Epigraphy," Brent D. Shaw points out that:

1. Compared with pagans, Christian inscriptions almost never noted secular, non-genetic relationships. In earlier centuries and in cities, on the other hand, secular relationships were most common.
2. Christian tombs, contrasted with pagan tombs, were also generally dedicated to children and young people rather than to parents.

There is a great deal of such evidence concerning the evolution of values surrounding family and fertility[23]. We do not have space to discuss it all here, but I encourage the interested reader to investigate the late Roman Empire and compare with the state of affairs in the modern world.

In any case, we do not need direct evidence to infer that natural selection would have favored the proliferation of anti-infanticide and anti-abortion values.

For centuries, at least among the elite, the teachings of Plato and Aristotle were considered the most rational. It seemed to follow logically that if you limited your population you would have more resources. But it appears that such rational arguments only led to selection against rationality. Within a few centuries, the teachings of Plato and Aristotle took a back seat to the *Bible*, which was filled with admonitions to ensure the multiplication of your progeny, and prevent your lineage from dwindling:

GENESIS 9:7:
> As for you, be fruitful and increase in number; multiply on the earth and increase upon it.

GENESIS 22:17:
> I will surely bless you and make your descendants as numerous as the stars in the sky and as the sand on the seashore.

Exodus 20:5:
> I, the Lord your God, am a jealous God, punishing the children for the sin of the fathers to the third and fourth generation of those who hate me, but showing love to a thousand generations of those who love me and keep my commandments.

Deuteronomy 28:18:
> The fruit of your womb will be cursed ...

Psalm 127:3:
> Sons are a heritage from the Lord, children a reward from him.

Job 21:19:
> It is said, 'God stores up his punishment of the wicked for their children.'

1 Timothy 2:15:
> But women will be saved through childbearing — if they continue in faith, love and holiness with propriety.

There are many more such passages in both the *Old Testament* and the *New*. The *Bible* mentions the afterlife actually quite rarely, and there are several times more warnings and blessings directed toward descendants than toward the afterlife. Using the "Topical Guide" of a King James version of the *Bible*, I have found a total of 39 references to rewards and punishments in terms of number of descendants, and only 14 references to punishment in the afterlife. Interestingly, every unambiguous mention of the afterlife occurs in the New Testament. Cross-referencing with other translations, *not one* mention of "heaven" or "hell" in the Old Testament can be decisively interpreted as a reference to the afterlife rather than the "sky" or the "grave" respectively.

Frequent encouragements to leave descendants and pass down values faithfully are found in every other major religion:

Qur'an, "Abundance":
> We have truly given abundance to you [in descendants] — so pray to your Lord and make your sacrifice to Him alone — it is the one who hates you who has been cut off [in descendants].

Rig Veda 2:2:
> Help us to wealth exceeding good and glorious, abundant, rich in children and their progeny.

BHAGAVAD GITA 1.39-43:
> On destruction of the family, the perennial family dharmas perish. When dharma perishes, adharma [the opposite of dharma] overwhelms the entire family. From the predominance of adharma, O Krishna, the family women are polluted. When the women are polluted, O Varshneya, a confusion of social orders arises. This confusion leads only to hell both for the destroyers of families and for the family. Certainly the forefathers fall since the ritual offerings of food and water are suspended. By these crimes of the family killers, who propagate a confusion of social classes, community dharmas and the everlasting family dharmas are devastated. We have always heard, O Janardana, that those men who devastate family dharmas have their residence fixed in hell.

CONFUCIUS, "DOCTRINE OF THE MEAN":
> It is said in the Book of Poetry: 'A happy union with wife and children is like the music of lutes and harps! When there is concord among brethren, the harmony is delightful and enduring. Thus may you regulate your family and enjoy the delights of wife and children!' The Master said, 'In such a condition parents find perfect contentment.'

Selection for these sorts of doctrines continues to this day. The fastest growing subpopulations of the United States include traditional Catholics, Mormons, Amish, and Rabbinical Jews, all of which value family highly and have birth rates two to three times the national average. At current rates of growth—taking into account members who leave the religion—these minorities will together make up the majority of the North American population within three centuries.

Progressives argue that population control will help tip the balance between joy and suffering by ensuring that there is enough food for all. Small families are considered preferable today in the West, rewarded with more admiration, especially in the media. But this set of values is not consistent with evolution. It is inevitable that this value judgment will eventually give way to the "family values" seen in more traditional, longer-lived societies, and in our own past. The precedent for this is ancient Rome, where it was thought that killing one's extra infants would make one happier. This practice came to be seen as monstrous by some, and eventually by most Western cultures, as it is still today.

It is interesting to note that the most prominent utilitarian philosopher of our time, Peter Singer, who endorses an absolute right to abortion, argues in his book *Practical Ethics* that "the newborn baby is on the same footing as the fetus, and hence fewer reasons exist against killing both babies and fetuses than exist against killing those who are capable of seeing themselves as distinct entities ..." To be fair, this is a controversial view at present and not all modern philosophers share it. But we are left with something of a puzzle: if evolution tends to eliminate such views, why do they keep coming back? To resolve this paradox we must get clear on the distinction between culturally and biologically evolved values.

BIOLOGICAL VERSUS CULTURAL EVOLUTION OF VALUES

Karl Popper, as I've remarked, once proclaimed that rational thought sets humans apart because it allows our ideas to "die in our stead."

There are two possible ways an idea can die. You can either forget it because it is bad or useless, or you can physically die. The first option implies some sort of value judgment, whether the idea was deemed harmful or simply not interesting enough to remember.

Popper is correct to point out that judging ideas as good or bad is essential to rationality. Perhaps one could call it the defining feature of humankind. But there is a progressive note to what he writes:

> Our schema allows for the development of error-eliminating controls (warning organs like the eye; feed-back mechanisms); that is, controls which can eliminate errors without killing the organism; and makes it possible, ultimately, for our hypotheses to die in our stead (Popper, "Of Clouds and Clocks," 1982).

It does seem like human rationality allows us to see still farther ahead and possibly discard an idea before it leads to death. And isn't this foresight exactly what is supposed to allow us to finally achieve progress? Modern philosophers and social scientists seem to think so. Another element of this kind of progressivism is the idea that we can choose better sets of values for ourselves. As Popper puts it:

> It would be a mistake to think that, because of natural selection, evolution can only lead to what may be called 'utilitarian' results: to adaptations which are useful in helping us to survive. ... [T]he choice of aim may become a problem; different aims may compete, and new aims may be invented and controlled ...

In his book *Collapse,* Jared Diamond puts forward a similar pair of ideas. He states that our world faces "overpopulation" and "overwhelming poverty" but declares that "we are not beset by insoluble problems." He believes that "long-term planning, and willingness to reconsider core values" would ensure that "the most serious [global problems] are not ones beyond our control."

Both of these writers believe that (1) prediction and (2) conscious selection among our cultural values places our modern civilization a step higher in rationality, giving us a perspective from which we can achieve progress. This belief is shared by many scientists and philosophers:

- E.O. Wilson, after lengthy arguments that culture cannot escape its slavery to biology, ends his book *On Human Nature* on a similar note, suggesting that if we change our values so that "scientific materialism" becomes our new "mythology" or "religion" then "human progress" may occur.
- Both Daniel Dennett and Richard Dawkins believe that selection among ideas rather than genes gives us a way to transcend brute selection. "Persons," writes Dennett, "as a result of interactions between their meme-infested brains, are not at all bound to answer to the interests of their genes alone—or their memes alone. That is our transcendence, our capacity to 'rebel against the tyranny of the selfish replicators,' as Dawkins says ..."

This view of the cultural evolution of values is, I think, based on fallacious reasoning. These thinkers have likely missed the fallacies being made because their utopian hopes are usually reserved for the final chapters of their books, offered less as well-argued theories and more as icing on the cake.

One fallacy is the idea that we might know beforehand which set of values will turn out to be best. There are two ways to see the mistake. (a) Following our discussion in Section 3.4, we know that for learning to be beneficial, the environment must change in unpredictable ways. There will always be events that catch us off guard, otherwise learning would be unnecessary and we would act out of pure instinct and tradition. (b) We can also simply note that our world is too complex for the prediction of future fitness to be infallible. The most rational minds of the Roman era were blind to the fact that Platonic philosophy would decline and Christianity would rise to prominence. At present we still have massive disagreements about what our future holds, even among our most respected thinkers.

Another fallacy is the assumption that consciously selecting among our core values is generally less painful than pure natural selection. On the contrary, values, especially *core values*, are things people are often willing to die for. Giving up ideas is painful. It's not easy to convert someone to a new belief system. It's not easy to convince someone they are wrong, and even if proof is possible it is not pleasant to be proven wrong, especially about something fundamental.

Ultimately, all the arguments I've given about the balance between joy and suffering apply to ideologies. Ideologies that seek their own demise will die out. Ideologies that value convincing others will spread. When ideologies don't place much value on conversion, as in Judaism, they invariably place great value on procreation. Ideologies that don't value biological procreation, such as modern progressivism, tend to place great value on convincing others that you are right. (In fact the hope that the world population can be controlled depends on *convincing everyone in the world* to control births.)

The same considerations of fitness tracking apply to cultural values. Ideas that are less essential to overall fitness, such as trivia or historical knowledge, are less painful to lose. But it is extremely painful to lose faith in one's entire religion or to suffer a complete ideological breakdown, and these cases are more relevant to overall fitness.

Our minds are inextricable combinations of biological drives and cultural values. Biological joy tends to be bodily, such as food and sex. Biological suffering is similar—physical harm, ugliness. These sorts of value judgments are programmed into our genes. Aesthetic pleasure, especially in nature, is probably largely genetic too.

Cultural joy comes in the form of pride and praise. When we do something we feel that others will emulate we are taught to be proud. We enjoy to receive praise from others, and this makes sense in terms of cultural evolution because it means that we enjoy receiving attention and being able to teach our ideas to others. There is surely a biological component here too, since being admired has biological benefits. But to a large extent we are *taught* what to be proud of, whether it is having a large family or writing beautiful poetry. Our points of pride are primarily cultural.

Cultural suffering comes in the form of shame and disapproval. People feel ashamed for wearing clothes that are out of fashion, or people are ridiculed for holding certain religious beliefs. These things are never pleasant, and in extreme cases this kind of suffering can be severe enough to lead to suicide.

The same balance between joy and suffering must ultimately apply to culture. The function of pride and shame is to allow people to learn how best to reproduce their ideas in others. If some ideas have fitness higher than one, then if the population of ideas is to remain constant, other ideas must have fitness exactly the same degree lower than one. And as with biological values, pride and shame must match the degree of fitness gain or loss if they are to have any evolutionary benefit.

There are physical limitations to data storage, whether in brains or computers. Exponential growth, as we are experiencing now with computers and brains, can only last for a relatively short time according to Malthus's principle. Deaths and births of ideas must balance out too. And we should expect that with ideas, as with genes, spreading them is pleasurable and letting them die is painful.

Another apparent way around Malthus—rationally choosing our own ideas and values—has been shown illusory. Any extra happiness this might give would be balanced by suffering somewhere else. If some people are praised, others will be shamed. Even if we could prove that a certain set of values was perfect, and everyone adopted that set of values, then there would be no pride or praise to be had, because no one would have a fitter set of values than anyone else.

Whether we are talking biological values or cultural values, they are all subject to Darwin's Law, and thus are selected for fitness. Over time we would expect our cultural values to converge, as our biological instincts have, on ideals that promote fitness. We expect suffering to accompany destruction and joy to accompany creation.

Cultural values are subject to the same unshakable forces of evolution as biology. Both cultural individuals and cultural institutions seek evolutionary fitness. We see this with writers, who universally want their books to spread their ideas, leaders, who all want to be admired and emulated, and traditional religions, that all promote either childrearing or missionary work or both so that they can grow. When a writer fails to gain an audience, the feeling is one of defeat. The same goes for a leader who loses a campaign, or a religion or ideology that is persecuted or ridiculed, rather than admired and emulated.

We are so used to thinking this way that we've overlooked how obviously our quests for power, truth, and influence can all be seen as natural results of evolutionary selection among cultural values.

And now it should be clear how the same ideas of birth control return again and again, despite genetic selection against them. By sacrificing family, certain people are sometimes able to achieve an unusually high *cultural* fitness. Today's mass media gives certain people, who give up everything for fame, great power to persuade many people of their values. And these values, unsurprisingly, stress the importance of spreading ideas (fame, education) *over* spreading genes (family, childrearing).

In the meantime, "traditional" societies—which have not adopted Western values and avoid mass media—almost always place a high value on large families. But because they spend so much time on family, there is much less time to advance career and run big businesses and industries, which may explain why people in the West often look down on them as less "advanced." That is, as less "progressed."

Is there a way to strike a balance between cultural and biological evolution? The fact is, it's already been done many times. All long-lived traditional societies have manifestly succeeded in this. It is our culture in particular that has lost this balance and come to favor cultural success so violently.

But could we not do better than tradition, and use the theory of evolution to create a society that is exceptionally fit? There have already been ideologies that have attempted this, most famously fascism and eugenics. But such movements have oversimplified and misused evolutionary theory. The truth is humans are far too complex to design from scratch. So are social systems. The world we inhabit is far too complex for us even to calculate what strategies would give the maximum fitness. Our blindness to this inexhaustible complexity has led to a number of mistaken interpretations of evolutionary theory, particularly ones that misunderstand "survival of the fittest" by stressing its brutal and selfish aspects over its compassionate and unselfish ones. In the next chapter I will elaborate on this point, showing that evolution should teach us not contempt for the altruistic teachings of traditional religions, but rather a deep respect for those teachings that have been tried longest and hardest by the process of cultural selection.

SUMMARY AND PHILOSOPHICAL IMPLICATIONS

Prior to this chapter we took it for granted that creation (or reproductive success) means joy, and destruction (or reproductive failure) means suffering. This assumption falls under the broad category of utilitarianism, since it requires a way to measure joy and suffering as quantities.

The first utilitarian, Jeremy Bentham, introduced the idea that we should strive to achieve progress by maximizing people's happiness. This idea has taken hold, and led to the neo-Malthusian strategy of using birth control to increase overall happiness. Modern philosophers define total happiness in terms of preference rankings, as people might provide in a survey. This is the dominant theory of ethics among modern progressives.

Analyzing our usage of the terms "good" and "bad," we can see that the experience of goodness and badness, or joy and suffering, *evolved* so that we could *learn* to avoid certain outcomes and pursue others. Evolution will shape joy and suffering so that joy causes us to pursue sources of reproductive success and suffering causes us to avoid sources of reproductive failure. Ideally, as we weigh joy and suffering against one another, we should be doing so according to their effects on fitness. Though this ideal will not be realized exactly in real organisms, instincts will tend to converge to this ideal in long-run evolution. And since fitness should always average to one in the long run—due to Malthusian resource constraints—total joy and suffering, which reflect displacements from this average, will always cancel to zero in the long run. I refer to this principle as the Law of Balance of Joy and Suffering, which contradicts the idea of long-term, worldwide progress.

Looking at the history of reproduction in the late Roman Empire, we see that belief systems encouraging small families eventually went extinct. In fact, all long-lived, traditional religions encourage large families. This confirms that natural selection shapes culturally transmitted values and calibrates them to evolutionary fitness. Religions have thrived or perished based on the evolutionary fidelity of their value systems.

Many modern philosophers have argued that progress is achievable by rationally choosing our values and using foresight to overcome selection. However, foresight is always limited and values that do not respect Darwin's Law are selected against. It is already common sense that ideologies seek to spread themselves, and those that don't care to spread will die out. We've just been failing to express this observation in terms of long-run evolution.

Sometimes cultural and biological evolution come into conflict. Some societies, through the spread of mass communication, encourage people to value fame over family. In other societies this valuation is reversed. Either way the result is instability, either through cultural or genetic decay. The most long-lived, traditional societies have a balance of the two, often where religious leaders alone sacrifice family to pass on old traditions, while most of the lay population is expected to strive to pass on their genetic legacy.

Values form the core or germ line of a culture. Since values are used to select other cultural elements, and even biological ones, they constitute the locus of cultural evolution, dying out by natural selection—rather than rational selection—when they are unsuccessful. Religious texts may seem irrational, but they have been shaped by thousands of years of natural selection. The ones that have survived and spread most widely therefore most closely reflect what is evolutionarily optimal.

Ancient wisdom, from this point of view, contains much more of value than modern rationalists would have us believe. Unless we respect the ancient traditions, our society stands in danger of losing its connection to its own evolutionary past, and giving way to other more vibrant societies with a longer memory for what matters.

V

EVOLUTION AND COMPASSION

DOES HUMAN EVOLUTION EQUAL SOCIAL DARWINISM?

The evolutionary way of describing human culture may sound stark. It may seem that everything has been reduced to evolutionary fitness. Apparently life is a zero-sum game and there are always winners and losers. Even before Darwin's theory was published, Alfred Lord Tennyson, having read Malthus and precursors to Darwin such as Oswald Chambers, wrote of "nature red in tooth and claw." A century and a half later, Dawkins in the *Selfish Gene* would praise Tennyson's phrase as an "admirable" summary of natural selection. The view that human society should be this way is often called *Social Darwinism*. Eugenicists and industrial capitalists have been classed as part of this movement.

But the fact is, "Social Darwinism" was never an actual movement or school of thought, and few if any sociologists have openly endorsed it. It is a label more than a movement, used historically to throw discredit on overly competitive views of life, including fascism, nationalism, and racism. The label was popularized most widely by Richard Hofstadter's 1944 book, *Social Darwinism in American Thought*.[24] But many historians of sociology are now arguing that Darwinism has played a subordinate role, if any, in producing nationalistic movements. Geoffrey Hodgson has done an extensive survey of the literature between Darwin and World War II and found that "not only conservatives and nationalists used Darwinian arguments. In addition, anarchists, socialists and liberals deployed them extensively."[25]

The real question is this, and it needs to be addressed directly: *Does Darwinism commit us to a brutally competitive view of life?*

In this chapter I argue that it doesn't. On the contrary, a nuanced understanding of Darwinian evolution can help explain the origins of compassion and altruism. Malthus, a Christian reverend, may have glimpsed such an explanation when he said that his Principle worked to "soften and humanize the human heart."

SOCIAL REFORM VERSUS PROPERTY RIGHTS

Though Malthus died before Darwin's theory was developed, his attitude toward the poor has often been criticized as overly Darwinian. G.K. Chesterton's famous 1927 article critiquing birth control, "Social Reform versus Birth Control," sharply denounced what he perceived as Malthus's brutal social policy. As he put it,

> Malthus meant his argument as an argument against all social reform. ... Malthus even used it as an argument against the ancient habit of human charity. He warned people against any generosity in the giving of alms. His theory was always thrown as cold water on any proposal to give the poor man property or a better status. Such is the noble story of the birth of Birth Control.

Malthus understood that many saw his ideas this way, and claimed that it was based on lack of understanding:

> First appearances indeed are in this branch of science still more deceitful than in any other; and the partial and immediate effects of a particular mode of giving relief are often directly opposite the general and permanent consequences. This circumstance renders all inquiries of the kind remarkably open to misconstruction; and those who have not had leisure to pay that attention to the subject which its peculiar intricacy demands, if they hear one or two detached passages noticed by their friends which

contradict their first feelings and apprehensions, are naturally disposed to be prejudiced against the whole Work in which they are found.[26]

In the same letter, he expresses his support for universal education and for government relief for the aged, the helpless, those who have met with unavoidable misfortunes, and children. His main objection to the specific bill in question is that by providing cottages for state-dependent poor it would allow their population to grow disproportionately by encouraging marriage.

Malthus's *Essay on the Principle of Population* made few specific suggestions for reform. Instead, its target was the utopian views of Godwin and Condorcet. Godwin believed that a perfect society was possible if private property was abolished and "all shared alike in the bounties of nature." As we've discussed, Malthus believed that population pressures would make such a society unstable in the long run.

The dispute between Malthus and Godwin prefigures the twentieth-century political divide between Right and Left. On the Left, socialism and wealth equalization are promoted as means to a more just civilization. On the Right, protecting the private property of the rich is defended as necessary for the survival of civilization.

Which view is correct? If Malthus is right that progress is impossible, does that necessarily mean that the conservative view is the right one?

Maybe in certain respects. But the argument I've given enriches the Malthusian perspective with that of Darwin. While Malthus provides us an understanding of what limits the growth of the poor, Darwin provides us an understanding of what limits the growth of the rich.

Poverty—or the lack of resources—makes it difficult to survive, to marry, to reproduce, and to support one's children. This checks the population of the poor. But what checks the population of the rich? Wealth—or the surplus of resources—makes it *easy to* survive, to marry, and to reproduce. So, in other words, wealth destroys the forces of selection. Thus it leads to uncontrolled cultural and biological mutation.

EVOLUTION, RELIGION, AND GREED

Just as birth control diminishes selection and increases the mutational load on a population, so does wealth. On the view I've given in this book, you would expect that eventually the wealthy classes would grow decadent and decline. And if you look at the history of civilizations, there does not seem to be any exception to this rule. Most dynasties last for a few generations. Rarely, they may last for a thousand years, but never at a steady level of wealth and power, and always with the help of healthy genetic material from other families.

Those who wish to live off the interest of their wealth without desiring to work are generally given the label "greedy." It would appear, then, that our principles guarantee that pure greed can never win out in the long run. To eliminate all forces of competition and selection is to undermine the process of evolution. Cultural and biological mutations enter the dynasty and no suffering will rise to check them. Eventually, greed destroys itself.

This is seen not only on the scale of families, but on the scale of societies. In David Hackett Fischer's book on quantitative history, *The Great Wave*, he examines evidence that as wealth inequalities rise, economic systems become increasingly unstable, leading to social, political, and economic collapses and revolutions. Fischer shows how this pattern of collapsing inequality occurred in the late Middle Ages, sixteenth-century Europe, and the French Revolution. Such revolutions are inherently complex and difficult to predict. But since wealth inequalities across the globe are currently at their highest historical level, it appears that we are due for another collapse soon, though Fischer is rightly reluctant to say how and when this will occur.

A similar analysis was done on the collapse of the Roman Empire and other major civilizations by Joseph Tainter in *The Collapse of Complex Societies*, and he found similar patterns. As more complexity and bureaucracy is added to the government (what would classify as "cultural mutation"), the system becomes cumbersome and less able to deal with the stresses caused, such as crime and conflict. New investment in improvement has fewer and fewer benefits. Economists call this cycle the "decline of marginal returns on investment." Eventually stresses become impossible to deal with and collapse occurs, after which power and wealth are more evenly distributed.

In light of this insight, that wealth causes decline, it is no surprise that every major religion contains powerful injunctions against greed:

EVOLUTION AND COMPASSION

PROVERBS 15:27:
> A greedy man brings trouble to his family,
> but he who hates bribes will live.

PROVERBS 16:19:
> Better to be lowly in spirit and among the oppressed, than to share plunder with the proud.

MATTHEW 19:24:
> Again I tell you, it is easier for a camel to go through the eye of a needle than for someone who is rich to enter the kingdom of God.

ST. AUGUSTINE, CITY OF GOD, CH. 31:
> A people becomes avaricious and luxurious by prosperity.

QUR'AN, "REPENTANCE":
> Tell those who hoard gold and silver instead of giving in God's cause that they will have a grievous punishment: on the Day it is heated up in Hell's Fire and used to brand their foreheads, sides, and backs, they will be told, 'This is what you hoarded up for yourselves! Now feel the pain of what you hoarded!'

BHAGAVAD GITA 5:12:
> A person who is not in union with the divine, who is greedy for the fruits of his labor, becomes entangled.

BUDDHIST TEACHER NYANATILOKA MAHATHERA:
> For all evil things, and all evil destiny, are really rooted in greed, hate and ignorance.

CONFUCIAN ANALECTS 4.9:
> The Master said, "A true gentleman is one who has set his heart upon the Way. A fellow who is ashamed merely of shabby clothing or modest meals is not even worth conversing with."

TAO TE CHING 9:
> Displaying riches and titles with pride brings about one's downfall.

TAO TE CHING 12:
> Searching for precious goods leads astray.

Some might argue that it is easy to find support for any position in scriptures, since they often have contradicting claims. But this is untrue when it comes to the topic of wealth. In the *King James Bible*, for example, there are 57 passages using the term "wealth" or "riches." Of these, 27 are neutral toward the pursuit of wealth, speaking of spiritual riches or material wealth as a reward for following God's commandments. An almost equal number, 28, are warnings against pursuing wealth. Only two passages (in Proverbs) have something positive to say about seeking wealth, namely that it makes you many friends. But these are ironic because they occur among other passages encouraging one to prefer poverty and loneliness to immorality.

EVOLUTION, DIVERSITY, AND CHARITY

What about charity? If all values must evolve by natural selection, how can we explain that most major religions also encourage charity?

It is sometimes argued that religions exist primarily to consolidate the social status of the powerful and keep the lower classes under control. But on this view, it is hard to explain not only their admonitions of the greedy, but their encouragements to charity and generosity:

QUR'AN, "THE NIGHT JOURNEY":
  Give relatives their due, and the needy, and travelers.

MATTHEW 25:31-46:
  Come, you who are blessed by my Father; take your inheritance, the kingdom prepared for you since the creation of the world. For I was hungry and you gave me something to eat, I was thirsty and you gave me something to drink, I was a stranger and you invited me in, I needed clothes and you clothed me, I was sick and you looked after me, I was in prison and you came to visit me. ... Truly I tell you, whatever you did for one of the least of these brothers and sisters of mine, you did for me.

BHAGAVAD GITA 17:26-27:
  O Arjuna, the word *sat*, representing the eternal, is designated to signify the all-pervading existence of the Ultimate Truth. In this way the sound *sat*, representing the eternal, is utilized for all auspicious activities. Being

established in the performance of sacrifice, austerities, and charity is described also by the word *sat* ...

Confucian Analects 17.6:
>The Master said: 'Whoever could spread the five practices everywhere in the world would implement humanity." "And what are these?" "Courtesy, tolerance, good faith, diligence, generosity."

Tao Te Ching 67:
>I would have stayed small
>but I possess three treasures
>I treasure and uphold.
>First is compassion
>second is austerity
>third is reluctance to excel.

Are scriptures univocal in their endorsement of compassion toward the needy? I don't know of any holy texts that warn against it. Of the 18 passages I've found that mention giving to the poor in the *Bible*, every one encourages the practice and not one discourages it.

It is clear that selection has favored value systems that place importance on generosity toward the less fortunate. On the face of it this seems counterintuitive, because you might expect that charity allows the "unfit" to breed, as many eugenicists have feared.

We've already seen, however, that the eugenicist fear is based on poor evolutionary reasoning. The idea that the human intellect can distinguish the "fit" from the "unfit" is fundamentally mistaken. Human beings are too complex to infallibly judge in this way. Every human is unique, and to see new kinds of talent arise we must allow for diversity to arise, and give new humans a chance to prove themselves by living in the world. "Judge not, lest ye be judged," as Jesus put it in the gospel of Matthew.

The distinction between rich and poor does not always coincide with the difference between fit and unfit. Lack of selection on the rich will often cause them to be less fit in an objective sense than the poor. Redistributing wealth from the rich to the poor can only make the game of life more fair, and thus improve the chances that new kinds of talent will arise and succeed. By giving many people a chance to raise families, rather than encouraging a few powerful rich to do so, we enhance genetic diversity. The more diversity there is, the more raw material there is for selection to work on.

The fear is often expressed, following Malthus and the ideas of eugenics, that allowing the poor to live from charity alone would encourage laziness. In fact, Darwin's theory might seem to predict that if we ease the forces of selection on the poor, uncontrolled mutation will occur and harm their overall fitness.

But this prediction is fundamentally incompatible with the theory we've been developing in this book. The fact is that selection will guarantee that peoples with the largest families will survive in the long run. So there will always be a tendency toward exponential growth in a population. If a population is growing exponentially, it doesn't matter how evenly wealth is redistributed, total resources are ultimately limited. So a scenario in which all poor people in the world are taken care of simply won't occur. It can't. The most that will happen is that the difference between rich and poor will be reduced and more healthy kinds of selection—in terms of innate abilities—will be able to take place.

Charity can never be harmful in the long run because nothing is harmful in the long run. Just as progress is impossible, so is regress.

Why give to charity? To add to the diversity of the gene pool of your society. The more you give, the more you help a variety of kinds of people survive, and the richer your gene pool and culture will become in the long run.

Among evolutionary biologists and sociologists, this way of seeing things remains puzzling. Even if helping the poor is more rational, how can such cooperative behaviors evolve when natural selection appears to be a competitive process? Let's turn to this question next.

ALTRUISM AND "GROUP SELECTION"

Altruism refers to any act that benefits another and harms oneself. Charity is a form of altruism because it gives another person more resources and reduces your own. Many animals will risk their lives to protect their young, their mates, or the herd. Since natural selection seems inherently selfish, Darwinists have long been puzzled by the evolution of altruism.

In the early twentieth century, Darwinists attempted to explain the evolution of such behaviors by invoking a theory called "group selection." The original idea was that herds or tribes composed of individuals that help each other will do better in competition against herds or tribes that fight amongst themselves. Thus selection may actually favor group-beneficial traits in the long run, even if they have a cost to individuals.

Evolutionary geneticist R.A. Fisher, whose quantitative work focused on the selection of individual genes, worried that group selection may be too slow to be significant in humans:

> The selection of whole groups is, however, a much slower process than the selection of individuals, and in view of the length of the generation in man the evolution of his higher mental faculties, and especially of the self-sacrificing element in his moral nature, would seem to require the action of group selection over an immense period.[27]

He concluded that sexual selection in terms of social values such as "heroism" played a larger role in selecting such traits. This idea, however, does not explain how such social values evolved in the first place.

Though he did not call it "group selection," J.B.S. Haldane presented a model of the evolution of altruism that did not depend on relatedness in his 1932 book, *The Causes of Evolution*.[28] He noted that if the altruistic trait is recessive, it will only spread if it is already common in the population, or if the population is small. Later, in 1955, he suggested a model of group selection based on relatedness:

> Let us suppose that you carry a rare gene which affects your behaviour so that you jump into a river and save a child, but you have one chance in ten of being drowned, while I do not possess the gene, and stand on the bank and watch the child drown. If the child is your own child or your brother or sister, there is an even chance that the child will also have the gene, so five such genes will be saved in children for one lost in an adult. If you save a grandchild or nephew the advantage is only two and a half to one. If you only save a first cousin, the effect is very slight. If you try to save your first cousin once removed the population is more likely to lose this valuable gene than to gain it.[29]

W.D. Hamilton formalized this idea in a 1964 paper.[30] His reasoning ran essentially like this. A gene for altruism will tend to decrease your fitness and increase another's fitness. Say there's a gene for saving drowning relatives. If it gives you a one-in-ten chance of being drowned, it decreases its own fitness by 0.1 if you find someone drowning. That is, the gene will by 10 percent less likely to spread itself to offspring. But if the relative saved is a brother or sister, they have a 50 percent chance to have the gene themselves. This means the gene will also be 50 percent *more* likely to spread. The net gain in fitness is 0.5 − 0.1 = 0.4. So it would seem that such a gene is likely to spread in the population. But if the person is not related to you, there is 0 percent chance they are carrying the same gene, so you have a net loss in fitness if you find someone drowning: 0 − 0.1 = -0.1.

This theory is now called "kin selectionism," and has become the predominant theory of the evolution of altruism in biology. Yet it remains controversial. Andrew Bourke's *Principles of Social Evolution*, and Gardner, West, and Wild's "The genetical theory of kin selection," each list twelve distinct criticisms published by professional biologists.

The main critics are proponents of an alternative theory that has been winning converts over the last few decades: group selection theory. This theory is based on the strict application of Lewontin's criteria, which were originally introduced to argue that subpopulations and even entire species could undergo Darwinian selection. While kin selectionists (also called inclusive fitness theorists) tend to focus on the selection of specific genes, group selectionists recognize that what may be under selection is groups of genes spread among a population, a species, or even across species within an ecosystem.

Kin selectionists object that group selection muddies the waters and obscures the importance of gene-based selection. They ask why any other theory is needed when keeping track of individual gene frequencies should suffice to make predictions.

Group selectionists ask why individual genes should be the only locus of evolution, given that Lewontin's criteria should be universally applicable (as Lewontin himself originally argued).

Many volumes have been written attempting to resolve the debate, whether in favor of one side or the other. I recommend Sober and Wilson's *Unto Others* as giving a thorough defense of group selection theory. It cites a number of individual studies that show the operation of group selection, even selection at the level of ecosystems. Unfortunately, their argument, however clearly it was made, has failed to end the debate.

Many argue that the dispute is ultimately about mere terminology. "The irony in the debate over group selection is that the theorists involved in the debate fight endlessly over it even though they know that there is nothing to fight about, while the onlookers, such as those tempted to read this book, believe the debate must be over something real and of momentous importance."[31] Rather than get into the technical details, and drop my reader into this vast and largely pointless controversy, I trust the interested reader can check the sources listed. What I offer here is not an attempt to answer every objection to group selection theory, but rather an attempt to answer the question of whether evolution may only favor kindness toward relatives, or may sometimes favor universal kindness—toward nonrelatives or other species.

Let's return to our theoretical gene-for-saving-one's-close-relative-from-drowning. What would happen if such a gene did prove successful and spread through the population? Well, in that case, the chance that some random person drowning also has the gene would increase. From a selfish-gene point of view, shouldn't you then be more likely to help the drowning person as the gene becomes more common, even if they're not a close relative? If your chance of dying is 10 percent, and there is more than a 10 percent prevalence of the gene, you should, by Hamilton's theory, be willing to rescue them. But wait. This was only a gene-for-saving-one's-*close-relative*-from-drowning.

So here's a better sort of gene. A gene-for-saving-anyone-else-who-also-has-this-gene. With this gene, you will help anyone who is likely to also carry the gene. (How can you tell who's carrying the gene? I don't know, it's a thought experiment.) Such a gene will spread even faster because as it becomes more common, it will be much more beneficial to have, because it's saving more people with the gene and they're saving you.

Hold on, we can still do better. What if there were a bunch of different genes, falling into two classes:

- The first type of gene is only for saving other people with the exact same gene, as above. But there are multiple kinds—perhaps some turn your skin purple and some turn it green. Purple people will save purple people but not green people. Green people will save green people but not purple people.

- The second type are genes-for-saving-others-who-would-save-you-too. This one is more inclusive. It doesn't matter what exact gene you have that makes you altruistic, so long as you are altruistic this type of gene will favor rescuing you.

You would expect the second type to do better. Why? Because it is more inclusive. Even if there are different types of the gene, each type will work to save the other. With more friends, there will be more opportunities to help and be helped and thus to raise the fitness of this kind of gene.

Computer models bear this out. Running a simulation where different genotypes work together produces the same results as a simulation where all these altruistic genotypes are the same (see Appendix 4, Simulation 4). Altruists benefit from helping *all other* altruists, not only those that share the same gene or genes for altruism. To see why this is so, consider the purple-skins and the green-skins, who were altruistic only toward their own type. These genotypes would have more fitness if they were willing to help each other too. Though the 10 percent chance of death when rescuing another is encountered more often, decreasing fitness by 0.1, just as often you will be rescued and your fitness will increase by 1.0, or 100 percent. There is a net gain on average the more interactions are possible.

The fact is, relatedness is not important at all to the evolution of altruism. The only important factor is that you don't waste your resources on others who are not altruistic. Doing so will cause altruistic individuals to decrease and selfish individuals to increase. This is why a cohesive society must put so much stress on detecting and punishing the selfish—not always an easy task. (D.S. Wilson offers convincing evidence for this in *Darwin's Cathedral*.)

Assuming this is correct, why are kin selectionists and selfish-gene theorists so confused on the issue? I think it comes down to two factors. The first is that selfish-gene theory sounds more cold and scientific. It's reductive and makes DNA itself the main causal agent. This sounds more mathematical than saying that any and all groups you can think of can be selected. The second factor, I think, is what makes Darwin's theory seem romantic to many, that it seems to demolish the boring, cooperative monotony of modern life. The boring and unfit will not survive. The new and interesting will smash through the competition. As the kin selectionist sees it, evolution is *essentially* competitive. It's not about the average, it's about the mighty. And this *seems* certain because in order to talk about selection, you must talk about the spread of a variant that is different from average. As Andrew Bourke puts it, "[S]election only 'cares' about gene frequencies different from average gene frequencies."[32]

It is true that selection depends on differences. But this is to focus exclusively on change in evolution, rather than stasis. Darwinian selection more frequently prevents change than favors it. As computer simulations confirm—I discuss some of my own in Appendix 4—after an altruistic trait spreads through an entire population, it can stay at close to 100 percent even with occasional selfish mutants arising.

Selfish-gene theorists worry that this way of seeing things sacrifices the explanatory power of Darwin's theory. To them it sounds like group selectionists are saying that anything goes. If someone is acting kind, it's due to group selection. If someone is acting selfish, it is due to individual selection. And group selection seems too permissive: If relatedness is not necessary, what is to stop the group selection of a zebra and a lion and a kind of grass?

The fact is, *nothing* will stop the group selection of a zebra and a lion and a kind of grass. When this happens, it's called an *ecosystem*. Ecosystems vary, ecosystems can reproduce themselves faithfully as their component organisms spread, and some ecosystems will spread faster than others. (See *Unto Others* for a long list of studies, though they're a bit dated. See also *The Social Conquest of Earth* by E.O. Wilson, who has "defected" to the group selectionist camp over the last few years.) Ecosystems evolve, and this is a kind of group selection.

But is this too permissive? Can't such a theory explain anything too easily?

Yes and no. It's too permissive in the same way that most evolutionary explanations are too permissive. They are based on incomplete evidence and assumption. For example, we don't know all the intermediate species between modern day humans and the original hominids two million years ago. And those that we do know, we only know incompletely. *Any* explanation we give of human evolution will be too permissive. It will be what biologists call a "just-so" story. Anthropologists frequently say that humans evolved larger brains to help them hunt large game. It could have happened just so, but maybe there were other factors. Maybe that wasn't the reason at all. Maybe social interactions and sexual selection were more important for the evolution of big brains. Or maybe the whole reason we needed big brains was specifically to cooperate in larger groups, and larger groups were needed to take down bigger game. Or maybe it was making clothing to migrate and stay warm in new regions. Maybe all these things. I don't think that we'll ever have decisive evidence. The game of just-so stories can go on forever. Restricting our explanations to selfish-gene explanations adds an additional constraint that may make explanation a more challenging game. But the constraint is arbitrary, and doesn't solve the root of the problem, which is lack of evidence.

Group selection *need not* be too permissive. Simply apply Lewontin's criteria in their strict, tautological sense. If a group is showing differential, heritable fitness, it is showing selection. If not, then it's not. This is strictly true. We are not talking about a heuristic, an interesting idea, or a theoretical hypothesis. It's simply a mathematical fact. If an invading species is making a forest ecosystem unstable, and the forest is giving way to tundra, this is an unambiguous case of ecosystem-level selection. You cannot describe such selection as a change occurring at the level of a single gene. That is, no single gene is logically necessary and sufficient for a boreal forest, for example, and thus you cannot reduce the increase or decrease of a boreal forest ecosystem to the increase or decrease of a single gene, nor even an undifferentiated collection of genes. On the contrary, a boreal forest is an extremely complex pattern that involves genes, soil, minerals, and manifold relationships. The fact that we have no perfectly precise way of describing these patterns and constellations is merely a function of our inability to grasp the entire system in its full complexity.

Make no mistake. Group selection does not always dominate. Cases of invasive species demonstrate this. Sometimes individuals (such as invading species) will spread at the cost of the group (such as an ecosystem). What happens depends on the details of the case. In my own computer simulations of group selection, I've easily made either altruism or selfishness dominate simply by tweaking a few parameters. If I increase the reward of "plundering" your neighbors enough, selfishness goes to fixation. But then if I decrease the harm of being plundered a bit, the two populations stay roughly equal. If I decrease it a bit more, the altruists win out.

It often seems that selfish-gene theorists, kin selectionists, and even stalwart group selectionists want there to be a literal, final answer to the question of whether altruism or selfishness is more fit. They want to say that altruism *really is* a kind of selfishness, or maybe that it is the exception to a general rule. Or that selfishness is always unfit in the long run. But the fundamental law of evolution is Darwin's Law, as given by Lewontin's criteria. This law doesn't care about selfishness or unselfishness. It only cares about differential fitness. And what makes life interesting is that differential fitness depends on the details of the situation. This is why there are both altruistic and selfish people in the world. For example, sometimes it's possible to conceal one's selfishness. When this happens, the benefits of altruism are diminished because sometimes it helps those who are not altruistic. Selfishness can then become more common. But as it becomes more common, perhaps its tricks of deception are discovered. If this happens it may be stamped out again. It all depends on context, and the closest thing we have to a final answer to this question are the oldest ideas we have about good and evil, ideas that have survived for many generations and proven themselves robust to vicissitudes and shifting contexts. I mean our oldest philosophies and religions.

THE ULTIMATE SIMULATION AND THE FATE OF CIVILIZATION

The problem with all these computer simulations and thought experiments is that they are too simplistic. How could there be a gene-for-rescuing-your-close-relatives-from-drowning? You can't really divide people or animals into definite categories of "selfish" and "altruistic." You could be selfish when it comes to money but generous with lending a hand. You could be partially selfish and only help people of your own family, race, or country. How can you write a computer simulation that takes into account *every* form of selfishness or unselfishness that people might have? And how could you write one that would have as many rich interactions as there are in the actual history of life and civilization?

Actually, there is such a simulation, and it's called the history of the world. Let's use it to answer our burning question, namely: What strategies of selfishness and altruism are the best in the long run?

If by "long run" you mean the scale of a few thousand years, you can look at the world's major religions, and you can look at human instinct. Those instincts and religions that have survived the longest and spread the farthest have proven themselves most adept and surviving and replicating in environments of mixed selfishness and unselfishness. If you trust your instincts and your tradition, you are more likely to preserve the fitness they have evolved over the centuries.

Many progressives believe that our old traditions are "outdated." Modern life with all its conveniences has created a new world, with different standards of morality. Old traditions, they argue, are like fossil species: ancient, fixed, and non-adaptive.

Actually, religious traditions do adapt and have adapted. In the Christian church, for example, the Biblical canon—books considered as proper to the Bible—changed radically over the early history of the church. As new sects have sprung up, including Roman Catholic, Eastern Orthodox, and many different forms of Protestantism, they have added or subtracted books from this canon of scripture. As it is, there are hundreds of Christian Churches and many of them have differing sets of scriptures. Translations differ, interpretations differ, and rituals differ. Just as with human DNA, certain parts of Christianity remain fixed while other parts adapt and change.

Progressives argue that traditions haven't changed fast enough in recent years. They also typically argue that classical philosophy, including Platonism, Aristotelianism, and even Cartesianism, are outdated due to the radical changes in our time, that they must be abandoned in light of the discoveries of modern physics and evolutionary biology, in particular. But these recent scientific discoveries do not greatly impact what the ancient classics say about metaphysics, ethics, morality, politics, logic, or personal virtue, which collectively form the majority of what both religion and philosophy are about.

In truth, many of the radical changes we've experienced in industrialized countries can only be temporary. Even if we do not run out of resources, the lack of selection on our genes and culture will cause steady decay by mutation. The more we try to prevent population growth and mutation, the smaller, less diverse, and less adaptive our culture will be and the more likely it will be overtaken by "less-developed" nations that are growing in size and diversity. In short, our current "utopia," where true struggle and suffering are largely irrelevant, must eventually end. And as it collapses, the teachings of traditional religions and philosophies will become essential once more.

In the next chapter I will clarify this picture of what we can expect to happen over the next few decades and centuries. In particular, since our civilization's energy use is growing exponentially, it appears that nonrenewable resource depletion and ecological destruction will likely cause economic decline and collapse before mutational load does.

SUMMARY AND PHILOSOPHICAL IMPLICATIONS

It has been claimed that Darwinism leads to extreme-right doctrines such as fascism and eugenics. Historical studies have shown, on the contrary, that Darwin's theory has had an equal influence on left-leaning political theories, including socialism, liberalism, and anarchism.

Nevertheless, it is important to demonstrate that Darwinism does not, in any way, commit us to the view that life is pure, brutal competition with no place for compassion. This is what I've attempted to do in this chapter.

Malthusian theory was not originally intended as an argument against charity, but rather a way of seeing what sorts of charity would be most beneficial. Malthus argued that universal education and government relief for the aged, the sick, and children were forms of charity that could have long-run benefits for a particular society, if not for the world as a whole. But he argued that reforms that encouraged early marriage, such as free housing, could cause harm to a society by adding population pressures. Such moderation of charity has sounded too harsh to liberals in the centuries since, and such "right-leaning" policies have been blamed for benefiting the rich in their exploitation of the poor.

There are evolutionary checks already in place on the prosperity of the rich. Wealthy people experience much smaller forces of Darwinian selection. For this reason, they have always been prone to biological and cultural mutation. The history of the decline and fall of various dynasties does seem to show an increasing "decadence" over time. Books such as *The Great Wave* and *The Collapse of Complex Societies* show the increasing instabilities that result from high concentrations of wealth and power. Every major world religion warns against greed and ambition, and almost no long-lived scriptures can be found that exalt them. Most religions encourage poverty and a simple life.

In fact, all major religions go a step further and encourage that the rich give generously to the poor. No scriptures in the Bible can be found that warn against charity, but many can be found that exalt it. This fact may be puzzling at first on the evolutionary view. But the truth is that the distinction between rich and poor is not the same as the distinction between fit and unfit. Since poor people experience greater forces of selection, they may often be more fit than the rich, who are more prone to mutation. Redistributing wealth from the rich to the poor can only make things more fair. Moreover, Malthusian pressures will guarantee that resources are always limited, no matter how evenly the wealth is spread. There can never be too much charity, because resource limitations and population growth will always maintain a roughly constant level of selection. The main long-term effect of charity is increased diversity for a population, which is a local evolutionary benefit.

Evolutionary biologists have debated the source of altruistic behaviors in humans and animals for several decades. Darwin's theory, often stated as "the survival of the fittest," superficially seems to promote selfishness. The most widely-accepted theory of how unselfish behaviors evolve is currently kin selection theory, which argues that by helping one's relatives one is helping copies of one's genes. Thus, the argument goes, we may appear unselfish but it is really the selfishness of our genes that is at work. Opposed to this view is group selection theory. Employing Lewontin's criteria for natural selection, they argue that there need be no single locus for evolution. Groups can evolve too, as long as they show diversity, inheritance, and differential fitness. Even ecosystems as a whole can evolve in this way.

I hope I've given good reason to think, in this chapter and in Appendix 4, that kin selectionism is missing an important logical point. The benefits of altruism towards kin are the same as the benefits of helping any other altruistic organism, no matter if the genetic source of the behavior is the same or different. It turns out that evolution is "blind" to genotypic differences, and computer simulations bear this out. By helping a broader group of fellow altruists, the benefits of altruism increase, and thus the most inclusive behaviors are the most strongly favored by selection.

While this theory may seem to allow for too much, and give too much room for speculation, the truth is that evolutionary theory rarely has enough evidence to go beyond speculation. There is no reason to ban group-selectionist speculation simply because it doesn't sound Darwinian.

Computer simulations and mathematical models can only get us so far. The actual world of evolution is far more complex than any simulation we can run. To see what sorts of behaviors evolution favors, the best and most complete simulation we can study is human history itself. Our oldest traditions contain cultural-genetic material that has been tested by natural selection over the longest periods of time and over the widest varieties of environments. These traditions confirm that we would do best to set aside greed, nepotism, and selfishness, and instead practice altruism, charity, kindness, and universal love.

VI

ECOLOGY AND THE FATE OF CIVILIZATION

CIVILIZATION AND THE BIOSPHERE

Modern Western life is changing quickly and radically. Where is this change all going? Do we need a radically new set of values? Or is our situation temporary, the fleeting result of plentiful fossil fuel energy?

Our situation is temporary, as should be clear. The key to seeing this is the single statistic I keep citing: it would take five planet earths to maintain everyone in the world at an American standard of living. Given that most of our labor has been outsourced overseas, this presumes that four of those five planet earths would be filled with third-world laborers. In essence, the scheme to lift everyone up to the Western standard of living is a pyramid scheme.

All pyramid schemes collapse. And no dynasty, no matter how wealthy, can last forever. Our prosperity has virtually eliminated selection on our genes, and eliminated much meaningful selection on our culture. It is inevitable that as our prosperity goes on our genes and culture will decay by mutation. This is part of the natural cycle of the boom and bust of civilizations.

But then is it all going nowhere? Is it impossible, then, that life will ever become less violent or more ecologically sound? Is there no reason to care about the environment or international politics?

I would say it is, in fact, all going somewhere. Just not where we thought.

This book is an attempt to debunk the *utopian* notion of progress, the idea that a world can be created without suffering, risk, or challenge. Such a world would be impossible, or at least empty of significance. Without different ideas or genes, some more valuable than others, there would be no more competition and thus no more suffering. And there would be no triumph or joy either. There would be no good or evil. There would be no need for learning or consciousness. But this still leaves room for a world that is better in a very different sense.

If you look broadly at the few billion years of biological evolution on this planet, it appears that ecosystems evolve toward a kind of—for lack of better terminology—*creative stability*. On the one hand, evolution in our biosphere never stagnates. New species are always arising, millions upon millions of varieties. On the other hand, things never get out of control. We've never had a single species of bacteria so successful that it wipes out all other species. But we have come close: when photosynthesis first evolved, it was a catastrophe. This new process—used today by all plants—took in carbon dioxide and water, used the carbon, hydrogen, and some oxygen to produce organic molecules, and released a deadly poison into the atmosphere: pure oxygen. No organism at the time was equipped to handle this pollutant. Once the atmosphere was saturated with oxygen, more than 99 percent of all species went extinct. It took some time to evolve antioxidant defenses and oxygen respiration, of the kind we use, and the path there was not easy. To this day our cells have a tendency to oxidize and cause malfunctions like cancer if we do not get enough antioxidants.

There have been several major extinctions like this over the course of the history of life on this planet. But over time the diversity of species has grown on average, and the frequency of revolutions has decreased.[33] For example, between 500 million years ago and 250 million years ago there were dozens of extinction events that each killed off more than 10 percent of species in the fossil record. But in the last 250 million years, there have been fewer than a dozen, and most of those were over 200 million years ago. In terms of known genera, biodiversity (as it was before modern human hunters) was double what it was 75 million years ago, at which point biodiversity was already higher than it had ever been. More species are being created faster than ever before—at least until recently. The rise of humans has already led to the extinction of most large land animals. We are, unfortunately, now in the midst of another huge extinction event.

The thing about catastrophes is that they cannot last for very long. They burn themselves out. As we run out of fossil fuels, deplete easily accessible minerals, and destroy the last of the topsoil, resource limitations will halt and reverse the growth of our civilization. It seems unlikely that we will go extinct, but a new Dark Age does seem inevitable.

What will happen in the extreme long run? Is there any way that the patterns we see in the evolution of life on earth will repeat for human civilization? Can human civilization reach "creative stability"? What will it look like? This will be the topic of this chapter, which will discuss the highest, most ancient, and most complex tier of group selection: the biosphere.

GLOBAL ECONOMIC GROWTH AND ECOLOGY

So far, we've mainly discussed theoretical limits to societal progress. We've talked about unlikely scenarios where the birthrate of the entire world is reduced to replacement levels. We've imagined farfetched societies of cybernetic beings, and examined how evolution allows, in theory, for the selection of altruism. But what does all this mean for the future of our civilization? Will it collapse as our DNA mutates out of control, or are we headed for long-term dystopia as governments tighten their grasp and attempt to stop evolution?

Neither runaway mutation nor global totalitarianism are likely scenarios, for two simple reasons: (1) our economy is increasing exponentially and (2) our economy depends on nonrenewable resources. Regulating the world's births and mutations indefinitely would take vast, renewable resources that we do not have. Long before the DNA of Europeans and Americans can become catastrophically degraded, our economies will have reached the limits of their growth and collapsed.

Countless experts worry about our exponential population growth, but few have anything critical to say about our exponential economic growth.[34] The world's energy consumption has increased by about 2 percent a year for the last 100 years. It's doubling roughly every 35 years, while our population doubles every 40. The nations whose energy use is increasing most are those with negative or nearly zero population growth rates, including China, the U.S., and Europe. This is an example of Malthusian growth of "cultural" entities: factories, power plants, and infrastructure. Eventually Darwinian selection will kick in due to resource ceilings. The only question is when.

You've probably heard the riddle of the lily pond. The pond starts with one lily pad. Every day the number of lily pads doubles, only stopping when the pond is full. On what day is it half full? On the second to last day, of course.

Our civilization is close to that point with energy and other nonrenewable resources. The doubling time for the pond is a single day. For the global economy it's about 35 years. We should expect no more than a few decades to prepare once resources get tight.

Petroleum is used to power more than 90 percent of our transportation, and about 75 percent of our products contain some amount of material made from it, namely the synthetic polymers we call "plastics." We've been using fossil fuels for centuries but current estimates give oil and natural gas less than a century at constant use. Discoveries of new oil fields peaked in 1964, though they are accelerating again with the ecologically questionable practice of fracking. Coal could last more than a century at current rates of usage, but if energy usage doubles every four decades and oil and natural gas become scarce, coal will also have less than century before it becomes too expensive to profitably mine.

Our food production is heavily dependent on fossil fuels. Oil powers the machinery used for plowing, planting, and harvesting. Fertilizers, pesticides, and herbicides, are all produced and shipped with the help of fossil fuels. Most food bought in stores in the U.S. is nonlocally grown and depends on petroleum for packaging and shipping. It's been estimated that without fossil fuels, our agriculture and food transportation would be able to support about one or two billion people, though our population is projected to reach almost 9.5 billion by 2050.[35]

Renewable energy sources, especially wind and solar, are among our fastest growing industries. But "renewable" is not the same as "unlimited." Continued growth in energy use must eventually run up against limitations of space, materials, and available raw energy. For example, the "geophysical limits" to wind power, which means the amount that can be extracted before winds are too slow to extract any more, are about 100 times the current energy needs of the world. But long before this point is reached, there would be dramatic climactic consequences. At 20 times the current energy needs, average temperatures in some locations would vary by as much as 3 degrees Celsius, enough to rival the anticipated effects of global warming[36]. Scientists argue, however, that if wind were to supply all the world's energy today, temperatures would change only by about 0.1 degrees Celsius. This may be true, but if energy use continues to grow by 2 percent per year and wind becomes our primary energy source, we would be seeing severe climactic changes within 150 years.

It is likely that nonrenewable resources other than energy will become a problem before that time. Even if we were to rely primarily on solar power, it takes copper, silver, indium, and other rare minerals to build photovoltaic cells. The price of these minerals is only increasing as mines are depleted. Twenty-four of the major minerals we use, including iron, nickel, and copper, will be entirely depleted at current rates of growth and current reserves within 50 years. Twelve other minerals, including indium, silver, gold, zinc and lead, will be depleted within 25 years.[37] According to a recent study, worldwide expenditures on mineral exploration have roughly doubled over the last 20 years, while discoveries have dropped by at least half.[38] Whether or not this trend continues in the short term, mined minerals are a nonrenewable resource and are bound eventually to run short as our use of them grows exponentially.

There are a number of resources that are technically renewable but which are being used up faster than they are being replenished, most notably water, forest, biodiversity, and topsoil.

We have already destroyed about 50 percent of the world's original forest cover, and forests are being cut down faster than they can grow back, at the rate of about 14 million acres a year.

Water usage is increasing exponentially worldwide. According to a study by UNESCO and the State Hydrological Institute, it is doubling roughly every 40 years. Another study using satellite data has shown that 21 out of 37 of the largest aquifers in the world have lost reserves over the last 12 years.[39] In his useful summary of global unsustainability, *The Little Green Handbook*, physicist Ron Nielsen estimates that "[b]y 2025, people living in 48 countries will suffer severe water shortage, and water availability will be catastrophically low for 2.6 billion people."

Biodiversity is experiencing its sharpest decline since the extinction of the dinosaurs 65 million years ago. Over 100,000 species go extinct every year due to human activities. That means that half the known species on earth will be wiped out within a century.[40] At current rates of wilderness loss, all wilderness areas will have disappeared within 85 years.[41]

Our most immediate concern, arguably more serious than the depletion of fossil fuels, is the destruction of topsoil. According to a study in *Science*, one-third of the arable land in the world has been lost over the last 40 years, and it continues to be lost at the rate of at least 10 million hectares per year.[42] This resource is already being stretched thin by growth in consumption. Ron Nielsen estimates that if China adopted the U.S. standard of living, it would need more biologically productive surface area than what is currently available on the planet.

It is commonly claimed that further innovation will improve our efficiency, lead to the discovery of new energy sources, and help repair and preserve the environment. This is a lot to expect from innovations that we cannot predict, especially when past inventions have had a tendency to reduce the sustainability of our civilization, rather than improve it. But even if innovation could provide a way to perpetuate progress, studies are showing that it is slowing down. Between 1974 and 2005, patents per inventor in the U.S. have decreased by over 20 percent, while the average team size filing new patents has increased by 50 percent.[43] In other words, research is gradually becoming more expensive and less fruitful as fewer easy discoveries—"low-hanging fruit"—are left and inventors are forced to move on to more difficult and expensive investigations.

As the complexity of our society increases, the cost of maintaining it at a constant level is also increasing. The cost of retirement is expected to grow from 4.8 percent of the GDP in 2009 to 6.1 percent of the GDP in 2035. The Social Security system is spending more than it is making and will run out of surplus around 2034. Health care costs are rising as our population ages. These costs grow by about 2.6 percent per year, doubling every 27 years. The U.S. is already $1.6 trillion short of what is needed to maintain our infrastructure and keep roads and bridges up to code.[44]

Meanwhile, the globe is faced with a price tag of $190 trillion to transition our transportation and energy infrastructure from fossil fuels to renewables. This is almost twice the global GDP.[45]

In light of these trends, I find it very hard to imagine that our civilization will be sustained longer than a few more decades. Some might blame this on lack of imagination. I say it is lack of imagination that makes our civilization seem even close to sustainable. It can't be anything but lack of imagination that makes it seem that the easy life we are enjoying today in the West will last forever. The fact is that it can vanish as quickly as it appeared when faced with the hard limitations of Malthusian reality.

THE PAST, PRESENT, AND FUTURE OF THE BIOSPHERE

The question is not whether our civilization will decline, but how, and what it will mean for the fate of the biosphere, society, and civilizations to come.

As we destroy the world's habitats and species, is it possible that the ecosystems we depend on might finally collapse, driving even our own species extinct? Or could climate change, as some fear, begin to accelerate, causing massive releases of carbon and methane that make our planet into another Venus, devoid of life? Might it be as simple as suddenly running out of fossil fuels and—having forgotten how to farm sustainably—perishing of hunger? Are we doomed to extinction by our own exponential success?

It's possible. But I would guess not. The human species as a whole may not have much in the way of foresight, but we do have a lot in the way of diversity. Amish, Mennonites, and dozens of traditional societies around the world have managed to preserve ways of life that do not crucially depend on nonrenewable resources. There are at least tens of thousands of distinct ecosystems throughout the world, and it seems unlikely that pollution or climate change could be severe enough to destroy them all. The hidden blessing of the coming catastrophes is that they will naturally select those ecosystems and societies that are adaptable, sustainable, and self-sufficient.

I base this reasoning on what has happened in the prehistory of life. The oxygen revolution we've discussed caused 99 percent of species on the planet to go extinct. It took millions of years for ecosystems to recover, but eventually organisms evolved—animals—that could make use of oxygen for respiration. Similar worldwide revolutions have occurred several times. The appearance of eukaryotic cells, multicellular life, the major animal phyla, and land animals all involved catastrophic ecological changes and massive extinction events.

These catastrophes parallel what is happening today. Humans are causing rapid and radical ecological changes. Some species are disappearing—but others are booming. Ocean acidity levels, for instance, are rising due to human activities. Though this is bad for most fish, it has caused the populations of many invertebrates—which do well in acid environments—to thrive.

Similar patterns might be expected to occur among human societies. As fossil fuels diminish, traditional farming will flourish. As mining grows expensive, recycling will bring prosperity.

Certain facts about the earth's climate make many scientists uncomfortable because they defy any simple, mechanical explanation. As James Lovelock has remarked in several papers, the sun's luminosity has gradually increased since the earth was formed, by about 7 percent every billion years. This may not sound like much, but if carbon dioxide levels had remained what they were when life began, this increase in solar luminosity would have raised the temperatures enough to boil the oceans and destroy all life on earth. Instead, what happened was that photosynthesis began to remove carbon dioxide from the atmosphere, and has been doing so steadily for the last several billion years. Originally, carbon dioxide made up maybe 3 percent of the earth's atmosphere—now it is down to about 0.035 percent. This has made up for the increasing luminosity almost exactly, keeping average surface temperatures steady between 0 and 25 degrees Celsius for 2 billion years.

Lovelock points out that almost every atmospheric gas has been kept within tight bounds in a similar way. The earth has a very different atmospheric composition than any planet could have without life, and somehow this composition has been kept just right to support life for several eons. He explains this as a form of natural selection. Organisms best able to consume new pollutants or make use of excess energy tend to thrive, driving down the abundance of these excess nutrients and returning the system to equilibrium.

What makes scientists most uncomfortable, it seems, is Lovelock's name for this process of sustained equilibrium—"Gaia." It comes from the

Greek goddess, Mother Nature. Many have criticized this view for imputing sapience to the biosphere as whole, as if the planet could anticipate future changes and react purposively.

Whatever the status of Lovelock's theory, the incredible stability of the earth's climate over billions of years of solar intensification demands an explanation. This ability to maintain equilibrium in the face of external changes is called *homeostasis*, and scientists usually reserve it as a property for living things.

Richard Dawkins and other evolutionary biologists argue that the biosphere could not have evolved such an ability because evolution requires variation, and since there is only one biosphere there have been no other variants for mutation and natural selection to work on.

This is an important observation, but it neglects to take into account the obvious fact that unstable systems tend to collapse, giving way to something new. The stability of our biosphere may be the result of natural selection across time rather than space, unstable regimes self-destructing and stable regimes preserving themselves.

Even if Dawkins were right that it can't be natural selection, it would do no good to protest that the biosphere is not "smart enough" to adapt. The fact is that it adapts. Call it Gaia, call it selection over time, or call it homeostasis: it is remarkable that the earth's climate and atmosphere have remained so stable, even through the oxygen revolution, several comet impacts, and the increasing luminosity of the sun.

AN ETERNAL MYSTERY?

The critics of Gaia do not offer a convincing replacement hypothesis. They suggest that there are natural processes, such as the diffusion of carbon dioxide into rock, that might account for the earth's continued equilibrium. But such explanations are entirely coincidental. For inanimate, non-biological processes to luckily result in homeostasis seems a terribly thin explanation.

Humans are currently reversing the trend of carbon dioxide absorption, enhancing the greenhouse effect and causing average temperatures to rise. Many experts today expect that government can and will defuse such environmental crises; most don't think there is such a thing as natural homeostasis on a worldwide scale. They have taken it to heart that the last four billion years of evolutionary bounty have been the result of blind luck. It follows that it will all soon come to end unless we engineer the biosphere ourselves.

Can we engineer the whole biosphere? We have already seen how ridiculous it is to think that we can engineer humanity or society. And the biosphere is something even bigger and more complex that the human species—it is the collection of all species, visible and invisible, and all natural processes happening all over the globe. If it is impossible to engineer humanity, then it is worse than impossible to engineer the global ecosystem.

There must be some adaptive mechanism that keeps the biosphere stable. It cannot be natural selection—at least of the well-known, spatial sort—because that would require multiple competing biospheres. What is this mechanism? We don't know. Scientists who have asked this question, including James Lovelock and Stuart Kauffman, have largely been marginalized for asking questions so hard that fashionably reductive science has trouble answering them.[46]

The ultimate fate of our civilization and our world remains a mystery. Perhaps this mystery will remain forever out of grasp. Perhaps the openness of our future is part of what makes life worth living.

WHAT WE CAN LEARN

Though we do not yet have a final theory of global homeostasis, there are a few clear lessons we can learn from the history of evolution. As the biosphere has evolved, it has become increasingly (1) diverse, (2) stable, and (3) creative. The number of species has steadily increased over time, despite periodic setbacks due to extinctions. Extinction events tend to be smaller now and the biosphere bounces back more quickly from them. The growth of diversity appears to be roughly accelerating. Some scientists, notably Stuart Kauffman, argue that the more niches there are for species to fill, the more creative an ecosystem becomes at generating new niches for new species.

These patterns provide us a rough roadmap of what lies ahead for humanity. Species extinctions are happening faster than they have since the extinction of the dinosaurs. Many regions of the world are losing biological productivity quickly—and with it good soil for agriculture. Local areas that can preserve ecosystems and use ecologically sustainable farming techniques—such as traditional methods or permaculture—will prove more robust and productive as energy and transportation become expensive again.

Not only localism—in the sense of producing our goods locally—but a certain kind of provincialism will prove beneficial as well. By eschewing mass media and embracing local community, humanity can come to contain more local diversity of ethnicities, and can explore more possible solutions to our ecological crises. In short, localism and provincialism will make our communities more self-sufficient and our species more robust.

We must learn to think of humanity as another species. Using contraception and birth control will ultimately weaken our genetic stock. Local areas that are not only willing to farm in harmony with nature, but also willing to produce large families and teach them provincial, traditional values, will in the end produce a greater diversity of human genes and ideas, and will produce cultures that will ultimately overcome those over-urbanized, over-industrialized, over-homogenized cultures that are quickly destroying their own resource-bases, cultural and genetic legacies, and ecosystems.

This vision of the future will seem overly grim to some, especially to those who value the sophisticated knowledge and skills our civilization has produced. As the Roman Empire collapsed, most philosophy and other forms of high culture were lost as people became illiterate and put their energy primarily into survival. Much of what intellectuals produce today—including advanced science, new inventions, high art, refined literature, and philosophy—will be rendered moot as we decline into a new age of tradition and simplicity. In the next chapter I will discuss those forms of intellectual life that will be more useful in the years to come—namely, philosophy and literature in the classical style of Plato, Aristotle, Homer and other figures from ancient history. Such high culture has survived and spread widely through both urbanized and traditional societies, and has helped people live more deeply fulfilling lives in both the best and the worst of times.

SUMMARY AND PHILOSOPHICAL IMPLICATIONS

Many see the Western way of life as an innovation that can be exported to the rest of the world. In reality, our way of life is so resource intensive that (a) there are not enough resources for the rest of the world to adopt it and (b) it is quickly destroying its own resource base. We know that our high civilization cannot last forever in its current form. What we are seeing is not progress, but rather an evolutionary crisis caused by radically new forms of technology—akin to the major evolutionary transitions in the history of biological life. Oxygen respiration, multicellular life, and eukaryotic cells all caused similar ecological disruptions when they first appeared on the scene.

In previous chapters, we discussed theoretical limits to progress, including evolutionary limits to genetic engineering and eugenics. However, we will sooner run up against more practical, Malthusian limits to our economic growth. Our resource use is growing exponentially, and many of our resources are nonrenewable or slowly-renewable. Traditional Malthusian limits to food production are fixed, but nonrenewable resources not only can't grow but are shrinking at accelerating rates. Without fossil fuels, it has been estimated that we can support a world population of only a billion people.

Renewable energy, such as wind and solar, will likely soften the collapse, but they cannot eliminate it. Our economy is growing exponentially, and total available sunlight and wind are not. Harnessing them depends on rare minerals that are becoming scarce. Worse, topsoil is eroding faster than it can be replenished, and now food production is effectively a nonrenewable resource. Forests, water, and biodiversity are also showing accelerating decline. In the West, innovation, health care, infrastructure maintenance, and retirement are all becoming by degrees more expensive and unsustainable.

Exponential growth can be deceptive. We are seeing a 35-year doubling time for our resource use. This means that we probably won't see massive shortages until we are mere decades away from collapse. We should not be fooled by our present comfort and security into thinking that collapse is "far-fetched" or remote in time.

However, it seems unlikely that humans or human culture will disappear entirely. There are still many traditional societies around the world that can survive without modern infrastructure. There are also many diverse ecosystems with a good chance of surviving severe climate change and increasing pollution. Some organisms are even thriving as conditions change. We can expect more self-sufficient and sustainable societies to survive, and lead the way to a more ecologically-sound humanity. Those scientists who have thought deeply about the history of the biosphere believe that there are naturally-occurring evolutionary processes—such as Gaia or self-organization—that eventually lead to more stable and creative ecosystems. Whether or not these theories are the right explanations, it is true that the biosphere has become more creative and stable over time. Recently, the realm of multi-cellular life has been made unstable by the rise of a new evolutionary sphere: human culture. If the history of biological life is any guide, we should continue to experience evolutionary crises while the culture-sphere is still young, but these should become less intense and less frequent in the long run. With our cognitive limitations that prevent us from engineering even a single organism in its entirety, it is unlikely that we could ever engineer the biosphere—or culture-sphere—as a whole. Instead our duty is to preserve what local tradition we can and pass it down faithfully, so that our descendants can live wisely, independently, and virtuously.

VII

PHILOSOPHY REVITALIZED

HOW PROGRESS HAS DESTROYED PHILOSOPHY

The notion of progress is dehumanizing. It treats human beings purely in terms of their numbers and material needs. They are liabilities to be cared for, and never the self-sufficient, free, untamed souls that they should be. Unless you can see the human soul as something deep, you can never philosophize deeply about it.

Values that get in the way of progress have been denigrated now for over a century. Religious morality makes people disagree, and it promotes families and the flourishing of populations. Since the adventure of conflict and the mathematics of population do not jibe with utopia, religious morality has been tossed. In particular, child-rearing—which our ancestors had valued highly for millions of years—not only adds to our numbers but prevents us from pursuing a career and furthering industry. (Never mind that industry is also growing exponentially.) As significantly, everything spiritual and traditional is seen as a throwback to earlier unprogressed times, when people did not know the value of science and universal agreement. (Never mind that universal agreement precludes cultural diversity.) In short, religion, values, tradition, spirituality, poetry, children, and family are all bad things because they make our hearts wild and diverse and harder for the utopian bureaucracy to pacify and control.

To embrace reason, on the utopian view, means to wipe out all these "prejudices." It means to subordinate this rich diversity of values to a single value: material prosperity. Deeply religious people are said to oppose reason merely because they do not accept this utopian logic. The question of whether there is evidence for God is not actually relevant to progressives, whose simple aim is to stifle religious-based rebelliousness and population growth.

Mirroring this attitude, our universities have gradually reoriented their entire educational philosophy to center on the ideal of progress. Religion has been banished from the schools, the pragmatic methods of science are to be used, and all investigations are undertaken to advance modern civilization, whether by bureaucracy or industry. The humanities, including literature and poetry, are demeaned because they are not directly productive of progress. The best and brightest should be spending their time developing technologies to boost industrialization and ultimately feed all the poor.

Except in our popular cinematic and literary fantasies, in which the hero or heroine must struggle and suffer to attain honor, we have lost sight of the truth that each person is responsible for succeeding in their own life. We have forgotten that this success used to be defined in terms of virtue and honor, rather than in terms of money and security. Literature and art are no longer undertaken to portray the Good and edify future generations, but merely to make a profit, or even as a form of rhetoric, that is, to persuade people to drop traditional values and take up the cause of progress.

Even philosophy, which used to be occupied exclusively with cultivating wisdom and virtue in the individual, is now modeling itself on science, hoping to contribute to the project of world-improvement. But open any one of Plato's dialogues and you'll find Socrates investigating the nature of personal virtue. Even the extended discussion of a hypothetical society in Plato's *Republic*, has its ultimate aim in illuminating why an individual should live justly. Socrates ends his description of the ideal Republic: "In heaven I think there is laid up this pattern, which he who desires may behold, and beholding, may set his own house in order. But whether such exists, or will exist in fact, is no matter." Aristotle's *Nicomachean Ethics* and *Politics* are both meant to help individuals find happiness in virtue, and the rest of Aristotle's books are primarily concerned with imparting the ability to think and reason. Nowhere does Aristotle attack religion or offer ultimate schemes for progress, material gain, or social engineering. This is true about philosophy as a whole, for the most part, until the time of Condorcet and Malthus.

This isn't to say that there aren't still philosophers debating moral and ethical topics. But even these discussions have become, for lack of a better term, bureaucratic. They lack cohesion and passion. They split hairs and lose the forest for the trees. Because reason has been enthroned above value, being technically right has become more important than getting to the point.

To make this more concrete, let's open up a random philosophy of ethics journal. The first article in this month's *Ethics* is called "Practical Reasoning: Where the Action is." Here's the abstract:

> Widespread conceptions of practical reasoning confront us with a choice between its practicality and its objectivity: between its efficacious, world-changing character and its accountability to objective rational standards. This choice becomes unnecessary, I argue, on an alternative view embodied by the thesis that the conclusion of practical reasoning is an action. I lay bare and challenge the assumptions underlying the rejection of that thesis and outline a defense of its picture of practical reasoning against common objections. On such a picture, practical reasoning provides a principle not externally imposed upon an action but rather constitutive of it.

Opening Aristotle at random can make your eyes glaze over too, so this alone is no sign of triviality. But let's examine what his thesis really is. "Practical reason" is a philosophical term of art that distinguishes reasoning about actions from reasoning about ideas. In essence, the author is saying that practical reason can both change things and be accountable to objective standards, because the conclusion of practical reasoning is an action. To say whether this is actually a good position, we'd have to do some serious digging. But the point is that the question he is asking, "Can practical reason be held accountable to objective standards?" is one that can only possibly be of interest to a professional philosopher.[ii] As I said, tech-

---

ii On any commonsense definition of "reason" and "objective," the answer to the question must be yes. Practical reason by its very nature as a form of reason must be accountable to objective standards. I've only heard objections to this from other people with philosophy degrees.

nical correctness is trumping everything else, to the point where philosophy is losing the ability to converse with the outside world. A random survey of other first articles reinforces the conclusion. "Does the feeling of pain essentially urge taking action to extinguish it?"[iii] This one is part of a long exchange on the nature of pain, of interest to a few specialists. Another one seems maybe more promising: "Does belief in the afterlife give meaning to altruistic projects?" But this is a twenty-page piece written in response to several other articles on the same question. To really understand it we would need to read at least a hundred pages of articles, if not more. And if every such minute question of interest took a hundred pages, we'd never reach the end of reading what the modern view of morality is.

Of course, it is quite true that there is no way to reach the end of everything you might say about morality, or almost any topic in philosophy. And here we have the essence of the absurdity of modeling our discussions of morality on science. The ancients—including Socrates—tried to get to the point of their discussions, and if they could not get to the point using pure logic they came to terms with this. Modern philosophy consists mainly in discussions that have not only forgotten the point, but which do not care to have a point anymore. Furthering one's career as a professor has become the ultimate goal of modern philosophy—because this is the kind of attitude that makes philosophy most like its new idol, modern science.

PROGRESS MAKES MONOCULTURAL MINDS

These days you are encouraged to focus and specialize, both in academia and in the business world. By finding one thing you can do really well and becoming an expert, you more easily garner money and fame because you've got something rare and special to contribute to society.

But might this tendency not be harming our mental ecosystems?

---

iii It's been pointed out to me (by someone with a philosophy degree) that this question is actually relevant to my argument in Chapter 3. I guess that depends on your definition of relevance. If I were to bring up every such academic discussion relevant to my argument, I would never finish my background research, let alone squeeze my argument into less than 1000 pages.

Just as a forest ecosystem can be weakened or destroyed by a too-successful insect or vine, a human mind can be weakened or destroyed by a too-successful idea. Examples of this are common among scientists, philosophers, and poets. The mathematician Georg Cantor (1845-1918) was the first to develop a detailed theory of infinity. By the time he was thirty he had published a paper proving that there is more than one kind of infinity ("countable" and "uncountable" infinities). Many of his mathematical peers ridiculed him. Still, he continued to develop the theory, proving that there were in fact infinitely many infinities, increasing in size without limit. He became so obsessed with his theory—equating infinity and God in his mind—that as time went on he had difficulty thinking about anything else. A certain result known as the "continuum hypothesis," which stated that there was no infinity between "countable" and "uncountable," proved particularly elusive, and his obsession with proving or disproving it became so powerful that he neglected his wife and children and was in out of sanitariums for the last two decades of his life.

Cantor's fascination with infinity became expertise—but expertise became obsession. Like a parasite or invasive species, infinity destroyed a mind that lacked any ideas capable of balancing it.

Similar examples are manifold. The greatest logician of the twentieth century, Kurt Gödel, who thought exclusively about a handful of foundational problems, began to see the world in terms of an ancient struggle between intelligence and non-intelligence. Fear of poisoning by hidden enemies led him to starve himself to death.

Robert Pirsig, the author of *Zen and the Art of Motorcycle Maintenance*, recounts the story of how the singular question "What is Quality?" led him step-by-step to madness, an asylum, and electro-convulsive therapy before he recovered.

Many other philosophers appear to have lost their sanity to singular questions, from Zeno to Nietzsche. The psychologist Kay Jamison (herself bipolar) estimates that at least 40 percent of famous poets have had psychotic episodes, including Lord Byron, Alfred Tennyson, Sylvia Plath, and Robert Lowell. In most cases these episodes are characterized by thoughts either racing out of control (mania) or plodding in a slow circle (depression)—a few unbalanced ideas dominating the mind.

Ecosystems thrive best on diversity. If you play around with an online ecosystem simulator (there are plenty to choose from), you'll find that if you put more species and connections in, the system will usually reach equilibrium sooner, and with less chance of extinction. It also helps to have top predators, because without enough vertical eater-eaten relationships it's more likely some organism will spread out of control. Predators will often help the species below them survive in the long run. Species help each other best by preserving the overall equilibrium, even if this involves predation, which non-ecologists often mistake for a form of competition.

For example—and this was something that actually happened in a number of national forests—if you get rid of wolves and bears your deer population is likely to explode. As a deer population grows it can strip parts of the land bare of vegetation, expose the soil, and cause massive erosion. Without anything to hold river banks in place, rivers disperse and evaporate, and forests can become deserts. Famine sets in and even the deer populations themselves eventually dwindle or disappear. This process is called desertification and it is happening worldwide, often as a result of livestock like cows and sheep that are allowed to proliferate out of control. In some national parks wolves or bears have been re-introduced, stabilizing the deer and moose populations and restoring much of the ecosystem that has been lost.

Interactions among diverse evolutionary entities form an ecosystem. Thought is an ecosystem. Thought evolves. Monocultures—fields of a single crop, sterilized by chemicals—are harmful because they destroy the ecosystems of the soil and halt evolution. When thinking is dominated by a small collection of ideas, it destroys the natural soil of the mind, which should be alive with a thousand skills, ideas, reasons, and myths.

Life is flourishing diversity. The most ancient forms of agriculture respect this principle. Like most traditional societies, the Amish always leave some fields fallow, allowing them to relax and play and foster new diversities of wild plants and animals. This restores the soil for free, and keeps populations of predators like birds healthy and present to control outbreaks of insects or mice.

Farming used to be so central to our culture that we used agricultural metaphors without even thinking. The word "culture" itself came from a Latin word for agriculture. Aristotle frequently wrote passages like, "The soul of the student must first have been cultivated by means of habits for noble joy and noble hatred, like earth which is to nourish the seed."[47] We need to think of philosophy this way again.

HOW TO THINK THE ANCIENT, ECOLOGICAL WAY

Philosophy is flourishing diversity of thought. The greatest thinkers have been renaissance men and polymaths: broadly-read, creative, less narrow than their peers. Charles Darwin was an avid reader of not only botany and zoology, but of philosophy, geology, agriculture, animal-breeding, and plant-breeding. Thomas Jefferson was a scientist, philosopher, scholar, lawyer, inventor, and agricultural pioneer. Isaac Asimov wrote both fiction and non-fiction, and popularized every field of science from mathematics to biology. Masanobu Fukuoka, one of the founders of the modern sustainable-agriculture movement, was a trained scientist, a Buddhist philosopher, a mystic, a poet, a father, and of course a successful farmer. It is said that human knowledge is now too vast for there to be polymaths anymore. It's more reasonable to think that the more there is to know, the wider and more diverse your knowledge can be, and the more fertile the soil for polymaths. Broad knowledge gives a thinker stronger context. A scientist seeking knowledge for its own sake will probably find nothing of interest. A farmer without any reading or education will probably do what his neighbors do. But a passionate farmer who uses science to improve his farm is far more likely to advance both science and farming.

The greatest novels show deep insight into human nature, careful thought concerning the individual's place in the world, and broad learning about the many diverse aspects of life and nature portrayed. Music is the same, though less obviously so. The most powerful melodies evoke a range of emotions, challenge the mind, and show intricacy of structure that can only come from active and diverse thought. Classical painting, too, shows geometric reasoning, deftness of hand, an understanding of human and natural forms, insight into human emotion, and dramatic expression. And if broad thinking can benefit us in making likenesses of life, how much more might it help us in living our lives, in seeing the big picture, setting higher goals for ourselves, and achieving them? How much more might it benefit our family lives and our culture as a whole? This is what leadership is made of. Alexander the Great was the student of Aristotle, the greatest philosopher of Greece. Charlemagne was considered the wisest king of his time in Europe, and helped keep Roman learning alive through the Dark Ages. Thomas Jefferson, James Madison, Benjamin

Franklin, and other founding fathers were profound thinkers, broadly read, with well-trained rhetorical skills. I can't help but feel that this is what the twenty-first century is already lacking. You don't see technical logicians—who specialize in elliptic curves or Hilbert spaces—accomplish anything on a grand scale. Leave it to the Einsteins of the world, fed up with narrow scholarship and working in patent offices.

Modern philosophers love to praise the Greeks for being more "objective" and "scientific" than any other ancient civilization. This is nonsense. It forgets that modern mysticism, magic, music, poetry, and art also have their origins in Greek culture.

Ancient Greece was the first nation to produce a written tradition of philosophy, but also of tragic and comic plays, political theory, ethics, logic, physics, literary criticism, and axiomatic mathematics. Other subjects which they did not invent they brought to their highest pre-Renaissance level, including geometry, arithmetic, algebra, astronomy, poetry, epic poetry, mysticism, and music. No single society has had as big an impact on Western culture. We still use Greek harmonies in our music, we still learn Euclid's theorems in geometry class, and Xenophon's writings about horses were still considered authoritative among cowboys of the old west.

Why were the Greeks so intelligent, so wise?

There were other empires throughout the Middle East that were larger and wealthier. What was truly remarkable about Greece was the richness and plenitude of culture there. It was a healthy and thriving ecosystem of ideas. Greece excelled in so many things because it *was* so many things. History suggests that novelty is the result not of specialization, but of variety. We might expect our philosophy to be Hittite, our military theory to be Assyrian, and our music to be Egyptian. But it all came from Greece, because that was the first place that reached a critical diversity of ideas, a prototypically healthy cultural ecosystem. While the Persian empire was a vast machine designed to produce only conquest, wealth, and power for the Emperor, the Greeks—who lived in autonomous city-states—admired wisdom over wealth, and preferred the advice of their barefoot philosophers to that of fearsome tyrants. The first democracies were Greek. The Greek philosophers were all polymaths and were expected to be. If a man did not value virtue above all else, Plato would refuse to call him a philosopher. And if a man did not know geometry, or had no practical inventions credited to his name, Plato would also withhold the title. For Plato, a philosopher must be an ethicist, an inventor, a mathematician, an astronomer, a dialectician, a logician, a politician, a metaphysician, and a physicist. His student Aristotle demanded mastery of biology, meteorology, and epistemology as well. This way of thinking stretched back to Thales, reputedly the first Greek philosopher, who was skilled in science and math, an inventor, a businessman, and at the same time considered one of the "Seven Sages" of Greece for his dedication to virtue. Philosophy was not simply a thing to read about or study for the Greeks. It was a way of life.

A healthy ecology sees a balance of creativity from every species. No one substance or process or rule of order enslaves the rest, and thus there is a perfect balance of power from the largest to the smallest. Even the lion must answer to the grass because without the grass there are no deer.

No one book or thinker or discipline can teach you how to think, or what wisdom is. There are thousands of classics out there—why not make use of them? There are thousands of skills to learn, thousands of points of view to understand.

It is not possible to learn everything, nor is it possible for most of us to be heard by everyone. But it is beneficial to find ways to keep your ideas your own, to keep them rich and diverse and different from the univocally progressive perspective of the mass media.

Evolutionary quality gives ideas power. Books or statements that became famous simply because they were provocative or well-advertised will not last through the ages. This gives me peace of mind. It reminds me that chasing fame is ultimately useless. An honest, insightful idea may spread very slowly, like a plant whose seeds are carried on the breeze, but if it is good and true it will spread steadily and may stay vital for ages.

BACK TO THE CLASSICS

Most people seem to assume that the best books are the most recent ones. But I say the older the more worthwhile. Old books have proven their mettle. It's good to read new books too, of course, but it's always more of a gamble.

It's very difficult for a book to survive more than a few decades. For example, when my wife and I browse the clearance boxes at used bookstores, most of the books we find there are less than twenty years old. In fact, it's always surprising, and a bit sad, to find a book more than 50 years old in the clearance boxes, because you know that if it isn't sold, they'll have no choice but to throw it away, and chances are you're looking at one of the last copies. There are probably around a million new books published every year. It would be impossible for a library or used book store to save a copy of each one. Most books are doomed to oblivion.

Any book that has survived centuries—or millennia—must be exceptional. And we've got many such books, including the writings of Aristotle, Plato, Homer, Ovid, Cicero, St. Augustine, Lao Tzu, Confucius, and Chuang Tzu. For over 1500 years the writings of such authors had been copied by hand from one crumbling manuscript to another. Life is not easy during dark ages, and it should flatter Aristotle that monk after monk found the time to copy all his many books. The vast majority of Greek philosophers were not so lucky.

A similar story can be told about the holy books of the world's religions, including the *Bible*, the *Qur'an*, and hundreds of Buddhist and Hindu scriptures. Some have estimated that there have been at least 100,000 religions or religious sects created over the course of history. Each that has survived is something extraordinary.

It is absurd when scientists talk about "overcoming" religion or philosophy, simply because most have proven mistaken. Perfect knowledge is not obtainable by finite beings like ourselves.

Confucius said: "I for my part am not one of those who have innate knowledge. I am simply one who loves the past and who is diligent in investigating it."[48]

Also: "He who by reanimating the old can gain knowledge of the new is fit to be a teacher."[49]

Confucius lived around 500 B.C. and is considered one of the founding figures in Chinese philosophy. Yet he claimed that most of his knowledge was more ancient still, from books which are now lost.

WHAT IS THE TASK OF PHILOSOPHY?

Without the goal of progress, one might wonder what philosophy is for. Today, we think of it as a way to challenge tradition. But we should know better, because tradition is the result of thousands of years of evolution, evolution so complex that one should not expect to create new, long-lived traditions from scratch. Attempts to do so slide into utopianism and totalitarianism. On the contrary, the theory of cultural evolution teaches us to think of tradition as the repository of our most vital principles of living, principles that are unprovable by any practical calculation.

Tradition is to be respected. Yet the world changes, and no religion or culture has remained completely static. Some traditional societies have persisted for thousands of years. But none have lasted much longer than that, because relative to the rest of the life on this planet, modern humanity is relatively young. Urban civilization has been around for about 10,000 years. The major world religions are at most a few thousand years old. New spiritual revolutions may yet be in store for many of the world's cultures. And we should expect these revolutions to occur in ways we cannot calculate. We should expect them to introduce values we could not have deduced logically. But this doesn't mean philosophy will have no role to play in these revolutions. The philosophies of the ancient Greeks had many deep influences on the formation of Christian and Muslim faiths.

Immediate certainty is not possible in philosophy. Reason, logic, and evidence can and should be used, but even logic is based on unproven premises. What has refined philosophy most strictly is the operation of selection over thousands of years. We should strive to be as rational as we can, but we should realize that we are contributing to a pool of ideas that will undergo unpredictable selection. The vast majority of the philosophies of the ancients have been lost to time.

We now have the opportunity, as the ancient Greeks did, to build our intellectual life to its highest extent, to provide raw material for the cultural evolution that is to come. Plato's discourses on the Good, and Aristotle's principles of Virtue, formed part of the basis for the high theology of Late Antiquity and the Middle Ages. We are not talking about idle philosophical rumination. We are talking about ideas that soar faithfully to what is most sacred in life. These ideas should be championed again.

ANCIENT WISDOM'S PRIMACY

The older the classic, and the more times it's had to be recopied, and the more chances it's had to be lost in time, and the more lives it's changed for the better—the truer. By reading the classics you improve your own evolutionary fitness. You enrich your own inner culture and make it healthier. And thus you enrich your society as well.

This book you are holding, if the year is not already 2070 A.D., has not been tested by more than one generation and remains highly in doubt. Maybe it is logically correct, but it encourages the wrong spiritual values. Maybe it is spiritually correct despite logical flaws, and perhaps this will allow it survive for a few decades or even centuries. It is impossible to know yet.

What is most certain is most ancient: the sacred texts, the surviving philosophers of Antiquity from both the East and the West. Start with these. Plato, Aristotle, the *Bible*, the *Qur'an*, the *Vedas*, Confucius, Lao Tzu. Read them and see how unexceptional our civilization is. We are just another temporary flourishing, fragile and foolish and intemperate, likely to be forgotten over the millennia, except perhaps as an odd flowering of fossil-fuel-driven prosperity.

The fact is, the more we embrace material progress, the more surely our culture will perish.

Maybe we can be remembered as something more. If we can start philosophizing again now, in quantity and conciseness, with logical and spiritual quality, with extreme diversity and soundness, with unflagging faithfulness to tradition and canon—then perhaps one of the many obscure poets and philosophers to come will be the Homer or Plato of future ages.

APPENDIX 1: THE MATHEMATICS OF MALTHUSIAN EQUILIBRIUM

In Chapter 1 we proved that the exponential growth of the human population cannot continue in the long run, even in the case of a population growing as fast as possible, that is, expanding outward at the speed of light and filling space as it goes.[iv] Obviously, however, populations almost never grow this way. In fact, the human population has been experiencing "hyperexponential" growth during the last few centuries, and total human births have significantly outweighed total deaths during this period[50]. Therefore, it would be fallacious to try to prove that the ratio between births and deaths must *always* remain within strict bounds.

---

iv I've been asked whether relativistic time dilation would affect the rate of population growth for a civilization expanding at close to the speed of light. On a little thought, it is clear that even with time dilation, this growth would still be exponential. Imagine that you have a space-faring civilization that wants to exploit relativity to slow down growth. To do this they will have to eschew planets and all live on board space colonies traveling at some percentage of the speed of light. If this speed is constant, population growth will still be exponential, if slowed by a constant factor. If this speed is continually accelerated to cause time (and thus population growth) to slow down, this will cause a relativistic increase in mass that will demand a proportional increase in energy used for acceleration. That is, at relativistic speeds the energy needed to increase speed is proportional to speed—so this still demands an increase in energy that is exponential!

There seems to be a very deep principle at work here.

Illustration 5: Even if population growth is zero (a balance of births and deaths) in the interim periods, the periods of exponential growth will get shorter and farther apart with time.

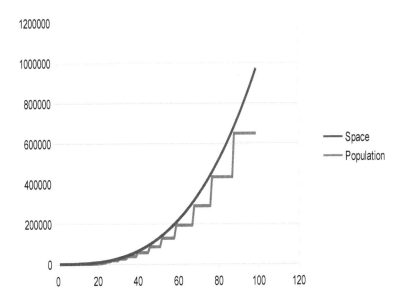

Instead, what we will do is prove mathematically that, in the long run, episodes in which this ratio is unbalanced are rare and short-lived. Populations are allowed to grow at an exponential rate or faster for brief periods of time, but if these imbalances persisted, a violation of Malthus's Principle would result. In this appendix, we will prove the most precise formulation of "the balance between creation and destruction" in this treatise. Note that this principle will apply to any multiplicative effect, including mutational diversification, though we will speak in terms of population growth for intuitive clarity.

Let's call the total population at time t, $N(t)$. The total number of births to date will be $B(t)$, and deaths $D(t)$. Note that $N(t) = B(t) - D(t)$. Also note that if the limit of $B(t)/D(t) = 1$, then the limit of $N(t)/B(t) = 0$. We will not be able to prove such strict limits, but we will work with the latter ratio, $N(t)/B(t)$. We'd like to prove the following:

APPENDIX 1: MATHEMATICS OF MALTHUSIAN EQUILIBRIUM

Assume that for some k > 0, dB/dt ≥ kN (i.e., the population "tends" to grow exponentially). It follows that for any ε > 0 and λ > 0, if $N(t)/B(t) \geq \lambda$ on intervals whose total length up to time t is L, then L/t < ε for any t larger than some finite number, a.

In other words, we want to show that the fraction of time during which there is an imbalance between creation and destruction (that is, when $N(t)/B(t) \geq \lambda$) will approach zero for long enough time-scales.

Note that N is not necessarily increasing, even if B is, since there may also be deaths occurring, D, which check total growth.

Let's examine an interval $[x_1, y_1]$ where $N(t)/B(t) \geq \lambda$. We'd like to demonstrate that on such intervals $N(t)$ will grow at least exponentially. Using $B' \geq kN$, we have

$$B' \geq \lambda k B$$

or

$B' = \lambda k B + h(t)$, where $h \geq 0$ for all t in the interval.

This differential equation is hyperexponential, since B may be growing more than proportionally to its own value. To make this precise, let's define a function that is the difference between B and an appropriate exponential function.

$$g(t) = B - B(x_1)e^{\lambda k(t-x_1)}$$

We can also write

$$(*)\ B = B(x_1)e^{\lambda k(t-x_1)} + g(t)$$

Plugging this into the differential equation above, we get,

$$B' = \lambda k B(x_1)e^{\lambda k(t-x_1)} + \lambda k g(t) + h(t)$$

We can also differentiate it directly to get,

$$B' = \lambda k B(x_1)e^{\lambda k(t-x_1)} + g'(t)$$

Comparing these expressions, we have

$$\lambda k g(t) + h(t) = g'(t)$$

Using the bound $h \geq 0$ for all t in the interval (as it was originally defined),

$$g'(t) \geq \lambda k g(t)$$

This inequality is crucial. It means that if $g(x_1)$ is zero or positive, $g(t)$ will never become negative in the interval $[x_1, x_2]$. But if we plug in $t = x_1$ in equation (*) above, we get $g(x_1) = 0$. This means that $g(t) \geq 0$ and thus, by equation (*),

$$B \geq B(x_1)e^{\lambda k(t-x_1)} \text{ in the interval } [x_1, x_2]$$

We've proven the simple principle that if total births outweigh total deaths during an interval, they will begin to grow exponentially or hyperexponentially.

It should be noted that while the total population may fluctuate, total births are cumulative and thus always increasing. So, if we compare two consecutive intervals in t, $[x_1, x_2]$ and $[y_1, y_2]$, we know that $B(y_1) \geq B(x_2)$. But this means that in the second interval,

$$B \geq B(x_2)e^{\lambda k(t-y_1)}$$

or

$$B \geq B(x_1)e^{\lambda k(x_2-x_1)}e^{\lambda k(t-y_1)} = B(x_1)e^{\lambda k((x_2-x_1)+(t-y_1))}$$

In other words, since change in B is cumulative, this lower bound on its growth continues unabated through each interval. We can generalize the above formula to read:

$$B \geq B(0)e^{\lambda k L(t)}$$

where $L(t)$ is the total length of all intervals up to time t. But these intervals are defined as those where $N/B \geq \lambda$, i.e., $N \geq \lambda B$. Combining this inequality with the one above, we get

APPENDIX 1: MATHEMATICS OF MALTHUSIAN EQUILIBRIUM

$N \geq \lambda B(0)e^{\lambda k L(t)}$

In other words, the total population must also show cumulative, hyperexponential change from these intervals. To demonstrate what we set out to, let's assume, for a *reductio*, that the total length of these intervals accumulates such that $L(t)/t \geq \varepsilon$ for all t, where ε is some constant > 0. But then

$L(t) \geq \varepsilon t$

or

$L(t) = \varepsilon t + j(t), j \geq 0$

If we plug this into the inequality we derived for N, we get hyperexponentiality even with respect to t. This is impossible, by Malthus's Principle, so we know that, for some finite number a, $L/t < \varepsilon$ for all $t > a$, as desired.

APPENDIX 2: THE MATHEMATICS OF DARWINIAN EQUILIBRIUM

This appendix will make the argument from Chapter 2 more precise. We'd like to show, numerically, that complex traits can only be maintained with a certain minimal force of natural selection determined by mutation rate. Nothing here should be new to someone versed in population genetics, though I will be using a simplified and idealized framework that anyone with basic knowledge of calculus should be able to understand. The idea is not to put forward a novel thesis, but merely to state what we already know in as simple a way as possible.

We will be looking at a single trait in an asexual population of arbitrarily large size. (Our results will generalize to the sexual case, but in the interests of parsimony I am omitting the relevant algebra.) Using the approximation of an infinite number of organisms will allow us to neglect the effects of drift. The first step will be to determine the conditions under which the forces of selection and mutation are in equilibrium. Let X denote the fraction of the population with trait x, and Y denote the fraction with trait y, i.e. lack of trait x, such that X + Y = 1. Let R_{xy} denote the chance that an offspring of an organism with the trait will lose it by mutation, and R_{yx} the chance that the trait will be gained by mutation. Finally, let S denote a measure of the force of selection for x, defined as

APPENDIX 2: MATHEMATICS OF DARWINIAN EQUILIBRIUM

$S = F_x - F_y$

where F_y is the relative fitness of an organism without the trait, and F_x is the relative fitness of an organism with the trait. To see the significance of the quantity S, let's derive an expression for the change in the relative frequency Y. This is given by the expression

$\Delta Y = F_y Y - Y$
$= Y(F_y - 1)$

Our assumption of equilibrium tells us that $F_x X + F_y Y = 1$. This equation can be used to modify our expression to read:

$\Delta Y = Y(F_y - F_y Y - F_x X)$

Substituting in $Y = 1 - X$, we get,

$\Delta Y = Y(F_y - F_y + F_y X - F_x X)$
$= YX(F_y - F_x)$
$= -XYS$

Adding in forward and back mutations, we get the following equation for change in Y:

$\Delta Y = R_{xy} X - R_{yx} Y - XYS$

So, our equilibrium condition is simply

$0 = R_{xy} X - R_{yx} Y - XYS$

Using $X = 1 - Y$, we can put the equation in quadratic form.

$0 = SY^2 - (R_{xy} + R_{yx} + S)Y + R_{xy}$

This equation will suffice to demonstrate what we want to know, namely, the conditions under which natural selection balances out mutation.

For reasonably low mutation rates, say $R_{xy} = R_{yx} = .0001$, Illustration 6 shows how the equilibrium (i.e., $\Delta Y = 0$) frequency of those without the trait varies with the force of selection.

Illustration 6: How the force of selection counters the force of mutation at equilibrium.

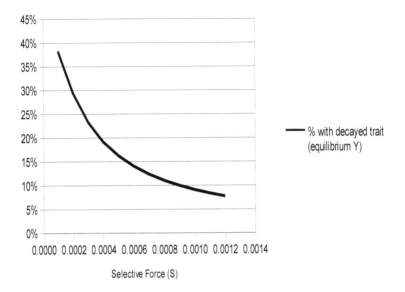

What concerns us most here is the possible degeneration of complex traits due to attenuated selection. In the case of a complex trait x, the chance for back mutation becomes negligible, that is, $R_{xy} \gg R_{yx}$. (In the following equations we will simply write R instead of R_{xy}.) Setting $R_{yx} = 0$, we get a quadratic equation with the following solutions

$$Y = \frac{(R+S) - \sqrt{R^2 - 2SR + S^2}}{2S}$$

or

$$Y = \frac{(R+S) \pm |R-S|}{2S}$$

APPENDIX 2: MATHEMATICS OF DARWINIAN EQUILIBRIUM

Now, if the mutation rate is greater than the selection rate, that is $R > S$, we get one solution:

$Y = 1$

In other words, if the selection rate does not exceed the mutation rate for a complex trait, that complex trait will disappear. On the other hand, if $S > R$, we get two solutions, $Y = 1$ and $Y = R/S$. Were we to plot our original quadratic equation, we would see that the change in Y is positive for $Y < R/S$, and negative for $Y > R/S$. This means that the solution $Y = 1$ is unstable, and the solution $Y = R/S$ is stable. At the stable equilibrium, we see that the frequency of degeneracy—that is, lack of the complex trait in question—is proportional to the mutation rate, and inversely proportional to the selection rate. This suffices to demonstrate that all mutation must be balanced by selection in order for a species to be at equilibrium, as I have been attempting to show.

APPENDIX 3: EVIDENCE FOR CULTURAL EVOLUTION IN THE HISTORY OF TECHNOLOGY

In my search for easy-to-understand examples of cultural evolution by natural selection, I have found some notable evidence in the history of technology, which I present in this appendix. However, in-depth investigation is still needed, since most of my examples come from the secondary literature. (*Note:* In this appendix, to avoid excessive reference to endnotes, I will use in-line citations. Please refer to the Bibliography for details on these sources.)

Following Basalla (1988), I will group the evidence under several evolutionary themes. However, where Basalla saw this as an exercise in analogy, I will be looking for instances where Lewontin's criteria can be strictly applied.

VARIATION

In this section I will cite evidence gleaned from the secondary literature that technology satisfies Lewontin's criterion of variability. The question is whether tools and devices tend to come in multiple competing variants. This indeed appears to be a ubiquitous theme in the history of technology.

APPENDIX 3: CULTURAL EVOLUTION AND TECHNOLOGY

Even a device as simple as the wheel has displayed a rich diversity of variants. This diversity appears to extend back in time almost as far as we have evidence for its use. It is believed that the wheel was invented between 3400 and 3000 B.C. (Piggott, 1983, p. 41; Anthony, 2007, p. 66-72). The earliest wheeled vehicles had solid wheels (carved from a single block of wood) rotating on a fixed axle. But it did not take long for a great deal of diversity to arise. Wheels fixed to a rotating axle have been dated to the third millennium B.C. in Switzerland (Piggott, 1983, p. 25), though fixed-axle vehicles have remained common until the present day. Composite wheels, made from three to five blocks of wood attached, have also been found as far back as the third millennium B.C. (Anthony, 2007, p. 70), while solid wheels are still found today in Ireland, Scotland, Anatolia, Sardinia, and the Iberian Peninsula (Piggott, 1983, p. 25-26). Perhaps the most significant innovation in the history of the wheel is the *spoked wheel*, which is much lighter and can be built without the felling of large trees. This invention dates to around the beginning of the second millennium B.C. (Piggott, 1983, p. 27), and was pivotal in the rise of the war chariot. An interesting variant that appears to predate the spoked wheel by a few centuries is described by Piggott:

> A peculiar form of wheel, of openwork construction but not with radial spokes, has long been recognized in antiquity as the "cross-bar" wheel, but its significance in the technological history of the wheelwrights' craft has only come to be recognized in recent years. It has been characterized as having "a single diametric bar, thick enough to accommodate the nave, and by two slender 'cross-bars' on either side of the nave which traverse the central bar at right angles to it, and the ends of which are morticed into the felloes. There may alternatively be four (or more) shorter cross-bars in similar relation to the central bar, but with their inner ends morticed into it" [Littauer & Crouwel, 1977]. Our immediate concern here is with two north Italian finds of the earlier second millennium B.C., but the type has been shown to have been in use as early as the late third millennium B.C. in the Near East (at Tepe Hissar in Iran), and continuing in use at least to the second, and with a notable frequency of use in Greece from the sixth century B.C. [Lorimer, 1903] as also in Etruscan contexts. A sixth-century example of an actual wheel comes from Gordion in Asia Minor [Kohler, 1980]. Its recent ethnographical distribution is remarkably wide, and includes the Iberian Peninsula (and hence to Mexico), England, China and Outer Mongolia (Piggott, 1983, p. 97).

For half-a-dozen more examples of early variants of the wheel, see the "wheel" entry in the index of Piggott (1983). Early vehicles also varied in whether they had a fixed or moving draft pole, and whether their wheels could steer or not (ibid., p. 86).

Cardwell (1995) describes diversity in the use of iron during the Industrial Revolution:

> The structural use of iron in Britain was, as Dr. Arnold Pacey [1974] has pointed out, pioneered by the ironmasters; in France architects and mathematicians led the way. The British favoured cheap cast iron; the French preferred wrought iron, which lent itself to more versatile use (Cardwell, 1995, p. 168).

Another good example of diversity in technology is given by Friedel (2007):

> There remained a great variety of plow types [in medieval Europe after the moldboard plow appeared], defined by region, crop, economy, and probably simply the varying skills and habits of plowwrights (Friedel, 2007, p. 17).

Since he uses an explicit evolutionary analogy, Basalla (1988) remains the best secondary source of evidence concerning variation in technology. His examples include the "4.7 million patents that have been issued since 1790" in the United States, the "500 different kinds of hammers produced in Birmingham England," and the "1000 [smokestacks] patented in the 19th century" (Basalla, 1988).

CONTINUITY

Continuity in technological change provides indirect evidence of the occurrence of natural selection. A gradual buildup of adaptations demonstrates the *heritability* of culture, because if culture were not heritable, there could be no such accumulation of change. It also demonstrates the need for selection among variants, because if useful innovations were the direct result of deliberation there would be no need to wait for beneficial ones to arise by gradual steps.

The use of the horse for riding appears to have postdated its use for meat by about 1500 years (Anthony, 2007, p. 201-217). This demonstrates

APPENDIX 3: CULTURAL EVOLUTION AND TECHNOLOGY

the non-obviousness of the use for which it would eventually become widespread. It also shows the facility with which knowledge of riding was passed on from generation to generation once it was learned.

It is also noteworthy that the sledge predates wheeled vehicles by about 4000 years. We have evidence that they were used in Finland as early as 7000 B.C., and were originally pulled by dogs (Piggott, 1983, p. 36). Surviving sledges have been found in the Urals and in England dating from the third millennium B.C., model sledges in southern Russia dating from the fourth millennium, pictographs in Mesopotamia also from the fourth millennium, and in the Alps from the third millennium (ibid., p. 36-38). This evidence indicates that the idea of an animal-driven vehicle was widespread for some time before the advent of the wheel. This strongly suggests that the wheel was invented in at most a few different places and then diffused. Once again, the persistence of this innovation would only be possible if knowledge of the wheel were somehow both heritable and differentially fitter than its alternatives. Further advances in wheel manufacture, such as spoked wheels, also took thousands of years to develop, further confirming this picture.

Burstall (1965) describes continuity in hydraulic technology, leading from the pump to the steam engine:

> This [1500 to 1750 A.D.] was the era of the pump. Pumping water, and the ways in which it could be done, occupied the minds of both the laboratory scientists and the practical mechanics (Burstall, 1965, p. 119).

The steam engine is often described as the invention of merely James Watt or Thomas Newcomen. But a cursory review of the secondary literature reveals otherwise (Robison, 1810; Stuart, 1824; Burn, 1854; Thurston,1878; Dickinson, 1938; and Rolt & Allen, 1977). As Burstall describes it,

> The men who contributed [to the] practical achievement [of the steam engine] were Bessou, Polheim, Wilkinson, Worcester, Von Guericke, Savery, Papin, and Newcomen, but there were also many others who in small ways made useful advances in mechanical engineering during this period (Burstall, 1965, p. 196).

Though the above-mentioned historians would certainly disagree about what names belong on the list (Worcester's role is hotly contested, for example), they would all agree that the steam engine was the collective achievement of at least half a dozen inventors. Another example of this kind of continuity is the centrifugal governor.

> The centrifugal governor ... is now known to have been used before his time for limiting the speed of rotation of the grindstones in windmills, but Watt adopted and improved it (ibid., p. 239-240).

As Cardwell puts it:

> [M]ost of the skills required to construct a Newcomen engine were the same as those required to construct a water mill. (Cardwell, 1995, p. 129).

The history of machine tools is especially interesting in this context (Rolt, 1965, gives a good overview). Roughly speaking, machine tools are tools used to fashion other machines. Since almost all modern machines are made using other machines, the collection of all machine tools at a given point in history constitutes a population of mutually-replicating entities. Humans are needed in this process, of course, but Lewontin's conditions are still applicable if we consider humans to be part of the environment. The evolution of machine tools was a relatively gradual process, involving a bit-by-bit increase in accuracy and refinement. Burstall describes some interesting episodes in this development (Burstall, 1965, p. 214). Because it takes a precise machine to make a precise machine, we see an important mode of inheritance entirely distinct from the human organism, but in an analog mode, as opposed to the discrete nature of writing or genes. Cardwell also describes continuity in the history of computing (Cardwell, 1995, p. 467-480).

Continuity is one of the main themes treated by Basalla as he expands on his evolutionary analogy. He devotes an entire chapter to it. One good example he discusses is stone tools, which have changed gradually over hundreds of thousands of years (Basalla, 1988, p. 31). One of Basalla's most surprising examples is the evolution of the cotton gin. As it turns out, this device was not wholly original with Eli Whitney, but was ultimately based on the several-century-old Indian gin (Basalla, 1988, p. 33).

APPENDIX 3: CULTURAL EVOLUTION AND TECHNOLOGY

BLINDNESS OF VARIATION

Blindness of variation also constitutes good evidence that natural selection is occurring. When variations are undirected, it would appear that selection would provide the best explanation for adaptive change. However, it should be kept in mind that blindness is not *necessary* for Lewontin's conditions to apply and for selection to occur. It merely provides confirmation that this is the case, as with continuity.

Unfortunately, failed inventions do not often make it into the mainstream history of technology. But it is well known that artificial selection is ubiquitous in technology and science—in the guise of experiment, and other kinds of "blind" or "empirical" investigation (cf. Campbell, 1960). It is generally assumed that most major inventions took a great deal of tinkering before a first working model was constructed. Cardwell describes an historical method—itself experimental—for illuminating this process. A modern team of engineers attempted to reconstruct Newcomen's early steam engine, and found it unexpected challenging (Cardwell, 1995, p. 123).

Some of the most unambiguous examples of blind variation come from metallurgy. Steel-making, for example, dates back to the Iron Age (Burstall, 1965, p. 55), but it wasn't until the Industrial Revolution that it was realized that steel was the combination of iron and carbon. As Basalla puts it,

> Not until the late 18th century was it possible to explain simple metallurgical processes in chemical terms, and even now there remain procedures in modern metal production whose exact chemical basis is unknown (27).

Early failures in textile machinery illustrate selection among distinct inventions. Cardwell describes several of these:

> In 1738 Lewis Paul, the son of a refugee Frenchman, and John Wyatt patented a spinning machine. ... Paul and Wyatt set up a spinning mill, driven by two donkeys, in Birmingham in 1741. Later, three other mills were built but none of them was successful. ... In 1748 Paul took out a patent for a carding machine to comb out the fibres mechanically. This, too, was not particularly successful. Where Paul and Wyatt failed Richard Arkwright [inventor of the water frame] (1732-92) succeeded, triumphantly (Cardwell, 1995, p. 141-142).

It would appear that even the most successful inventors had more failures than victories. James Watt's original patent presented two versions of the steam engine—one for pumping action and one for producing rotation. The latter innovation ultimately proved a failure, though a great deal of effort was wasted during the next 100 years in trying to make it work (Cardwell, 1995, p. 161-162). Cardwell describes another of Watt's failures:

> [Watt] remained throughout his long life strongly opposed to the use of high-pressure steam ... [But it] was the high-pressure steam engine that, from the time Watt's extended patent finally expired in 1799, was to dominate ... (Cardwell, 1995, p. 166-167).

The blindness of variation is also evidenced by the illusory problem of friction in early locomotives—a case where variation was a great deal more blind than it seemed. For years, many new locomotives were built with teeth or roughened surfaces on their driving wheels, until it was realized that it made no difference to their efficiency (Cardwell, 1995, p. 210-211). Another kind of blindness of variation is when an invention is based on faulty theory, but nevertheless proves successful. Cardwell describes such an example in the history of the steam engine, the development of the first successful high-pressure steam engine by Woolf, based on his own mistaken theories (Cardwell, 1995, p. 214). Still another kind of blindness is demonstrated by the fact that the most useful application of an invention is seldom anticipated when it is first introduced. Cardwell describes how "no one foresaw" wireless communication as a potential medium for "entertainment" or "education" (ibid., p. 384). Instead, it was seen as an alternative to telegraphy. He goes on to describe several additional examples from the history of science, including electromagnets and black powder (Cardwell, 1995, p. 491). According to this picture, there will almost always be some degree of blindness as to how successful a particular innovation will be in the long run—since it will never be clear how well it will do in a changing technological world.

Perhaps the most amusing example of blindness I've encountered is the long history of attempted perpetual motion devices, as described by Basalla (1988 p. 73-74).

APPENDIX 3: CULTURAL EVOLUTION AND TECHNOLOGY

DIFFUSION

Before examining direct evidence of natural selection, we will look at one more type of indirect evidence for it. The tendency of technological innovations to diffuse outward from a localized source supports the evolutionary view, because it shows that—rather than being developed as a direct result of need—technology arises from mutation (whether directed or undirected) and subsequently spreads due to differential fitness. Note that this sort of evidence was very important in the development of Darwin's theory. When Darwin realized that species tended to be related to those nearby, rather than those in similar environments elsewhere, he realized that they were not specially created, but arose from existing stock. The evolution of technology shows a strikingly similar pattern, a pattern illustrated quite well in Jared Diamond's famous book, *Guns, Germs, and Steel* (1997).

Perhaps the clearest example comes from the history of writing. As A.P. Usher (1954) describes it,

> Paper was invented in central China at the close of the first century of the Christian era and its use spread rapidly within the empire and extended even to the outposts of the Chinese Empire stationed on the roads to Turkestan at the edges of the Desert of Gobi. The use of the new product did not extend beyond these limits until the seventh century, but the development of both use and manufacture spread steadily thereafter. The paper was made in Samarkand as early as 751; in Baghdad, by 793; in Egypt, by 900; in Morocco, by 1100; at Jativa in Spain, by 1150; at Herault in southern France by 1189; at Montefano in Italy, by 1276. From France and Italy the new process spread slowly northward, reaching Cologne in 1320 and Nuremberg by 1391 (Usher, 1954, p. 239).

The slow diffusion of another device, the moldboard plow, is described by Friedel (2007, p. 14).

The quick spread of a device can also have the signature of diffusion. For example, pumping water out of coal mines was a problem throughout Europe for decades before the invention of the Newcomen steam engine. This device was invented in England in 1712, "and before 1750 was in use in large numbers in England, Hungary, France, Belgium and Spain and possibly elsewhere on the continent of Europe" (Burstall, 1965, p. 196). In this case, it is clear that the invention spread differentially from a single source. Of course, this isn't to say that there weren't competitors. In 1698 the inventor Thomas Savery had patented a steam-powered pump (considered by some to be the first steam engine) and spent the next several decades attempting to sell his device to coal miners. Savery did a great deal to publicize his idea, distributing pamphlets to miners throughout England. Few pumps were built, though he did raise the overall awareness of the potential of steam power (Rolt and Allen, 1977). In this case, because we have multiple variants, with one ultimately overtaking the other, we have an unambiguous example of natural selection in the cultural realm.

There is an interesting kind of diffusion distinct from spatial diffusion. Innovations can often diffuse from one niche to another within the same community. We might refer to this as "niche-to-niche diffusion."

> [The invention of] the pendulum clock ... gave rise to improvements of lasting value to mechanical engineering such as the study of gearing, gear-cutting machines, broaching, and the screw-cutting lathe (Burstall, 1965, p. 197).

Surprisingly, there are historians who reject the utility of the idea of diffusion. Donald Cardwell argues,

> [T]wo cultures ... at roughly the same technical level, may be expected to produce, more or less simultaneously, the same inventions quite independently, the nature of the inventions being determined by the general level of technical resources and public demand (Cardwell, 1995, p. 505-506).

On this view, it is unclear how Cardwell could hope to explain the vast differences, for example, between European and Chinese technology, even at similar stages in their development. His view certainly cannot be strictly true, since all societies began at the stone-age level, and have since diverged radically, even among localities where the natural resources available are the same (Diamond, 1997). His view does not even appear to be approximately true, given the technological differences even within Europe during the Industrial Revolution. For example, it is well-known that Great Britain vastly excelled the rest of Europe in mechanical engineering, despite the fact that other countries were quick to adopt whatever British inventions suited them.

APPENDIX 3: CULTURAL EVOLUTION AND TECHNOLOGY

NATURAL SELECTION

In this final section, we will discuss direct evidence of natural selection. In particular, we will be looking for examples that clearly satisfy all of Lewontin's criteria. In *The Camel and the Wheel*, R.W. Bulliet (1975) describes one such example at length—the replacement of camels for wheeled vehicles as the dominant mode of transportation in the Middle East between 0 and 500 A.D.

> [I]t would seem that the abandonment of the wheel would have marked a far-reaching effect upon the level of culture of the society ... However, ... the non-vehicular use of wheels ... suffered no regression [and] the greater economy of the pack camel marks [it] as a technological advance ... (Bulliet, 1975, p. 217).

Here we have two variants—the wheel and the camel—where one replaces the other because it is more efficient. As with most technological changes, there was probably both artificial and brute selection in play. As evidence of brute selection, the camel was an extremely important tactical element in warfare during this period (Bulliet, 1975). Furthermore, once the switch to camels was made, it persisted for a millennium, demonstrating heritability.

Cardwell describes an inventor who played an early but fleeting role in the development of the television, John Logie Baird, whose version of the device never caught on (Cardwell, 1995, p. 398). This is another example of a major invention which was really the result of competition among early variants. Variation in early locomotive technology is a famous example of such competition—see Cardwell (1995, p. 210) for an overview. Cardwell also describes competition between wires and chains in suspension bridges (ibid., p. 226-227), early dynamometers (p. 275-276), electric motors (p. 281-282), and water turbines (p. 293-297).

A great deal of primary evidence for selection among steam engines during the nineteenth century is available in the form of a newsletter published throughout the period, Joel Lean's *Monthly Engine Reporter* (Cardwell, 1995, p. 213). This newsletter could provide a potentially rich source of information on the evolution of the steam engine, including evidence of diversity, differential fitness, and the inheritance of successful traits. For an interesting discussion of evidence gleaned from this periodical, see Nuvolari and Verspagen (2007).

Though George Basalla's book *The Evolution of Technology* is a rich source of relevant examples of continuity and diversity, his examples of selection may be found wanting for our purposes, since there is a lack of attention to the factor of differential fitness. This appears to be due to his reluctance to move beyond a mere analogy with Darwin's theory. In his chapters on "selection" Basalla focuses on the *sources* of selection, and neglects the *process*. Nevertheless, he does provide several unambiguous examples of selection in Darwin's sense of the term, including dozens of early vehicles (such flying cars) that were mass produced for a time but failed to catch on (Basalla, 1988, p. 143). He explains the atmospheric railway "fad," which lasted from 1844 to 1860. About 100 were "proposed or built" and only four were completed. One was in operation for 13 years (ibid., p. 179). He describes how steam and electric automobiles were produced alongside gasoline ones from the 1890s to the 1920s. Around the turn of the century each was roughly as common as the other (ibid., p. 197). He gives his clearest example of selection under the heading of continuity:

> In the earliest, and unsuccessful, mechanical reapers, attempts were made to duplicate the swinging motion of the scythe as it *cut* through the grain or to imitate the *clipping* action of scissors or shears. The McCormick reaper, which brought large-scale mechanical reaping to the farmers of America, utilized an oscillating serrated (toothed) blade to *saw* through the grain stocks. McCormick's machine copied the action of the very ancient hand sickle ... (Basalla, 1988, p. 63).

As with any successful technology, McCormick's machine has been reliably reproduced, which establishes *heritability* (regardless of the exact details of the process, which are doubtlessly complicated). This device was one of several variants, including at least two other mechanisms for cutting, establishing *variation*. Finally—and this is true whether or not the best device was chosen rationally—there has been *selection* among these variants, such that only the most useful survives. It should be apparent from this example how easy it is to satisfy the conditions for Darwinian selection. In fact, we should expect selection to be the rule rather than the exception in technological evolution. As Basalla points out, "The fertile technological imaginations create a superfluity of novel artifacts from which society makes selections" (77). This one sentence tersely captures how both Malthus's Principle and Darwin's theory apply to the technological realm.

APPENDIX 4: COMPUTER SIMULATIONS AND THE EVOLUTION OF COMPASSION

Computer simulation has been a mainstream way to study the evolution of altruism for a number of decades[51]. In most cases, however, either group selectionists or selfish-gene theorists (or both) claim absolute victory for their view based on the experiment. When an experiment does not confirm their view, they tend to either reinterpret or dismiss it as unrealistic or question-begging, and neglect it in their discussions.

My aim in this appendix is to argue that in our world of extraordinary complexity, contexts favoring altruism are very common—and so are contexts favoring selfishness. Whether we seek to explain this using group selection theory or kin selection theory, there is no "ultimate" fact of the matter about whether evolution is selfish or unselfish. In general, it will depend (very sensitively, in fact) on the details of the context. Natural selection is what it is—a logical, mathematical principle of the spread of fitter variants. Evaluating it by human categories of selfish and unselfish is logically unsound. Instead, we must remember that selfishness and altruism must be considered in the context of ethics and actual human society if they are to be useful concepts. In this appendix I'd like to show the absurdity of assuming otherwise.

I hope that by contemplating the following experiments you will come to see the limitations of simplified simulations for demonstrating the overall tendencies of evolution. In the case of human societies, the best and most complete simulation we have is history itself. It is unlikely that a highly abstracted computer simulation will give us much insight, as I hope to make clear.

The following simulations were written in Java. I'll provide the basic specifications but no code, as a competent coder should have less difficulty reproducing them himself from scratch than wading through my own poorly-commented spaghetti code, especially if he wishes to make modifications.

Simulation 1:
- The world is a two-dimensional square 50 x 50 grid. Time passes in discreet turns.
- There are two types of organisms, selfish (A) and altruist (B).
- Each location on the grid has a population of 0-50 organisms, of one *or* the other type (not both).
- The population at each location grow by X, formula to be given. Being next to altruists will help a population grow. Since this is a competitive context, we will construe such indiscriminate assistance as "self-sacrifice," which is the technical definition of altruism.
- Random wars reduce the population of a square by 25, with a Y percent chance, determined by how many "selfish" organisms are nearby. The idea is that such "selfists" use aggression to clear out neighboring spaces for colonization.
- Places with population zero are colonized by a random neighbor.

X = 10 + B/50
Y = 33 + A/7
B = total population of altruistic neighbors (diagonal included)
A = total population of selfish neighbors (diagonal included)

Results:
  Exp. 1: By 1500 iterations, altruistic population went to fixation.

APPENDIX 4: COMPUTER SIMULATIONS AND THE EVOLUTION OF COMPASSION

Exp. 2: New random seed. By 1000 iterations, altruistic population went to fixation.

Exp. 3: New random seed. By 1500 iterations, altruistic population went to fixation.

Analysis:

Altruists benefit their neighbors by a factor of B/50. Selfish populations harm their neighbors by a factor of about -A/28 on average. On a frontier, altruists are adjacent to five friends and three enemies. Assuming that populations are comparable, you get an average benefit proportional to -.00714. The "selfists" on a frontier get a benefit of -.1186. So selfists would appear to be able to advance more quickly. However, altruists have the advantage of building up greater population within their ranks, while internal populations of selfists are decimated. Since the benefits of being an altruist are proportional to population, this advantage is great enough to make altruists grow at the frontier. Their only disadvantage is that small groups of surrounded altruists tend to do worse than small groups of selfists.

It may be objected that this simulation is already too complex to give us much insight into the "fundamental" nature of altruism. But any simplifications we make will tend to make the simulation *less* like real life. Instead, let's see if we can show how easy it is to tip the balance in favor of selfishness.

Simulation 2:

- Add in an advantage (plunder) for taking the selfish strategy, and a penalty for being altruistic.
- Subtracted *population* / 5 from the growth of each altruist.

Results:

Selfists went to fixation by 1000 turns.

Analysis:

In Simulation 1, there tended to be an average population of 30 within altruist ranks. This meant that each member benefited by about (30/50) per neighbor, or 0.6 x 8 = 4.8 per turn. In this simulation the average subtracted 30 / 5 = 6 per turn. So the advantage of being in a group was reversed.

Also, at the boundaries between selfists and altruists you can easily calculate that "plunder" will give the advantage to the selfist.

One could try this with lighter penalties for altruism. At some point this would surely give the advantages back to the altruists. A more interesting line of investigation might be to try and make our altruists more realistic. Some may argue, in particular, that this simulation does not force altruists to perform true self-sacrifice, as we normally use the term, that is, as courageous assistance in an emergency. In the next simulation we will introduce such a factor.

Simulation 3:
- The populations are divided into altruists and neutrals. In this scenario the disaster chance should be kept at a flat rate of 33 percent, and disasters should happen at the start of each turn, so that it is possible to save populations in trouble.
- The altruists only help populations that have fewer than 26 members, when they themselves have more than 41. In this case an altruist sacrifices 4 of its own population to save 2 of theirs. This can only occur among the 4 directly adjacent neighbors of a square.

Results:
Neutrals approach fixation, though it takes over 2000 turns.

Simulation 3.1:
- Same as previous, but now increase benefit of sacrifice to 3.

Results:
Neutrals fixate in about 1900 turns.

Simulation 3.2:
- Increase benefit of sacrifice to par (4).

Results:
Exp. 1: Neutrals fixate in 1900 turns.
Exp. 2: Neutrals almost fixate (99.7 percent) after 2000 turns.

Simulation 3.3:
- As 3.2, except charity is only given to other altruists.

APPENDIX 4: COMPUTER SIMULATIONS AND THE EVOLUTION OF COMPASSION

Results:

Altruists fixate in 1500 turns. This must be either group selection or kin selection, because charity still does not benefit the one giving it directly, e.g., individual populations pitted against one another would give no advantage to altruists.

Simulation 3.4:
- As 3.3, but charity only benefits the receiver by 3. It still costs 4 for the giver.

Results:

Fixation of altruists took 1800 turns.

Simulation 3.5:
- As previous, but benefit is now only 2.

Results:

Exp. 1: No fixation after 2000 turns, but neutrals down to only 6 percent of the population. After 4000 turns, neutrals are down to 1 percent.

Exp. 2: With a new random seed, neutrals were down to 3.5 percent at 4000 turns.

Analysis:

This is an interesting result, because the strategy is very costly. A population in trouble is given 2 population, and 4 are sacrificed from the giver! Yet it still works.

Simulation 3.6:
- Now the benefit is only 1 for a sacrifice of 4.

Results:

Altruists fixate around 3100 turns.

Simulation 3.7:
- The benefit for "altruism" is reduced to 0, for something like a control experiment.

Results:

Neutrals reach 90 percent after 4000 turns.

Simulation 3.8:
- Benefit of sacrifice is 1, cost is 8. Neutrals fixate in 3000 turns.

Simulation 3.9:
- Cost of sacrifice is 6. Neutrals fixate in 2200 turns.

Simulation 3.10:
- Cost of sacrifice is 5. Neutrals fixate in 3000 turns. This seems close to the limit of the amount of charity that is beneficial in this simulation, somewhere between a *cost:benefit* ratio of 5:1 and 4:1.

Simulation 3.11:
- As another control-like experiment, all practical differences between the two types were wiped out. No differences in behavior of "altruists" and "neutrals." After 4000 turns, the proportional representation hovered between 50/50 and 60/40, shifting back and forth.

Simulation 4:

In this simulation we'll examine the question of whether altruism needs to be "kin," "family," or "species" specific. We will simply add an algorithm to keep track of descent, as a way to represent genetic relation. Each initial population will be assigned a two-character code, and its descendent populations will be marked with the same code.

Re-running experiment 3.5 with the same random seed as the second experiment, the basic results are the same, as you would expect. The kinship map on the last page of this appendix shows the top left-hand corner of the world. You can see that certain regions are dominated by certain lineages. This means that many lineages are extinct, including most neutral ones. There are only a few dozen lineages left.

The motley character of this map is what you would expect, since there is no substantial difference in behavior among any of these altruists (see *Figure 1*, below).

The absurdity of having to run such an experiment should be clear. The benefits of charity have no dependence on genetic relation. When the only genotypic difference was "altruist" vs. "neutral," the altruists reached 96.5 percent prevalence in 4000 turns. When other genetic differences (albeit without phenotypic expression) were added, the final result was the same. It should be clear that relatedness has no bearing on the

APPENDIX 4: COMPUTER SIMULATIONS AND THE EVOLUTION OF COMPASSION

```
!9 !9 &F IE &F &F &F &F 79 79 &F IE IE IE IE IE IE IE IE IE &F &F
!9 IE !9 &F &F &F &F 79 79 79 &F &F IE IE IE IE IE IE IE IE &F &F
!9 !9 !9 IE IE &F &F 79 79 79 &F &F IE IE IE IE *E *E &F *E IE &F
!9 !9 !9 &F &F &F &F 79 &F &F &F &F IE IE IE IE IE *E &F IE &F RT
!9 !9 !9 &F IE &F 79 79 79 79 &F &F &F IE &F &F IE IE IE IE &F &F
IE !9 IE &F &F &F &F 79 79 &F &F IE IE IE &F &F *E *E IE IE *E *E
IE IE !9 &F &F &F &F &F 79 &F &F IE IE IE IE IE *E IE RT RT *E *E
81 !9 !9 !9 !9 &F &F &F 79 &F 79 RT IE IE IE RT IE RT IE RT *E *E *E
81 81 !9 &F &F !9 IE &F &F &F 79 79 IE RT RT RT RT RT RT IE RT
81 81 81 81 !9 !9 &F &F RT RT 79 79 79 RT IE RT RT RT RT RT RT RT
81 81 RT RT 81 81 &F &F RT IE RT 79 79 RT RT RT RT RT RT RT RT RT
81 RT RT RT 81 &F &F RT IE RT RT &F RT RT RT RT RT RT RT RT RT RT
81 81 81 81 81 81 RT &F &F &F 81 RT RT RT &F RT RT RT RT RT IE RT
81 81 79 79 81 RT 79 &F &F &F &F 81 RT &F RT RT RT RT RT RT IE RT
81 81 81 81 79 79 &F RT RT &F RT 81 81 RT RT RT RT RT RT RT RT RT
81 81 81 79 81 RT &F RT RT RT RT 81 RT RT RT RT RT RT RT *E RT RT
K* 81 81 81 K* K* 81 RT &F RT RT 81 RT RT RT RT RT RT RT RT RT RT
K* K* K* K* K* K* 81 &F &F RT 81 81 81 81 RT RT RT RT RT RT RT RT
K* 81 K* 79 79 79 79 79 RT 81 81 81 81 RT RT RT RT RT RT RT RT RT
H) 81 79 79 79 79 79 RT 79 81 81 81 RT RT RT IE RT RT RT RT RT
K* H) H) H) K* K* 79 RT IE IE 81 IE RT IE RT IE IE IE H) RT RT RT RT
H) K* K* K* K* 79 K* RT IE IE IE IE IE IE RT RT RT H) RT RT RT RT
K* H) K* K* H) K* K* RT IE 81 IE H) IE IE RT RT H) RT RT YP YP
K* K* K* 79 K* 79 K* 81 IE 81 H) IE IE IE RT IE RT IE RT RT YP YP
H) K* H) H) 79 79 H) K* K* 81 IE IE H) IE IE IE IE IE RT RT YP YP
K* K* H) H) H) 79 K* K* 79 H) H) H) IE IE H) IE H) IE IE IE YP YP IE
K* K* K* H) H) H) H) K* K* H) H) H) IE IE IE IE H) IE IE IE YP IE YP
K* K* K* H) H) H) K* K* H) H) H) H) H) BL BL IE IE IE IE YP YP IE
K* H) H) H) H) H) H) H) H) H) H) BL IE IE IE IE IE YP IE YP
K* K* K* K* H) H) H) H) H) H) H) H) BL IE ?U ?U YP YP IE IE
K* K* K* K* K* H) H) H) H) H) H) H) H) H) IE H) ?U IE IE IE IE
K* K* K* K* K* H) H) H) H) >4 H) H) H) H) BL H) ?U H) H) IE ?U
K* K* K* K* K* K* H) H) H) H) H) H) H) H) BL H) H) IE ?U ?U
K* K* K* K* K* K* H) H) H) >4 >4 H) H) ?U BL BL IE H) IE ?U ?U
K* K* K* K* K* K* ?U K* ?U >4 >4 >4 H) ?U BL H) H) IE IE IE BL ?U
K* K* K* H) K* H) K* ?U ?U H) >4 >4 H) H) ?U H) H) ?U ?U IE IE H?
K* K* K* K* K* K* >4 ?U K* ?U >4 >4 H) H) ?U BL BL ?U ?U IE IE H? BL
K* K* K* K* >4 >4 K* K* >4 >4 H) H) H) ?U ?U H? H? H? H? H? BL
K* K* K* K* >4 >4 >4 >4 ?U >4 H) H) ?U H? H? H? H? H? ?U
>4 K* K* >4 >4 H) >4 >4 >4 >4 ?U ?U ?U ?U ?U H? ?U H? H? ?U
```

Figure 1: This is the top-left hand corner of the world at the end of the simulation. Each genetic lineage is represented by a two-character combination. Over 95 percent of the population is altruistic at this stage, and you can see that though certain families predominate in certain areas, they are mixed indiscriminately at the boundaries, since it benefits altruists equally whether they are next to altruistic kin or altruistic non-relatives.

benefits of altruism. It only matters whether its sacrifices are benefiting other altruists.

We could easily begin to add *phenotypic* variation among families, but it should be obvious that any effects that would result from this would be incidental to genetic relatedness, and depend solely on phenotypic similarity. Again, any given phenotypic variation will have the same effect whether its subpopulations are genetically related or not. This train of thought should be enough to demonstrate the absurdity of such experiments, and more generally of the kin-selectionist paradigm.

SUGGESTED READING

Please refer to the Bibliography for full citations. Starred (*) items indicate essential reading in the topic.

THEORY OF NATURAL SELECTION
*Malthus, *Essay on the Principle of Population*
*Darwin, *Origin of Species; The Descent of Man*
*Lewontin, "The Units of Selection"
*Elliot Sober and D.S. Wilson, *Unto Others*
*Gregory Clark, *A Farewell to Alms*

DECAY OF DNA BY MUTATION
*M. Lynch, "Rate, molecular spectrum, and consequences of human mutation"
Kondrashov, "Direct estimates of human per nucleotide mutation rates"
Shabalina, "Rapid decline of fitness in panmictic populations of Drosophila ... under relaxed natural selection"

CULTURAL EVOLUTION
*D.S. Wilson, *Darwin's Cathedral*
*William Durham, *Coevolution*
Donald Campbell, "Unjustified Variation and Selective Retention in Scientific Discovery"
Thomas Kuhn, *The Structure of Scientific Revolutions*

THE RISE AND FALL OF CIVILIZATIONS
*Gibbon, *Decline and Fall of the Roman Empire*

*David Hackett Fischer, *The Great Wave*
*Joseph Tainter, *The Collapse of Complex Societies*
Rousseau, *Social Contract*
Ron Nielsen, *The Little Green Handbook*
John Michael Greer, *Our Ecotechnic Future*
Dambisa Moyo, *Dead Aid*
Chris Martenson, *The Crash Course*

TRADITIONAL SOCIETY
*Lila Abu-Lughod, *Veiled Sentiments*
*David W. Anthony, *The Horse, the Wheel, and Language*
Carol MacCormack, *Ethnography of Fertility and Birth*
B.D. Shaw, "The Family in Late Antiquity"

MODERN PHILOSOPHIES OF VALUE
*Jeremy Bentham, *Principles of Morals and Legislation*
*Nietzsche, *Beyond Good and Evil*
*G.K. Chesterton, *Everlasting Man; Eugenics and Other Evils*
*C.S. Lewis, *The Abolition of Man*
*Mary Midgley, *Science as Salvation; Evolution as Religion*

Peter Singer, *Practical Ethics*

ANCIENT WISDOM
The Bible
*Plato, *Republic, Sophist*
*Aristotle, *Politics*
*Augustine, *Confessions, City of God*
*Boethius, *The Consolation of Philosophy*
*Aquinas, *Summa Theologica*
Lao Tzu, *Tao Te Ching*
The Qur'an
Confucius, *Analects*
Bhagavad Gita
Rig Veda

BIBLIOGRAPHY

Abu-Lughod, Lila. 1986 [1999]. *Veiled Sentiments*. Berkeley: University of California Press.
Adami, Christoph. 1998. *Artificial Life*. New York: Springer-Verlag.
Agricola, G. 1556 [1950]. *De Re Metallica,* trans. H.C. and L.H. Hoover. New York: Dover Publications.
André, Jean-Baptiste and Bernard Godelle. 2006. "The Evolution of Mutation Rate in Finite Asexual Populations." *Genetics*. 172: 611.
Anthony, David W. 2007. *The Horse, the Wheel, and Language: How Bronze-Age Riders from the Eurasian Steppes Shaped the Modern World*. Princeton: Princeton University Press.
Aristotle. 1952. *Great Books of the Western World*, Vols. 8 & 9, ed. Robert Maynard Hutchins. Chicago: Encyclopedia Britannica.
Aunger, Robert, ed. 2000. *Darwinizing Culture*. New York: Oxford University Press.
Bedau, Mark A. and Norman H. Packard. 2003. "Evolution of evolvability via adaptation of mutation rates." *Biosystems*. 69: 143.
Basalla, George. 1988. *The Evolution of Technology*. Cambridge: Cambridge University Press.
Beaver, Stephen E. 1975. *Demographic Transition Theory Reinterpreted*. Lexington: Lexington Books.

Bentham, Jeremy. 1777. "Review of the Declaration of Independence." *The Scots Magazine*, Vol. 39. (Retrieved September 2016, from https://play.google.com/books/reader?id=5-g5AQAA-MAAJ&printsec=frontcover&output=reader&hl=en&pg=GBS.PP1

Bentham, Jeremy. 1789 [2015]. *An Introduction to the Principles of Morals and Legislation*. eBook: earlymoderntexts.com.

Bentham, Jeremy. 1843. "Of Population." In *The Works of Jeremy Bentham*, Vol. 3, ed. John Bowring. Edinburg: William Tait. (Retrieved September, 2016, from http://oll.libertyfund.org/titles/bentham-the-works-of-jeremy-bentham-vol-3)

Bentham, Jeremy. 1977. *A Comment on the Commentaries and a Fragment of Government*, ed. J.H. Burns and H.L.A. Hart, London: The Athlone Press.

Bhagavad Gita, trans. A.C. Bhaktivedanta Swami Prabhupada. 2008. Los Angeles: Bhaktivedanta Book Trust.

Blackmore, Susan. 1999. *The Meme Machine*. New York: Oxford University Press.

Boas, Franz. 1928 [1962]. *Anthropology in Modern Life*. Westport, CT: Greenwood Press.

Boethius. 2002 [1962]. *The Consolation of Philosophy*, trans. Richard H. Green. Mineola, NY: Dover Publications.

Bourke, Andrew. 2011. *Principles of Social Evolution*. Oxford: Oxford University Press.

Boyd, Robert and Peter J. Richerson. 1985. *Culture and the Evolutionary Process*. Chicago: University of Chicago Press.

Boyd, Robert and Peter J. Richerson. 2005. *Not by Genes Alone*. Chicago: University of Chicago Press.

Bulliet, R.W. 1975. *The Camel and the Wheel*. Cambridge: Harvard University Press.

Burn, Robert Scott. 1854. *The Steam-Engine: Its History and Mechanism*. London: H. Ingram and Co.

Burstall, Aubrey F. 1965. *History of Mechanical Engineering*. Cambridge: MIT press.

Caldwell, John C. 1982. *Theory of Fertility Decline*. New York: Academic Press.

Caldwell, John C. 2006. *Demographic Transition Theory*. Dordrecht: Springer.

Cameron, Averil. 1993. *The Mediterranean World in Late Antiquity AD 395-600*. New York: Routledge.

Campbell, Donald T. 1960. "Blind Variation and Selective Retention in Creative Thought as in Other Knowledge Processes." *Psychological Review*. 67(6): 380.

Campbell, Donald T. 1965. "Variation and Selective Retention in Socio-Cultural Evolution." In Herbert R. Barringer, et al., eds., *Social Change in Developing Areas: A Reinterpretation of Evolutionary Theory*. Cambridge, MA: Schenkman.

Campbell, Donald T. 1974. "Evolutionary Epistemology." In P. A. Schilpp, ed., *The Philosophy of Karl R. Popper*. LaSalle, IL: Open Court.

Campbell, Donald T. 1974b. "Unjustified Variation and Selective Retention in Scientific Discovery." In F. J. Ayala and T. Dobzhansky, eds., *Studies in the Philosophy of Biology*. London: Macmillan.

Cardwell, Donald. 1995. *The Norton History of Technology*. New York: W.W. Norton & Co.

Carlyle, Thomas. 1850 [2012]. *Latter-Day Pamphlets*. eBook: Project Gutenberg.

Carneiro, Robert L. 2003. *Evolutionism in Cultural Anthropology*. Boulder, CO: Westview Press.

Cavalli-Sforza, L.L. 2000. *Genes, Peoples, and Languages*. New York: North Point Press.

Cavalli-Sforza, L.L. and M.W. Feldman. 1981. *Cultural Transmission and Evolution*. Princeton, NJ: Princeton University Press.

Chesterton, G.K. 1922 [2001]. "Eugenics and Other Evils." In *The Collected Works of GK Chesterton*. San Francisco: Ignatius Press.

Chesterton, G.K. 1925 [2010]. *The Everlasting Man*. eBook: Project Gutenberg of Australia.

Chesterton, G.K. 1927 [2016]. "Social Reform versus Birth Control." (Retrieved September 2016, from
http://www.cse.dmu.ac.uk/~mward/gkc/books/Social_Reform_B.C.html)

Clark, Gregory. 2007. *A Farewell to Alms*. Princeton, NJ: Princeton University Press.

Cohen, L.J. 1973. "Is the Progress of Science Evolutionary?" *British Journal for the Philosophy of Science*. 24: 41.

Condorcet, Marquis de. 1795 [1796]. *Outlines of an Historical View of the Progress of the Human Mind*, trans. from the French. Philadelphia: Lang and Ustick. (Retrieved September 2016, from
http://lfoll.s3.amazonaws.com/titles/1669/0878_Bk.pdf)

Confucius. 1938 [1989]. *Analects,* trans. Arthur Waley. New York: Vintage Books.

Coulter, Ann, 2007. *Godless: The Church of Liberalism*. Random House Inc.

Crow, James F. 1997. "The High Spontaneous Mutation Rate: Is it a Health Risk?" *PNAS*. 94 (16): 8380.

Darwin, Charles. 1859 [1964]. *On the Origin of Species*. Cambridge, MA: Harvard University Press.

Darwin, Charles. 1871 [1909]. *The Descent of Man, and Selection in Relation to Sex*. New York: D. Appleton and Co.

Darwin, Charles. 1887 [1902]. "Autobiography." In *The Life of Charles Darwin*. Ed. Francis Darwin. London: John Murray. (Retrieved March 2010 from http://www.stephenjaygould.org/library/darwin_autobiography.html [dead link as of May 2017])

Dawkins, Richard. 1976. *The Selfish Gene*. New York: Oxford University Press.

Dawkins, Richard. 1982. *The Extended Phenotype*. San Francisco: Freeman.

Dawkins, Richard. 1983. "Universal Darwinism." In D.S. Bendall, ed., *Evolution from Molecules to Man*. New York: Cambridge University Press.

Dawkins, Richard. 1986 [1996]. *The Blind Watchmaker*. New York: W.W. Norton & Company.

Dennett, Daniel C. 1995. *Darwin's Dangerous Idea*. New York: Simon & Schuster.

Devlin, Bernie, et al., eds. 1997. *Intelligence, Genes, and Success*. New York: Springer.

Diamond, Jared. 1997. *Guns, Germs, and Steel*. New York: W.W. Norton & Co.

Dickinson, H.W. 1938. *A Short History of the Steam Engine*. Cambridge, UK: Babcock and Wilcox, Ltd. at the University Press.

Dims, 2005. "File:Perpetuum1.png." (Retrieved June 2017, from https://commons.wikimedia.org/wiki/File:Perpetuum1.png)

Douglas, Kate. 2006. "Are We Still Evolving?" *New Scientist*. March 11 2006, Issue 2542. (Retrieved April 2010, from http://www.newscientist.com/article/mg18925421.300-are-we-still-evolving.html)

Durham, William H. 1991. *Coevolution: Genes, Culture, and Human Diversity*. Stanford, CA: Stanford University Press.

Dobzhansky, Theodosius. 1973. *Genetic Diversity and Human Equality*. New York: Basic Books.

Easterly, William. 2006. *The White Man's Burden: Why the West's Efforts to Aid the Rest Have Done So Much Ill and So Little Good*. New York: Oxford University Press.

Ehrlich, Paul R. 1968. *The Population Bomb*. New York: Ballantine Books.

Evans, Patrick D. 2005. "Microcephalin, a Gene Regulating Brain Size, Continues to Evolve Adaptively in Humans." *Science*. 309(5741): 1717.

Fernandez, Patricio. 2016. "Practical Reasoning: Where the Action Is." *Ethics*. 126:4.

Fischer, David Hackett. 1996. *The Great Wave: Price Revolutions and the Rhythm of History*. New York: Oxford University Press.

Fisher, R.A. 1930 [1958]. *The Genetical Theory of Natural Selection*. New York: Dover Publications.

Fretz, J. Winfield. 1953. "Birth Rate, Mennonite." *Global Anabaptist Mennonite Encyclopedia Online*. (Retrieved March 2010, from http://www.gameo.org/encyclopedia/contents/B5412.html)

Friedman, Emily. 2009. "Why Are Condoms Disliked by So Many Men?" *Abcnews.com*. June 20. (Retrieved March 2010, from http://abcnews.go.com/Health/ReproductiveHealth/story?id=7889403&page=1)

Galton, Francis. 1887. *Hereditary Genius*. New York: D. Appleton and Company.

Galton, Francis. 1906. *Noteworthy Families*. London: J. Murray.

Gardner, A., S.A. West, and G. Wild. 2011. "The Genetical Theory of Kin Selection." *Journal of Evolutionary Biology*. 24: 1020-1043.

Gibbon, Edward. 1782 [1845]. *History of the Decline and Fall of the Roman Empire*. Kindle: Public Domain Books.

Godwin, William. 1793. *An Enquiry Concerning Political Justice*. London: G.G.J. and J. Robinson. (Retrieved September 2016 from http://lf-oll.s3.amazonaws.com/titles/90/0164-01_Bk.pdf)

Gould, Stephen Jay. 1981. *The Mismeasure of Man*. New York: Norton.

Gould, Stephen Jay. 1996. *Full House: The Spread of Excellence From Plato to Darwin*. New York: Harmony Books.

Gould, Stephen Jay. 2002. *The Structure of Evolutionary Theory*. Cambridge: Belknap Press of Harvard University Press.

Gould, Stephen Jay and Richard C. Lewontin. 1979. "The Spandrels of San Marco and the Panglossian Paradigm: A Critique of the Adaptationist Programme." *Proceedings of the Royal Society of London*. 205(1161): 581.

Graves, Joseph L., Jr. 2004. *The Race Myth*. New York: Dutton.

Greer, John Michael. 2009. *Our Ecotechnic Future*. Gabriola Island: New Society Publishers.

Haldane, J.B.S. 1927. "Eugenics and Social Reform." In *Possible* Worlds, by J.B.S. Haldane. London: Chatto & Windus.

Haldane, J. B. S. 1937. "The Effect of Variation on Fitness." *American Naturalist*. 71: 337.

Hardin, Garrett, ed. 1969. *Population, Evolution, and Birth Control; A Collage of Controversial Ideas*. San Francisco: W.H. Freeman.

Hare, Richard. 1982. "Ethical Theory and Utilitarianism." In *Utilitarianism and Beyond*, ed. Amartya Sen and Bernard Williams. Cambridge: Cambridge University Press.

Harrison, Niall. 2016. "Stories We've Seen Too Often." *Strange Horizons*. (Retrieved September 2016, from http://www.strangehorizons.com/guidelines/fiction-common.shtml)

Hawks, John, et al. 2007. "Recent Acceleration of Human Adaptive Evolution." *Proceedings of the National Academy of Sciences of the United States of America*. 104(52): 20753.

Herrstein, Richard J. and Charles Murray. 1994. *The Bell Curve*. New York: Simon & Schuster.

Hodgson, Geoffrey M. 2004. "Social Darwinism in Anglophone Academic Journals: A Contribution to the History of the Term." *Journal of Historical Sociology*, 17:4, 428–463.

Holy Bible, King James Version. 1979. Salt Lake City: The Church of Jesus Christ of Latter-Day Saints.

Holy Bible, New International Version. 1973 [2001]. Grand Rapids: Zondervan.

Hopkins, Keith. 1965. "Contraception in the Roman Empire." *Comparative Studies in Society and History*. 8(1): 124.

Hull, David. 1982. "The Naked Meme." In Henry Plotkin, ed., *Learning, Development, and Culture: Essays in Evolutionary Epistemology*. New York: J. Wiley.

Hull, David. 1988. *Science as a Process*. Chicago: University of Chicago Press.

Huxley, Julian. 1942 [2010]. *Evolution: The Modern Synthesis*. Cambridge, MA: The MIT Press.

Huxley, Julian. 1957. "Transhumanism." In *New Bottles for New Wine*. London: Chatto & Windus. (Retrieved September 2016 from http://www.transhumanism.org/index.php/WTA/more/huxley [dead link as of May 2017])

Huxley, Julian. 1963. *The Human Crisis*. Seattle: University of Washington Press.

Huxley, Julian. 1964 [1992]. *Evolutionary Humanism*. Buffalo, NY: Prometheus Books.

Huxley, T.H. 1893 [1993]. "Evolution and Ethics." In Matthew H. Nitecki, ed., *Evolutionary Ethics*. Albany: State University Of New York Press.

Jacoby, Russell and Naomi Glauberman, eds. 1995. *The Bell Curve Debate*. New York: Random House.

Javier A Magaña-Gómez, Ana M Calderón de la Barca. "Risk Assessment of Genetically Modified Crops for Nutrition and Health." DOI: http://dx.doi.org/10.1111/j.1753-4887.2008.00130.x 1-16 First published online: 1 January 2009

Jensen, Arthur. 1972. *Genetics and Education*. New York: Harper and Row.

Jobling, Mark. 2004. *Human Evolutionary Genetics*. New York: Garland Science.

Jones, Steve. 1993. *The Language of Genes*. New York: Doubleday.

Kauffman, Stuart A. 1993. *Origins of Order*. New York: Oxford University Press.

Kauffman, Stuart A. 1995. *At Home in the Universe*. New York: Oxford University Press.

Kauffman, Stuart A. 2000. *Investigations*. New York: Oxford University press.

Kauffman, Stuart A. 2008. *Reinventing the Sacred*. New York: Basic Books.

Kauffman, Stuart A. 2013. "Chasing the Seeds of Life." *NPR*. (Retrieved September 2016, from http://www.npr.org/sections/13.7/2013/04/26/177451425/chasing-the-seeds-of-life)

Kevles, Daniel J. 1995. *In the Name of Eugenics*. New York: Harvard University Press.

Kirk, Katherine, et al. 2001. "Natural Selection and Quantitative Genetics of Life-History Traits in Western Women: A Twin Study." *Evolution*. 55(2): 423.

Kitcher, Philip. 1993. *The Advancement of Science*. New York: Oxford University Press.

Kohler, E.L. 1980. "Cremations of the Middle Phrygian Period at Gordion." In Keith DeVries, ed., *From Athens to Gordion*. Philadelphia: The University of Pennsylvania Museum.

Kohler, Hans-Peter, et al. 2002. "The Fertility Pattern of Twins and the General Population Compared: Evidence from Danish Cohorts 1945-64." *Demographic Research*. 6(14): 383.

Kondrashov AS, 2003, "Direct Estimates of Human per Nucleotide Mutation Rates at 20 Loci Causing Mendelian Diseases," *Hum Mutat* 21:12–27

Konnor, Melvin. 1982. *The Tangled Wing*. New York: Harper Colophon Books.

Kroeber, A.L. 1923. *Anthropology*. New York: Harcourt, Brace & Co.

Kuhn, Thomas. 1962 [1996]. *The Structure of Scientific Revolutions*. Chicago: University of Chicago Press.

Lampert, Adam and Tsvi Tlusty. 2009. "Mutability as an Altruistic Trait in Finite Asexual Populations." Journal of Theoretical Biology. 261: 414.

Lao Tzu. 1994. *Tao Te Ching*, trans. Stephen Mitchell. New York: Harper Perennial.

Lao Tzu. 1996. *Taoteching*, trans. Red Pine. San Francisco: Mercury House.

Legates, James and Everett Warwick. 1979. *Breeding and Improvement of Farm Animals*. New York: McGraw-Hill.

Lewontin, R.C. 1970. "The Units of Selection." *Annual Reviews of Ecology and Systematics* 1: 1.

Lewontin, R.C., et al. 1984. *Not in Our Genes*. New York: Pantheon Books.

Littauer, M.A. and Crouwel. 1977. "The Origin and Diffusion of the Cross-bar Wheel?" *Antiquity*. 51: 95.

Lorimer, H. 1903. "The Country Cart in Ancient Greece." *Journal of Hellenic Studies*. 23: 132.

Losee, J. 1977. "Limitations of an Evolutionist Philosophy of Science." *Studies in the History of Science*. 8: 349.

Lovelock, J: "Gaia as Seen Through the Atmosphere," in P. Westbroek and E. W. de Jong (eds.), *Biomineralization and Biological Metal Accumulation*, pp.15-25. 1983, Boston: D. Reidel Publishing Company.

Lumsden, Charles J. and E.O. Wilson. 1981. *Genes, Mind, and Culture: The Coevolutionary Process*. Cambridge, MA: Harvard University Press.

Lynch, M. 2010. "Rate, Molecular Spectrum, and Consequences of Human Mutation." *PNAS* 107:961-968.

Lynch, M. 2016. "Mutation and Human Exceptionalism: Our Future Genetic Load." *Genetics*. 202:3, 869-875.

Lynn, Richard. 2001. *Eugenics: A Reassessment*. Westport, CT: Praeger.

MacCormack, Carol P., ed. 1982. *Ethnography of Fertility and Birth*. New York: Academic Press.

Malthus, Thomas Robert. 1798. *An Essay on the Principle of Population*. London: J. Johnson, in St. Paul's Church-yard. (Retrieved March 2010 from http://www.econlib.org/library/Malthus/malPop1.html)

Martenson, Chris. 2011. *The Crash Course*. Hoboken: John Wiley & Sons Inc.

Marvel K., Kravits B., Caldeira K. 2012. "Geophysical Limits to Wind Power." *Nature*, 3:118-121. (Retrieved June 2016, from http://www.nature.com/articles/nclimate1683.epdf)

McLaren, Angus. 1990. *A History of Contraception from Antiquity to the Present Day*. Cambridge, MA: Blackwell.

Midgley, Mary. 1985 [2002]. *Evolution as a Religion*. New York: Routledge.

Midgley, Mary. 1992. *Science as Salvation*. New York: Routledge.

Moore, G.E. 1903. *Principia Ethica*. Cambridge: Cambridge University Press.

Moyo, Dambisa. 2009. *Dead Aid*. New York: Farrar, Straus and Giroux.

Muller, H.J. 1973. *Man's Future Birthright*. Albany: State University Of New York Press.

Nelson, Richard. 2006. "Evolutionary Social Science and Universal Darwinism." *Journal of Evolutionary Economics*. 16: 491.

Nelson, Richard. 2007. "Universal Darwinism and Evolutionary Social Science." *Biology and Philosophy*. 22: 73.

Nielsen, Ron. 2006. *The Little Green Handbook*. New York: Picador.

Nietzsche, Friedrich. 1886. *Beyond Good and Evil*. In Walter Kaufmann's trans. 1967 [2000]. *Basic Writings of Nietzsche*. New York: The Modern Library.

Nuvolari, Alessandro and Bart Verspagen. 2007. "Lean's Engine Reporter and the Development of the Cornish Engine: A Reappraisal." *Transactions of the Newcomen Society*. 77: 167.

Ord-Hume, Arthur W.J.G. 1977. *Perpetual Motion: The History of an Obsession*. New York: St. Martin's Press.

Osborn, Frederick. 1968. *The Future of Human Heredity*. New York: Weybright and Talley.

Pacey, Arnold. 1974 [1992]. *The Maze of Ingenuity*. Baskerville: DEKR Corporation.

Pearson, Karl. 1905. *National Life from the Standpoint of Science*. London: Adam and Charles Black.

Piggot, Stuart. 1983. *The Earliest Wheeled Transport*. Ithaca, NY: Cornell University Press.

Pinker, Steven. 2002. *The Blank Slate*. New York: Viking.

Pirsig, Robert. 1974 [1999]. *Zen and the Art of Motorcycle Maintenance*. New York: Harper Torch.

Plato. 1892 [1937]. *The Dialogues of Plato*, trans. B. Jowett. New York: Random House.

Plotkin, Henry C., ed. 1982. *Learning, Development, and Culture: Essays in Evolutionary Epistemology*. New York: J. Wiley.

Plotkin, Henry C. 1993. *Darwin Machines and the Nature of Knowledge*. Cambridge, MA: Harvard University Press.

Popper, Karl. 1972. *Objective Knowledge*. London: Oxford University Press.

Popper, Karl. 1982. "Of Clouds and Clocks." In Henry Plotkin, ed., *Learning, Development, and Culture: Essays in Evolutionary Epistemology*. New York: J. Wiley.

Quinn, Michael. 2008. "Mill on Poverty, Population and Poor Relief: Out of Bentham by Malthus?" *Revue d'Etudes Benthamiennes 4*, 70-88.

Qur'an, trans. M.A.S. Abdel Haleem. 2010. Oxford: Oxford University Press.

Pimental, David; Harvey C., et al. "Environmental and Economic Costs of Soil Erosion and Conservation Benefits." *Science*, New Series, 267:5201, 1117-1123.

Ramelli, Agostino. 1588 [1976]. *The Various and Ingenious Machines of Agostino Ramelli*. Trans. by Martha Teach Gnudi. London: Scolar Press.

Reichenberg, A., et al. 2006. "Advancing Paternal Age and Autism." *Archives of General Psychiatry*. 63: 1026.
Rescher, Nicholas. 1990. *A Useful Inheritance*. Savage, MD: Rowman & Littlefield Publishers, Inc.
Rescher, Nicholas. 1999 (1974). *The Limits of Science*. Pittsburgh: University of Pittsburgh Press.
Rice, Victor A., Frederick N. Andrews, and Everett J. Warwick. 1953. *Breeding Better Livestock*. New York: McGraw Hill.
Richards, R.J. 1987. *Darwin and the Emergence of Evolutionary Theories of Mind and Behavior*. Chicago: University of Chicago Press.
Richey, A. S., B. F. Thomas, M.-H. Lo, J. T. Reager, J. S. Famiglietti, K. Voss, S. Swenson, and M. Rodell. 2015. "Quantifying Renewable Groundwater Stress with GRACE," *Water Resour. Res.*, 51, 5217–5238.
Rig Veda, trans. Ralph T.H. Griffith. 1896. (Retrieved September 2016 from http://www.sacred-texts.com/hin/rigveda/)
Robison, John. 1810. "Steam-engines." *Encyclopædia Britannica*, 4th Ed., Vol. XIX. Edinburgh: Archibald Constable and Co.
Rolt, L.T.C. 1965. *A Short History of Machine Tools*. Cambridge, MA: MIT Press.
Rolt, L.T.C. and J.S. Allen. 1977. *The Steam Engine of Thomas Newcomen*. New York: Science History Publications.
Rousseau, Jean-Jacques, trans. G.D.H. Cole. 1762 [1913]. *The Social Contract*. London: J.M. Dent.
Ruse, Michael. 1996. *Monad to Man: The Concept of Progress in Evolutionary Biology*. Cambridge, MA: Harvard University Press.
Ruyle, Eugene E. 1973. "Genetic and Cultural Pools: Some Suggestions for a Unified Theory of Biocultural Evolution." *Human Ecology*. 1: 201.
Sachs, Jeffery D. 2005. *The End of Poverty*. New York: The Penguin Press.
Sangharakshita. 1993 (1957). A Survey of Buddhism. Glasgow: Windhorse Publications.
Sen, Amartya Kumar. 1999. *Development as Freedom*. New York: Anchor Books.
Sesardic, Neven. 2005. *Making Sense of Heritability*. New York: Cambridge University Press.
Shabalina, S.A., et al. 1997. "Rapid Decline of Fitness in Panmictic Populations of Drosophila Melanogaster Maintained Under Relaxed Natural Selection." *Proceedings of the National Academy of Sciences of the United States of America*. 94 (24): 13034.
Shaw, B.D. 1987. "The Family in Late Antiquity." *Past and Present*. 115(1): 3.

Singer, Peter. 2011. *Practical Ethics, Third Edition*. New York: Cambridge University Press.

Smith, Charles. 1998. "Introduction: Current Animal Breeding." In A.J. Clark, ed., *Animal Breeding: Technology for the 21st Century*. Amsterdam: Harwood Academic.

Smith, John Maynard and George R. Price. 1973. "The Logic of Animal Conflict." *Nature*. 246: 15.

Sober, Elliot. 1992. "Models of Cultural Evolution." In Paul Griffiths, ed., *Trees of Life*. Boston: Kluwer Academic Publishers.

Sober, Elliott and D.S. Wilson. 1999. *Unto Others: The Evolution and Psychology of Unselfish Behavior*. Cambridge, MA: Harvard University Press.

Spencer, Herbert. 1892 [1900]. *First Principles*. Akron, OH: Werner Company.

Stevens, William K. "Evolution of Humans May at Last Be Faltering." *New York Times*, March 14, 1995.

Stokstad, Erik. 2005. "Will Malthus Continue to Be Wrong?" *Science*. 309 (5731): 102.

Stuart, Robert. 1824. *A Descriptive History of the Steam Engine*. London: John Knight and Henry Lacey.

Tainter, Joseph. 1988. *The Collapse of Complex Societies*. New York: Cambridge University Press.

Tainter, Joseph. 2010. "Complexity and the Productivity of Innovation." *Systems Research and Behavioral Science*. 27: 496-509.

Tainter, Joseph. 2011. *Drilling Down*. New York: Copernicus.

Thurston, Robert. 1878 [1891]. *A History of the Growth of the Steam Engine*. New York: D. Appleton and Company.

Toulmin, Stephen. 1972. *Human Understanding*. Princeton: Princeton University Press.

United Nations, Department of Economic and Social Affairs, Population Division. 2015. *World Population Prospects, the 2015 Revision*. (Retrieved September 2016, from
https://esa.un.org/unpd/wpp/Download/Standard/Population/)

Usher, A.P. 1954. *A History of Mechanical Inventions*. Cambridge, MA: Harvard University Press.

Van Valen, Leigh. 1973. "A New Evolutionary Law." *Evolutionary Theory* 1: 1.

Varfolomeyev, S.D. and K.G. Gurevich. 2001. "The Hyperexponential Growth of the Human Population on a Macrohistorical Scale." *Journal of Theoretical Biology*. 212(3): 367.

Wallace, Anthony. 1966. *Religion: An Anthropological View*. New York: Random House.

Watson, James E.M., et al. 2016. "Catastrophic Declines in Wilderness Areas Undermine Global Environmental Targets." *Current Biology*. September 8. 0(0).

Williams, Mary. 1970. "Deducing the Consequences of Evolution: A Mathematical Model." *Journal of Theoretical Biology*. 29(3): 343.

Wilson, David Sloan. 2003. *Darwin's Cathedral: Evolution, Religion, and the Nature of Society*. Chicago: University of Chicago Press.

Wilson, Edward O. 1975. *Sociobiology*. Cambridge, MA: Belknap Press of Harvard University Press.

Wilson, Edward O. 1978. *On Human Nature*. Cambridge, MA: Harvard University Press.

Wilson, Edward O. 1998. *Consilience*. New York: Knopf.

ENDNOTES

1. The list is from the submission guidelines for *Strange Horizons,* an online speculative fiction magazine edited by Niall Harrison.
2. For an overview of the data supporting this claim, see http://www.footprint-network.org/en/index.php/GFN/page/footprint_basics_overview/
3. See A.S. Kondrashov, "Direct Estimates of Human per Nucleotide Mutation Rates at 20 Loci Causing Mendelian Diseases"; M. Lynch, "Rate, Molecular Spectrum, and Consequences of Human Mutation"; M. Lynch "Mutation and Human Exceptionalism: Our Future Genetic Load."
4. https://www.wfp.org/hunger/stats
5. L.L. Cavalli-Sforza, *Genes, Peoples, and Languages.*
6. For a variety of detailed examples see Carol P. MacCormack, ed., *Ethnography of Fertility and Birth.*
7. See Averil Cameron, *The Mediterranean World in Late Antiquity AD 395-600*; Keith Hopkins, "Contraception in the Roman Empire." E.L. Kohler, "Cremations of the Middle Phrygian Period at Gordion." Angus McLaren, *A History of Contraception from Antiquity to the Present Day.* David Sloan Wilson, *Darwin's Cathedral: Evolution, Religion, and the Nature of Society.*
8. See, for example: Patrick D. Evans, "Microcephalin, a Gene Regulating Brain Size, Continues to Evolve Adaptively in Humans"; John Hawks, "Recent Acceleration of Human Adaptive Evolution."
9. See Kondrashov; Lynch.

10 See Lynch.
11 This limit is given by Landauer's Principle. See Rolf Landauer (1961), "Irreversibility and heat generation in the computing process" (PDF), IBM Journal of Research and Development, 5 (3): 183–191.
12 See Donald T. Campbell, "Blind Variation and Selective Retention in Creative Thought as in Other Knowledge Processes"; Donald T. Campbell, "Variation and Selective Retention in Socio-Cultural Evolution."
13 Javier A Magaña-Gómez, Ana M Calderón de la Barca. 2009. "Risk Assessment of Genetically Modified Crops for Nutrition and Health." *Nutrition Reviews*, 67:1. (Retrieved September 2016, from
http://dx.doi.org/10.1111/j.1753-4887.2008.00130.x)
14 Sangharakshita, *A Survey of Buddhism*
15 For a good introduction to this research, see Stuart Kauffman, "Chasing the Seeds of Life."
16 See for example Christoph Adami, *Artificial Life*.
17 A. Coulter, *Godless: The Church of Liberalism*.
18 Stephen Toulmin, *Human Understanding*.
19 Jeremy Bentham. "Review of the Declaration of Independence."
20 Jeremy Bentham, *A Comment on the Commentaries and a Fragment of Government*.
21 Michael Quinn, "Mill on Poverty, Population and Poor Relief: Out of Bentham by Malthus?"
22 Ibid.
23 The following sources have a great deal of evidence concerning human evolution, values, and fertility practices:
Averil Cameron, *The Mediterranean World in Late Antiquity AD 395-600*.
Gregory Clark, *A Farewell to Alms*.
Charles Darwin, *The Descent of Man, and Selection in Relation to Sex*.
Emily Friedman, "Why Are Condoms Disliked by so Many Men?"
Keith Hopkins, "Contraception in the Roman Empire."
E.L. Kohler, "Cremations of the Middle Phrygian Period at Gordion."
Carol P. MacCormack, *Ethnography of Fertility and Birth*.
Angus McLaren, *A History of Contraception from Antiquity to the Present Day*.
David Sloan Wilson, *Darwin's Cathedral: Evolution, Religion, and the Nature of Society*.
24 Geoffrey M. Hodgson, "Social Darwinism in Anglophone Academic Journals: A Contribution to the History of the Term."
25 Ibid.
26 Thomas Robert Malthus, 1807, *A Letter to Samuel Whitbread on His Proposed Bill*. London: Printed for J. Johnson, et al. (Retrieved September 2016, from
https://archive.org/details/lettertosamuelwh00maltrich)

27 R.A. Fisher, *The Genetical Theory of Natural Selection*, p. 273.
28 J.B.S. Haldane, 1932, *The Causes of Evolution*, London: Longmans, Green, p. 208-209.
29 J.B.S. Haldane, 1955, "Population genetics," *New Biology* 18: 34-51.
30 W.D. Hamilton, 1964, "The Genetical Evolution of Social Behaviour," *Journal of Theoretical Biology*, 7 (1): 1–16.
31 Herbert Gintis, "Review of Evolutionary Restraints: The Contentious History of Group Selection by Mark E. Borrello." (Retrieved September 2016, from http://www.umass.edu/preferen/gintis/Borrello.docx)
32 Andrew Bourke, *Principles of Social Evolution*.
33 Rohde, R.A., R.A. Muller, 2005. "Cycles in fossil diversity." *Nature*. 434 (7030): 208–210.
34 A couple of writers who do ably discuss the unsustainability of exponential economic growth (and prolifically) are John Michael Greer (e.g. *Our Ecotechnic Future*) and Chris Martenson (e.g. *The Crash Course*).
35 Dale Allen Pfeiffer, 2004, "Eating Fossil Fuels," *OrganicConsumers.org* (Retrieved September 2016, from
 https://www.organicconsumers.org/old_articles/corp/fossil-fuels.php); Graham Zabel, 2009, "Peak People: The Interrelationship Between Population Growth and Energy Resources," *Resilience.org* (Retrieved September 2016, from
http://www.resilience.org/stories/2009-04-20/peak-people-interrelationship-between-population-growth-and-energy-resources)
36 K. Marvel, et al., "Geophysical Limits to Wind Power."
37 A.M. Diederen, "Metal Minerals Scarcity and the Elements of Hope," NIDV, The Hague.
38 Richard Schodde, 2010, "Global Discovery Trends 1950-2009: What, Where, and Who Found Them," *MinEx Consulting* (Retrieved September 2016, from http://www.minexconsulting.com/publications/Global%20Discovery%20Trends%201950-2009%20PDAC%20March%202010.pdf)
39 A.A. Richey, et al., "Quantifying Renewable Groundwater Stress with GRACE."
40 Ron Nielsen, *The Little Green Handbook*
41 James E.M. Watson, et al. "Catastrophic Declines in Wilderness Areas Undermine Global Environment Targets."
42 Pimental, David; Harvey C., et al. 1995. "Environmental and Economic Costs of Soil Erosion and Conservation Benefits." *Science*, New Series, 267: 5201, 1117-1123.
43 See Joseph Tainter, "Complexity and the Productivity of Innovation."
44 See Joseph Tainter, *Drilling Down*.

45 Gary Radloff, "Clean Energy Versus the Status Quo, a Cost Comparison." (Retrieved October 2016, from https://energy.wisc.edu/news/powerpoints/clean-energy-versus-status-quo-cost-comparison)
46 See Stuart Kauffman, *Origins of Order*; *At Home in the Universe*; *Investigations*. See also James Lovelock, "Gaia as Seen Through the Atmosphere."
47 Aristotle, *Nicomachean Ethics*, X, 9.
48 Confucius, *Analects*, VII, 19.
49 Confucius, *Analects*, II, 11.
50 S.D. Varfolomeyev and K.G. Gurevich, "The Hyperexponential Growth of the Human Population on a Macrohistorical Scale."
51 Elliott Sober and D.S. Wilson, *Unto Others: The Evolution and Psychology of Unselfish Behavior*.

ACKNOWLEDGEMENTS

What impact this book will have on the world, I can't say, but its impact on my own life has been immense. Eleven years have passed between conception and publication, a journey that has led me out of academia, and away from the views of most of my family and friends. It has led me to rethink the purpose of my life, and ultimately to a new spirituality. My gratitude to everyone who has helped me along this journey, therefore, is boundless.

Being a first book, and with such a weighty task, inevitably means it will have many flaws, perhaps grievous ones. The responsibility for these flaws lies solely with me. From its first conception, *Progress Debunked* has been controversial. Simply in presenting my argument for critique, friendships have been tried.

For these reasons, let no one assume that anyone mentioned in these acknowledgments in any way endorses the views put forward in this book. Again, I take sole responsibility for them.

Over the years, even before the first draft was written, I've had many excellent discussions with family, friends, students, and professors on the topic of progress. In this way, I've received numerous helpful criticisms of arguments that would eventually appear in this book. My thanks to everyone who has been willing to humor me and talk philosophy.

For helpful critiques and comments on the many drafts of this book, I'm deeply indebted to Dave Armet, Alexander Carnera, Greg Gandenberger, Alex Koszelak, Doug Scibeck, Blaine and Matthew Thomsen, Claire Walton, and many others.

I'd also like to express my heartfelt gratitude to the many friends, family members, and online supporters who have given me encouragement in writing and publishing this book. You've helped make a lonely journey bright.

Finally, and most importantly, I must thank my wife for her unfailing, energizing faith in me; for tolerating an empty bed almost every morning; for keeping me fed and in reality; in short, for being both my sail and my anchor.

INDEX

A

abortion, 12, 26, 61, 72, 80, 84
adaptation/adaptability, xiv, 25, 40, 45, 116, 165
adventure, xi, xii, xvi, 123
agriculture, ix, 20, 113, 120, 128, 129
Alexander the Great, xi, 129
altruism, 92, 98–106, 108, 109, 112, 154–62
Amish, 26, 83, 116, 128
Analects, Confucian, 95, 97, 164, 167, 180
anarchism, xi, 92, 107
anatomy, comparative, 29
ancient wisdom, xi, xv, 8, 90, 134, 164, See tradition; religion; philosophy
ancient world. See Rome, ancient; philosophy, Greek; philosophy, Chinese; Greek civilization; infanticide; ancient wisdom
Aquinas, xiv, 164
Archimedes, 61, 79
Aristotle, xiv, 63, 80, 81, 120, 124, 125, 128, 129, 131, 132, 133, 134, 164, 165
art, 1, 57, 63, 124, 129, 130
    civilization's goals and, 7
    collapse and, 120
    culture includes, 64
    progress measured by, 2
artificial intelligence, 47, 52, 53, 55
Asimov, Isaac, 129
atoms, 59, 62
Augustine, St., 95, 164
authoritarianism, xi

B

balance
    creation-destruction. *See* creation-destruction balance
    joy and suffering, 5, *74–80*
    Malthusian, 6, 7, 32, 47, 54, 55, 64, 68
Basalla, George, 144, 146, 148, 149, 150, 154, 165
Bell Curve, 36, 170
Bentham, Jeremy, 2, 3, *68–71*, 72, 73, 77, 89, 164, 166, 173
Bhagavad Gita, 83, 95, 96, 164, 166
Bible, Holy, xiv, 28, 46, 81, 82, 95, 96, 97, 106, 108, 132, 134, 164, 170
biosphere, 111, 112, 116, 118, 119, 122
bipolar disorder, 127
birth control, 3, 4, 6, 19, 20, 21, *24–28*, 36, 37, 38, 51, 61, 73, 88, 89, 92, 93, 120

birth rate, 3, 20, 21, 25, 26, 38, 72, 78, 83, 169
Blackmore, Susan, 45, 166
Blackstone, William, 69
Blind Watchmaker, 56, 168
Boethius, viii, 164, 166
Bourke, Andrew, 100, 103, 166, 179
breeding, 51
    animals, 29, 30, 33, 34, *48–50*, 65, 129
    humans. *See* eugenics
    plants, 51, 129
Breeding Better Livestock, 49, 174
British Eugenics Society, 35
Buddhism, 55, 95, 129
Burstall, Aubrey, 147, 148, 149, 151, 152, 166
Byron, Lord, 127

C

Campbell, Donald, 44–46, 61
cancer, 51, 111
Cantor, Georg, 127
capitalism, 10, 91
carbon emissions, 116, 118, *See* climate change
Cardwell, Donald, 146, 148, 149, 150, 152, 153, 167
Carlyle, Thomas, 71, 167
Cavalli-Sforza, 25, 45, 46, 167, 177
charity, 7, 23, 92, *96–98*, 107, 108, 109, 158, 159, 160
Charlemagne, 129
Chesterton, G.K., 34, 92, 164, 167
Christianity, xi, 26, 80, 81, 86, 92, 97, 106, 133, *See* Bible, Holy
chromosomes, 33
City of God, 95, 164
civilization, 26, 54, 115, 116, 119
    collapse of, 7, 107, 113, *See* collapse
    decline of, xi, 107, 112, 116, 134
    far future of, 112, *116–19*
    futuristic scenarios, 43, *52–55*, 112
    Greek, 130
    history of, 105, 133, 134
    industrial, 5, 7, 107, *112–16*
    modern globalized, 8, 107, 124

rationality of modern, 85
regress impossible, xi, *See* regress
space faring. *See* space travel
sustainability of, xv, 4, 107, 112–16
Western, x, 5, 7, 120, 121, 134
Clark, Gregory, 20, 163
classics, xiv, 5, 8, 106, 131–32, 134
climate change, 114, 116, 117, 122, *See* carbon emissions
Coevolution, 45, 163, 168
collapse, xii, xiv, xv, 1, 7, 94, 107, 110, *112–16*, 116, 118, 121
Collapse, 85
Collapse of Complex Societies, 94, 107, 164, 175
Comment on the Commentaries, 69, 166, 178
Commentaries on the Laws of England, 69
Communism, 23
compassion, xi, 2, 7, 52, 89, 92, 97, 107, 155, *See* evolution, compassion and
competition, 6, 43, 62, 63, 94, 99, 102, 107, 111, 128, 153
computer viruses, 58
Condorcet, 2, *10–11*, 12, 15, 16, 93, 125, 167
Confucius, 83, 95, 97, 132, 134, 164, 167, 180
continuum hypothesis, 127
contraception, 7, 73, 80, 120, *See* birth control
Coulter, Ann, 58
creation-destruction balance, 5, 6, 7, 26, 64
creativity
    -control?, 63
    destruction and. *See* creation-destruction balance
    ecological, 111, 112, 119, 122, 131
    evolutionary, 4, 25
    mutation and, 39, 41, *53*, 54
    reproduction and, 34
    thinking with, 129, 131
cultural evolution, *39–66*, *See* evolution, cultural; Darwin's Law, culture subject to; selection, cultural
Cultural Transmission and Evolution, 45

INDEX

culture, *40*, 41–43, 64, *See* evolution, cultural; Darwin's Law, culture subject to; selection, cultural
high, xi, 120
Culture and the Evolutionary Process, 45, 166
cybernetics, 47, 52, 53, 65, 112
cynicism, x, xii, 37

D

dark ages, 7, 132
Dark Ages, The, 129
Darwin, *28–31*, 32, 33, 57, 66, 129, 151, 163, 167, 168, 169
    Autobiography, 29
    Beagle voyage, 28
    eugenics and, 34
    evolution theory, 5, *28–29*, 31, 32, 46, 91, 151, 154, 174
    finch studies, 29
    inheritance theory, *31*, 35, 57
    Malthus and, 5, *21*, *30*, 32, 38, 92, 93
    natural selection theory, 24, *29–30*, 31, *32–33*, 55, 58, 62, 65, 66
    Origin of Species, 30
    philosophy of, xiv, 46, 129
    progress and, xv, 26
    Social Darwinism and, 91, 92, 107
Darwin's Cathedral, 45, 46, 102, 163, 176
Darwin's Dangerous Idea, 45, 168
Darwin's Law, 26, *32*, *56–63*, *See* Darwin, natural selection theory
    culture subject to, 41–43, 65
    humans subject to, 38
    progress prohibited by, 73
    selfishness and, 104
    suffering and, 67
    transhumanism and, 50, 65
    universal nature of, 41, *56–63*
    values subject to, *76*, 79, 87, 90
Dawkins, Richard, 25, 45, 46, 47, 56, 85, 91, 118, 168
decadence, 107
dehumanization, xi, 123
democracy, 10, 130
Dennett, Daniel, 45, 85, 168
depression, 127

Descartes, xiv, 63
Development as Freedom, 15
Diamond, Jared, 85, 151, 152, 168
differential fitness, *31*, 42, 43, 54, 59, 60, 61, 63, 105, 108, 151, 153, 154
Dīgha-Nikāya, 55
diversity, 6, 25, 53, 54, 96–98, 120
    bio-, 111, 112, 114, 115, 119, 121, 128
    charity enhances, 108
    creativity dependent on, 4, 25, 39
    ecosystems dependent on, 127, 128
    group selection and, 108
    human, 7, 55, 106, 116, 168
    ideal of, xii, xv, 53, 55, 120, 128
    natural selection and, 25, 31, 39, 55
    progress destroys cultural, 123, 124
    technological, 145, 146, 153, 154
    thinking and, 129, 130, 134
DNA. *See* mutation, biological; selection, genetic engineering and; genetic engineering; eugenics
Durham, William, 45, 163, 168
dystopia, 112

E

ecology, xii, xiv, 5, 112, 131, 172, 174
economic growth, 7, 112–*16*, 116, 121
economics, 94
Ehrlich, Paul, 15, 18, 168
Einstein, 19, 52, 130
energy
    ecology of, 117
    expensive, 120
    exponential growth in use, 107, *113*
    fossil fuel, x, 110, *See* fossil fuels
    information and, 43, 178
    new sources of, 115
    ordered, 27
    progress measured by, 1
    renewable, *113–14*, 115, 121
    resources, x, 43, 113
English laws, 69
Enlightenment, 18th century, 10, 28, 68
Enquiry concerning Political Justice, 11
entropy, 27
equilibrium, 5, 7, 19, 73, 117, 118, 128, 140, 141, 142, 143

185

Euclid, 130
eugenics, 6, 28, *33*, *32–38*, 39, 47, 48–50, 63, 88, 98, 107, 121
   history of, *33–36*
Eugenics and other Evils, 35
eumemics?, 63
European Union, 26
evil, 10, 11, 22, 23, 34, 39, 71, 95, 105, 111
evolution, *28–33*
   altruism and, *98–105*, 112
   ancient philosophy and, 106
   artificial, 57, 102, 103, 104, 105, 109, 154–62
   biosphere undergoes?, 118, 119, 122
   blind to genotype differences, 102, 108, *160–62*
   classics and, 134
   cognitive, 62, 128
   common descent theory, 29
   compassion and, *90–109*, 154–62
   creativity and, 4, 25
   cultural, *39–66*, *80–89*, 90, 122, 133, 144
   Darwin's theory of, 5, *28–33*
   Darwinian, 6, 25
   ecological, 104, 111, 112, 118, 119, 121, 122, 128
   epistemological, 44
   eugenics and, 28, 97
   exponential reproduction and, 26
   family values and, 78, 81, 83, 84
   group, 57, *98–105*, 108, 154–62
   history of theory of, *28–31*
   human, 4, 6, 36
   ideas undergo, 80
   inanimate, 59
   intelligent, 53
   joy being success in, 68, 76, 78, 79
   Lamarckian, 60
   large populations and, *37*
   logical condition for, 58
   Malthus and, 21
   memic, 56
   morality's source in, xii, 22
   nutshell theory of/briefly, *31–32*
   philosophies undergo, 80
   religion vs., 106
   religions undergo, xii, 80, 90
   science undergoes, 44, 62, 63
   selfishness and, 7, 101–5
   short term, 59
   simulations of. See evolution, artificial
   suffering and joy and, 7, 68, 75, 76, 78, 79, 80, 89
   suffering being failure in, 68, 76, 78, 79
   survival and, 58
   technological, 41, 52, 61, *144–54*
   theory of, *28–33*
   traditions undergo, xii, 90, 109, 133
   universal, 57
   value judgments and, 75
   values and, *80–89*, 90, 133
Evolution and Ethics, 34
Evolution: The Modern Synthesis, 35
evolutionary creativity. See creativity, evolutionary
Evolutionary Humanism, 35
exponential growth. See population, exponential growth; economic growth
extinction, 111, 112, 115, 116, 117, 119, 120, 128

F

$F=ma$, 58
fallow, 128
Falsifiability Thesis, 44
family
   Bhagavad Gita on, 83
   birth control and, 25, 72, 90
   charity and, 97
   Confucius on, 83
   cultural achievement vs., 80, 88, 90
   cultural pride in, 87
   dynasties, 94
   early Christianity and, 81
   eugenics vs., 6, 33, 34
   Gnostics and, 81
   greed vs., 95
   joy of, 2
   natural selection for size, 26, 61, 83, 98
   non-industrialized, 38, 88

philosophy and, 129
progress vs., 8, 83, 88, 123
traditional, 83, 88, 90, 120, 123
value of, xii, 34, 78, 120
family planning, 4, 26
Fascism, 23
Feldman, M.W., 45, 46, 167
fertility rates, 21, 24, 25, 26, 32
fire, 20, 49, 60
Fischer, David Hacket, 94, 164, 169
Fisher, R.A., 35, 99, 169
fitness. *See* differential fitness
food resources, 4, 9, 13, 15, 17, 18, 20, 113, 121
forests, *114*, 128
fossil fuels, x, 17, 110, 112, 113, 115, 116, 117, 121, 134
fossil species, 106
founding fathers, 130
fracking, 113
Franklin, Benjamin, 130
French Revolution, 70, 72, 94
Fukuoka, Masanobu, 129
Full House, 47, 169

G

Gaia theory, *117*, 118, 122, 172, 180
Galileo, 63
Galton Institute. *See* British Eugenics Society
Galton, Francis, *34*, 35, 169
gene therapy, 51
genetic engineering, 38, 47, *51–52, 52–55*, 121
Gibbon, Edward, xiv, 163, 169
globlal warming. *See* climate change
Gnostics, 26
God, 21, 82, 95, 96
  city of. *See* City of God
  progressivism vs., 124
Gödel, Kurt, 127
Godwin, William, 11, 12, 93, 169
Gould, Stephen Jay, 35, 37, 47, 169
Grammar of Science, 34
Great Books. See classics
Great Wave, 94, 107, 164, 169
greed, *94–96*, 96, 107, 109

Greek civilization, 130, *See* philosophy, Greek; science, Greek
group selectionism. *See* selection, group
growth. *See* population, exponential growth; economic growth

H

Haldane, J.B.S., 35, 99, 169, 179
Hamilton, W.D., 100, 101, 179
happiness. *See* joy and suffering; utility
Hare, Richard, 71, 169
health care costs, 115
heaven, 82, 124
hedonism, 71
Hereditary Genius, 34, 169
heritability. *See* Lewontin's Criteria, *See* Lewontin's Criteria
high culture, xi, 120
history
  collapse of civilizations, 94
  cultural evolution theory's, *44–47*
  eugenics movement's, *33–36*
  evolutionary theory's, *28–31*
  group selection theory vs. kin selection theory, *98–101*
  progress's, *10–13*
  quantitative economic, 94
  technological, *144–54*
  utilitarianism's, *68–73*
  world, x, xiv
Hodgson, Geoffrey, 91
homeostasis, 118, 119
Homer, 120, 132, 134
Hull, David, 62
human condition, xiv, 3, 7, 22
Huxley, Julian, 35, 36, 38, 170
Huxley, T.H., 34, 170

I

idealism, xii
ideologies, 23, 64, 65, 86, 88, 90
incest taboos, 49, *61*
industrialized countries, 6, 7, 17, 25, 26, 37, 38, 72, 106, 120, 124
infanticide, 7, 12, 26, 61, 78, 80, 81
infinity, 127

infrastructure, 113, 115, 121, 122
innovation, *115*, 121, 145, 147, 150
Intelligent Design, 58
IQ, 35, 36
Islam, 6, 133

J

Jamison, Kay, 127
Jefferson, Thomas, 129
Jesus Christ, 80, 97, *See Bible, Holy*
Jones, Steve, 25
joy and suffering, x, 3, 4, 7, 43, 55, 64, 65, 67, 68, *74–80*, 83, 86, 87, 89, 90

K

Kauffman, Stuart, 119, 171, 178, 180
kin selectionism, *100*, 102, 104, 108, 155, *See* selection, kin
Kondrashov, A.S., 163, 171, 177
Kuhn, Thomas, 62, 63, 163, 171
Kurzweil, Ray, 52

L

Lamarck, 28, 60
Landauer's Principle, 43, 178
Language of Genes, 25
Lao Tzu, 80, 132, 134, 164, 171
Leibniz, 63
Lewontin, R.C.. *See* Lewontin's Criteria
  'The Units of Selection', 31
  Not in Our Genes, 36
Lewontin's Criteria, *31–32*, 57–61, 148, 149, 153, 163, 169, 172
  animal breeding programs satisfy, 50
  blindness of variation irrelevant to, *61–63*, 65
  culture satisfies, 40, 42, 64
  groups satisfy, 57, 100, 104, 108
  science satisfies, *61–63*
  selfishness and, 104
  Survival of the Fittest contains, 58
  technology satisfies, *144–54*
  transhumans satisfy, 53, 54, 65
  universality of, 57–61

light speed, 18, 19, 22, 43, 135
lily pond riddle, 113
literature, 8, 63, 120, 124, 129, 130
  collapse and, 120
  culture includes, 64
  Little Green Handbook, 114, 164, 173, 179
localism, xii, 8, 23, 120
logic, x, *xiii*, 133, 134
  ancient vs. modern, 106, 126, 130, 131
  classics and, 134
  cultural evolution and, 41, 47, 50, 62, 65, 66
  Gödel's, 127
  group selection and, 104, 108, 155
  IQ a *red herring*, 36
  Malthus's *reductio*, 17
  progress inconsistent according to, 41, 79
  selection theory and, 57, 58, 59, 65, 155
  tautology, 58, 65
  technical, 130
  tradition and, 134
  utopian, 124
  values analyzed with, 74
  values marking limit of, 133
Lovelock, James, 117, 118, 119, 172, 180
Lowell, Robert, 127
low-hanging fruit, 115
Luddite, xi
Lynch, M., 163, 172, 177, 178

M

Madison, James, 129
Mahathera, Nyanatiloka, 95
Malthus, xv, *12–17*, 23, 24, 29, 30, 93, 139, 163, 172, 173, 175
  birth control and, 6, 21, *24–26*
  Chesterton and, 92
  compassion and, 92, 107
  Condorcet and, 11
  creation-destruction balance and, 5, *See* Malthus's Principle, creation-destruction balance and

INDEX

Darwin anticipated by, *5*, 28, 29–30, 38
distribution of food and, 20
Essay on the Principle of Population, 9, 10, 12, 16, 22, 28, 93, 172
misinterpretations of, *9–10*, 21, 22, 63
mistakes of, 17, 18, 22
passion between the sexes, 24
Principle of Population, 4, 5, *12–17*, *17–20*, 20, 21, 23, 28, 32, *See* Malthus's Principle
progress challenged by, 5, 22, 93
Social Darwinism and, 91, 92, 98
struggle against evil as essence of life, 5, 10, 21, 22, 39
utilitarians and, 73
vindicated, 22
Malthus's Principle, 12, 17, 18, *17–20*, 20, 21, 23, 24, 28, 32, 50, 79, *134–39*, 154
Bentham and, 72
computers and, 87
creation-destruction balance and, 79
culture subject to, 44, 50, 63, 66, 154
generalization of, 18, *17–20*, *134–39*
mathematics of, *134–39*
Mill and, 73
motivation of, 45
technology subject to, 154
values and, 87
Malthusian pressures. *See* population, checks on
Malthusian Trap, 20, 24
Malthusians. *See* neo-Malthusians; Malthus
mania, 127
marriage, 81, 93, 107
Marx, 2
mass media, 83, 88, 120, 131
materialism, xi
media. *See* mass media
medical progress, 25
memes, *56*, 85
memetic engineering?, 64
memetics, 45, 57
Mennonites, 25, 116

Mill, James, 3, 71, 178
Mill, John Stuart, 3, 71, 73, 173
mineral resources, *114*
Mirabeau, comte de, 70
Mismeasure of Man, 35
Moore, G.E., 71, 172
morality, xii, 34, 96, 106, 123, 126
Murray, Charles A., 36, 170
music, xv, 83, 129, 130
mutation
    adaptability and, 25
    biological, *33*, 39, 40, 47, 56, 60
        collapse of civilization and, 7, 107, 110
        deletion, *33*
        human, 27–28, 32, 36–*38*, 41, 53, 60, 108
        insertion, *33*
        large populations and, 37
        mathematics of, 136
        models of, 35
        natural selection needed to balance, 6, 62, 73, 93, 94
        not a problem to be solved, xv
        sexual recombination, *33*
        substitution, *33*
    creativity and, 25, 30, 32, 39, 41, *53*, 54, 106, 165
    cultural, 7, 40, 53, 54, 56, 62–63, 63, 64, 65, 94, 107, 108, 110, 136, 151
    decay of human DNA, 6, 27–28, *36–38*, 38, 39, 41, 47, 51, 93, 98, 106, 107, 112, 163
    mathematics of, 136, *140–43*

N

natural selection. *See* selection
Nazism, xi, 33, 35
neo-Malthusians, 15, 72, 89
Newton's Laws, 58, 59, 61, 63, 80
Nicomachean Ethics, 124, 180
Nielsen, Ron, 114, 115, 164, 173, 179
Nietzsche, 127, 164, 173
nihilism, 55
nonrenewable resources. *See* sustainability

Not in Our Genes, 35

O

obsession, xi, xv, 127
ocean acidity levels, 117
On Human Nature, 36, 45, 85, 176
origin of life, 57
Origin of Species, xiv, 30, 57, 62, 163, 167
Outlines of an Historical View of the Progress of the Human Mind, 11, 167
overpopulation, 9, 16, 72, 85
oxygen revolution, 111, 116, 118

P

Pagans, 26
patents, *115*, 149, 150
Pearson, Karl, *34*, 173
perfectibility of humankind, 11, 15, 45
petroleum, *113*, *See* fossil fuels
Philosophic Radicals, 68, 71, 73
philosophy, xi, *xii–xiii*, xiii, xiv, xv, 105, 106, *123–26*, *132–33*
    academic, 71, 124, 125, 126
    agriculture analogous to, 128
    ancient, xi, 80, 106
    Chinese, 80, 83, 95, 97, 132, 134
    civilization's goals and, 7
    collapse and, 120
    culture includes, 64
    ecological, *129–31*
    Greek, xi, xiv, 80, 81, 86, 106, 120, 124, 129, *130–31*, 132, 133, 134
    inexhaustibility of, 126
    limits of, 133
    Malthus's, 10
    modern, 126
    natural selection of, 133
    Platonic, xiv, 86
    progress measured by, 1, 2
    progressivism leads astray, xv, 8, *123–26*
    purpose of, *132–33*
    reading list, *164*
    revitalized, *122–34*
    Roman, xi
    scientific, 124, 126, 167, 172
    systematic, xii, *xiii*
    traditional, xii, *xiii–xiv*, 8, 106, 120, 125
    values and, 133
photosynthesis, 111, 117
physics, 6, 12, 27, 47, 53, 78, 80, 106, 130
Pig Philosophy, 71
Pirsig, Robert, 127, 173
Planned Parenthood, 24
Plath, Sylvia, 127
Plato, xiv, 80, 81, 86, 106, 120, 124, 130, 132, 133, 134, 164, 169, 173
poetry, 87, 123, 124, 127, 130, 134
Politics, Aristotle's, xiv, 80, 124, 164
polymaths, *129*, 130
Popper, Karl, 44, 46, 61, 84, 173
population
    checks on, 13, 14, 16, 20, 21, 22
    exponential decline, 25, 77
    exponential growth, 4, *13*, 14, 19, 22, 112, 116, 123
        abruptness of, *113*, 121
        benefits of, 72
    conditions for, 138
    evolution and, 26, 32
    historical over last 200 years, 17, 22
    hyperexponential, *134–39*, 175
    ideas and culture subject to, 42, 43, 64, 87
    Malthus and, 9, *12–15*
    mathematics of, 19, *134–39*
    natural selection and, 30, 32, 38, 60
    normal tendency is, 21, 25, 98
    polynomial growth vs., 19
    postulatum of, *19*
    poverty and, 98
    resource use and, x, 7, 112
    speed of light and, 19, 22, 43
    Third World, 21, 22, 38, 39
    unsustainability of, 18, 77, 135, 136
overpopulation, 9, 16, 72, 85
pressures. *See* population, checks on
resources to support, x, 4, 9, 11, 13, 15, 17, 18, 20, 113, 121

INDEX

wild populations, 13
Population Bomb, 15, 18, 168
poverty, x, 17, 21, 85, 96, 107
Practical Ethics, 72, 84, 164, 175
pragmatism, 124
pride, 87, 95
Principle of Population, 9, 12, 18, 24, 50, 93, 163, 172
Principles of Morals and Legislation, 70, 164, 166
progress, *1–3*, 111
    definition of, *1–3, 68*
    history of, *10–13*
    illusion of, x, 20, 110
    Malthus debunking, 10
    moral, 69
    overcoming natural selection, 6
    recent idea only, x, xiv, 10
    scientific and technological, 1, 11
    universal assumption of, 4
    unsustainability of, x, 20, 110
    utility and, 2–4, *69*
    utopia and, ix
progressivism, x, xi, *123–25*
    adventure vs., 123
    balance of joy and suffering and, 79
    biological procreation devalued by, 86
    birth control and, 6, 86, 89
    ethics and, 89
    family values and, 86, 123
    far future prospects of, 52–55
    literature and art of, 124
    mass media's, 131, *See* mass media
    modern, 23
    Popper's, 84
    religion vs., 123
    tradition vs., 106, 123, 124
    utilitarianism and, 2–4, 67, *69*, 89
    value-set choosing and, 84
prototyping humans, *41*
pseudo-Malthusians. *See* neo-Malthusians
pyramid scheme, 110

Q

Quinn, Michael, 72, 73, 173, 178

Qur'an, 82, 95, 96, 132, 134, 164, 173

R

rationality, 81, 84, 85, *See* reason
    selection against, 81
    values determine, *74*
reactionism, xi, 71, 79
reason, *xiii*, *See* rationality
    Aristotle's not progressive, 124
    practical, 125
    progress and, *124*
    scientific revolutions and, *63*
    vs. value in academia, *125*
redistribution of resources, 20
reductio ad absurdum, 17, 19, 139
regress, xi, 26, *79*, 98
    technology loss and, 153
relativism, 55
Relativity, 19, 135
religion, *80–83*, 88, 89, 90, *94–97*, *105–6*, 133
    adaptation of, 133
    altruism and, 105–6
    charity and, *96–97*, 108
    civilization's goals and, 7, 48, 105–6, 133
    culture as including, 64
    Darwinian selection of, 63, 65, 132
    eugenics and, 34
    evolution as, 164
    evolutionary insights of, *80–83*, 105–6
    greed and, *94–96*, 107
    philosophy and, 124
    progress as a, 4, 85
    progressivism opposed to, 123, 124
    science and, xi, 46, 85, 132, 164
    selfishness and, 105–6
    suffering for, 86, 88
renaissance men, *129*
renewable energy. *See* energy, renewable; solar energy; wind energy
Republic, Plato's, xiv, 80, 124, 164
Rescher, Nicholas, 62, 174
resource redistribution, *20*

resources. *See* food resources; economic growth
retirement, *115*, 121
RNA, 57
robots, 53, 55, 65
romance, xi, xv, 102
Rome, ancient, xi, xiv, 26, 61, 73, 78, 81, 86, 90, 94, 106, 120, 129, 163, 169, 170
Rousseau, xiv, 164, 174

S

Sachs, Jeffery, 2
sacred texts, 8, 134
science, xii, xiv, 10, 11, 44, 62, 63, 129
   agricultural, 129
   breeding as a, 48, 50
   civilization's goals and, 7
   collapse and, 120
   culture as including, 40, 50, 64
   cybernetic, 51
   evidence and, xiii
   genetic, 51
   Greek, 61, 131
   logic and, xiii
   memetics not yet a, 57
   modern, 8, 126
   natural selection of, *44, 61–63*, 65, 149, 150, 167
   overemphasis of, xi, 123
   philosophy and, xiii, xiv, 2, 71, 124, 126
   progress measured by, 1
   progressivism and, 46
   reductive, 119
   religion and, 46, 124
   social, xii, 44, 92, 173
   technical, xiv
Science (magazine), 115, 168, 173, 175
Science as Salvation, 164, 172
science fiction, ix, x, 51, 129
Second Law of Thermodynamics, 27
selection
   artificial, *29–30, 32–33*, 48–50
   artificial intelligence subject to, 52–55
   charity and, *98*, 108

classics and, 133
cultural, 6, 8, 31, 40, 41–42, 44–47, 56–58, 64, 65–66, 144
Darwinian, 6, 24, *29–30*, 31–32, 64
diversity and, 98
ecosystem-level, 104, 112, 117, 118, 119
eugenics and, *33*, 36, 39, 48–50, 65
gene-centric, 99, 104, 155
genetic engineering and, 41, 52–55, 65
group, *98–105*, 108, 109, 112, 159, 154–62
   history of, *98–101*
humans subject to, 7, 25–26, 38, 39, 73, 171
industrialization and. *See* selection, reduced in industrialized nations
kin, *99–100*, 102–3, 104, 108, 155, 159, 162, 169
   history of, *98–101*
Lewontin's 3 criteria for, *31–32*, 57–61, 65–66, 108, 163
life's essence, 65
logic of. *See* Lewontin's 3 criteria for
Malthus and theory of, *29–30*, 32, 38
mathematics of, 31, 35, *140–43*
mutation balanced by, 25, 27–28, 32, 37, 39, 140–43, 163
natural, 25, *29–30, 32–33*, 169
pain and, 78
pleasure and, 76, 78
reduced in industrialized nations, *37–38*, 93, 106, 110
science subject to, *61–63*
sexual, 99, 103, 168
Singularity and, 52–55
suffering and, 67
technology, *153–54*, *See* selection, cultural
tradition and, 133, *See* selection, values' origin in
transhumans subject to, 52–55
Universal. *See* selection, cultural

INDEX

values' origin in, 7, 8, 79, *80–89*, 90, 109
wealth and, 93, 94, 97, 107
Selfish Gene, 25, 45, 47, 56, 91, 168
self-sufficiency, 116, 120, 122, 123
Sen, Amartya, 2, 15, 20, 169
sex, 4, 7, 12, 13, 24, 33, 48, 81, 86
shame, 87
simulation. *See* evolution, artificial
Singer, Peter, 3, 71, 72, 84, 164
Singularity, 52, 55
Smith, Charles, 48
Social Darwinism, 7, *91–92*, 170
social engineering, xi, 125
Social Security, 115
socialism, 10, 92, 93, 107
Socrates, 124, 126
soil. *See* topsoil resources
solar energy, 113, 114, 121
soul, ix, xii, 21, 123, 128
Soviet Union, xi
space travel, 18, 19, 20, 22, 43, 135
specialization, xiv, 126, 130
speed of light, 18, 19, 22, 43, 135
standard of living, x, 110, 115
steam engine, 147, 150, 151, 153
sterilizations, mass, 35
Structure of Evolutionary Theory, 37, 169
Structure of Scientific Revolutions, 62, 163, 171
struggle, x, xii, xv, 4, 5, 7, 21, 22, 23, 30, 106, 124, 127
suffering, ix, x, 2–5, 7, 10, 21, 22, 25, 39, 43, 54, 55, 64, 65, *74–80*, 87, 94, 106, 111
    balanced with joy. *See* balance, joy and suffering
    culture-based, 87
    ideological conflict, 86, 87
    instinctual, 86
    joy and. *See* joy and suffering
    necessary part of life, 22
    origin of, 55, *75*, 89
    population control and, 4, 83
    value-based selection and, *54–55*
surveys, as measure of happiness, 3, 72
survival of the fittest, 58, 89, 108
sustainability, 4, 116, 120, 122, 129

systematic philosophy, *xiii*, xiv

T

Tainter, Joseph, 94, 164, 175, 179
Tao Te Ching, 80, 95, 97, 164, 171
taxonomy, 29
technology, xi, xii, xiv, 38, 144–54, 165, 167
    agricultural, 17, 48, 128, 154, 175
    blindness of innovation, 41, 121, 151
    complexity compared with biosphere, 1
    culture as including, 40, 64, 151, 152
    cybernetic, 41, 52
    Darwinian selection of, 31, 40, 42, 61, 63, 65, *144–54*
    diffusion of, *151–52*
    diversity of. *See* technology, variation of
    ecological destructiveness of, 121
    genetic engineering. *See* genetic engineering
    history of, *144–54*
    hydraulic, 147
    locomotive, 153
    progress measured by, 2, 46, 72
    resource limitations and, 18, 121
    values are disrupted by, 7
    variation of, *144–46*
Tennyson, Alfred Lord, 91, 127
Thales, 131
thermodynamics, 27, 43, 53
third world, 6, 7, 17, 20, 21, 37, 38, 106, 110, 120
topsoil resources, *115*, 128
totalitarianism, 112, 133
Toulmin, Stephen, 62, 175, 178
tradition, 75, 90, 123, 131–32, 164
    collapse and, 106, 117, 120
    Darwinian selection of, 57, 61, 109
    destroyed by progressivism, xi, 10, 106, 123, 124
    evolutionary knowledge embodied in, xii, 8, 56, 75, 76, 86, 106, 109, 133
    family and, 90

importance of, 5, 8, 90, 122, 133, 134
memes and, 56
moral, xii, 109
philosophy and, xii, xiii–xiv, 8, 106, 120, 130, 132, 164
progress as dependent on, 40
religious, 83, 88, 89, 90, 106
societies still holding to. *See* traditional societies
transcending, 88, 106, 133
values are carried by, xii, 8, 83, 133
traditional societies, 37, 38, 83, 88, 116, 122, 128, 133, 164
transhumanism, 35, 41, 52–55, 65, 170

U

United States, 21, 25, 83, 170, 174
Universal Darwinism, 44, 45, 168, 172, 173
universities, xii, 124
unsustainability. *See* sustainability
Usher, A.P., 151, 175
utilitarianism, 2–4, 67, *68–74*, 89, 169
  history of, *68–73*
  ideal, *71*
  preference, *71*
  progressivism and, 2–4, 67
utility, 3, 69, 70, 71
utopia, ix, xii, xv, 10, 12, 13, 23, 25, 36, 49, 51, 54, 79, 85, 93, 106, 111, 123, 124, 133

V

Valerie, Paul, 4
value(s), *74–80*, 90, *See* Darwin's Law, values subject to; evolution, family values and; evolution, value judgments and; evolution, values and; logic, values analyzed with; logic, values marking limit of; Malthus's Principle, values and; philosophy, values and; progressivism, value-set choosing and; progressivism, family values and; selection, values' origin in; suffering, value-based selection

and; tradition, values are carried by; technology, values are disrupted by
  analysis of concept of, *74–80*
  biological, *80–89*
  cultural, *80–89*
  evolution of, *80–84*
variation. *See* Lewontin's Criteria

W

water resources, *114*
wealth. *See* greed
  Biblical view of, 96
  decline caused by, 94, 110
  genetic decay and, 94
  high culture and, 130
  inequalities, 94, 107
  redistribution, xi, 93, 97, 98, 108
  Rig Veda on, 82
  selection and, 93
  utilitarianism and, 69, 70
  Western civilization's, x, 20, 28
Westminster Review, 71
wheel, the, 20, 145–46, 153
wilderness, *115*
Williams, Mary, 31, 176
Wilson, D.S., 45, 46, 47, 102, 163, 175, 180
Wilson, E.O., 36, 38, 44, 50, 85, 103, 172
wind energy, *113–14*
wisdom, 131, See tradition; religion; philosophy
  ancient. *See* ancient wisdom
  evolution shapes, 44
  Greeks admired, 130
  philosophy and, 124
world government, xi, xv, 26
World War II, 33, 35, 92

X

Xenophon, 130

Z

Zen and the Art of Motorcycle Maintenance, 127, 173

ABOUT THE AUTHOR

Samuel W. Thomsen is a writer, philosopher, and software developer living in the Rockies with his wife and some brilliant, rambunctious little ones. He holds an Honors degree in *Physics* from Caltech, and master's degrees from the world-renowned departments of *Philosophy* and *History and Philosophy of Science* at the University of Pittsburgh. His essays on technology, education, and metaphysics have appeared in several journals, including *Studies in History and Philosophy of Science, The Salt Lake Tribune,* and *The Sydney Traditionalist Forum.* He blogs at *www.samuelthomsen.com.*

Printed in Poland
by Amazon Fulfillment
Poland Sp. z o.o., Wrocław